A FEW WELL-POSITIONED CASTLES
THE NORMAN ART OF WAR

A FEW WELL-POSITIONED CASTLES

THE NORMAN
ART OF WAR

STUART PRIOR

TEMPUS

For Luke Norrison (1974-1999), a greatly missed friend and comrade.

First published 2006

Tempus Publishing Limited
The Mill, Brimscombe Port,
Stroud, Gloucestershire, GL5 2QG
www.tempus-publishing.com

© Stuart Prior, 2006

British Library Cataloguing in Publication Data.
A catalogue record for this book is available from the British Library.

ISBN 0 7524 3651 1

Typesetting and origination by Tempus Publishing Limited
Printed in Great Britain

Contents

	Illustrations	7
	Acknowledgements	11
	Introduction	13
1	Architecturalists, landscapists, phenomenologists, strategists and Norman castles	19
2	Military considerations	39
3	Early castles in Somerset	68
4	Early castles in Monmouthshire	110
5	Early castles in Meath	165
6	A few well-positioned castles	223
	Appendix: A gazetteer of the castles studied	240
	Bibliography	244
	Index	251

Illustrations

TEXT FIGURES

1   The locations of Somerset, Monmouthshire and Co. Meath
2   Bodiam Castle, East Sussex
3   Trim Castle, Co. Meath
4   Diagram showing the various factors controlled by castles at each stage of a campaign
5   Stogursey Castle, Somerset
6   Montacute Motte and Bailey, Somerset
7   Warkworth Castle and 'New Town', Northumberland
8   The Norman world in the eleventh century
9   Chepstow Castle, Monmouthshire
10 John Speed's plan of the City of Winchester, Hampshire
11 Twyn-Bar-Lwm Castle, Monmouthshire
12 St Illtyd's Motte, Monmouthshire
13 Downend Motte and Bailey, Somerset
14 Fenny Castle, Somerset
15 Somerset's Norman castles
16 Table detailing Somerset's Norman castles
17 Somerset's earliest Norman castles (pre-1086)
18 The Norman Invasion of Somerset
19 Castle Neroche, Somerset
20 The landholdings of Somerset's principal Norman lords and the locations of the earliest castles
21 Table showing the proximity of castles and rivers in Somerset
22 Suggested stages of development for Cary Castle, Somerset

23 Somerset's Roman roads and Norman castles
24 O.S. map of 1811, showing Ilchester and the locations of Wimble Toot, Sock Dennis and the associated Roman roads
25 *Herepaðs* and castles around the city of Bath
26 Somerset's Hundredal Arrangements
27 Somerset's Anglo-Saxon burhs and towns and Norman castles
28 The Kingdoms of Early Medieval Wales
29 The Cantrefs and Commotes of Medieval Wales
30 The Cantrefs and Commotes of Monmouthshire
31 Topographical Map of Monmouthshire
32 Monmouthshire's Norman castles
33 Table detailing Monmouthshire's Norman castles – *Invasion Period*
34 Table detailing Monmouthshire's Norman castles – *Subjugation Period*
35 Table detailing Monmouthshire's Norman castles – *Welsh Offensive*
36 William fitz Osbern's Castles, 1066-1071
37 The militarily important 'pivotal points' in Monmouthshire's landscape
38 Navigable sections of rivers and associated Norman castles in Monmouthshire
39 Table showing the proximity of castles and rivers in Monmouthshire
40 Monmouthshire's Roman roads and sites and associated Norman castles
41 Table detailing the locations of castles associated with Roman roads in Monmouthshire
42 The Norman penetration of Monmouthshire, 1066-1093
43 Welsh stone castles in the commote of Machen and Norman castles in the lordship of Newport
44 Table showing the cantref, commote and lordship for castles constructed in Monmouthshire between 1066 and 1134
45 Monmouthshire's cantrefs and commotes and castles constructed between 1066 and 1134
46 Table showing the relationship between Norman Lordships and pre-Norman land divisions in Monmouthshire
47 Monmouthshire's Norman Lordships
48 Monmouthshire's Norman Lordships and castles
49 The political divisions of Ireland, *c.*1169
50 Ireland's political geography on the eve of the Anglo-Norman invasion
51 Genealogical table of the Ua Maelechlainn Kings of Meath
52 Ireland's physical features
53 Ireland's political geography under the Anglo-Norman colony, *c.*1210
54 The topography and rivers of Co. Meath
55 Meath's Anglo-Norman castles

56 Table detailing Meath's Anglo-Norman castles – datable
57 Table detailing Meath's Anglo-Norman castles – undatable
58 The militarily important 'pivotal points' in Meath's landscape
59 Meath's land-use capability and Anglo-Norman castles
60 Meath's motte and bailey castles
61 The distribution of mottes with baileys in Meath and Oriel
62 The rivers of Meath and associated Anglo-Norman castles
63 Table of factors associated with Meath's Anglo-Norman castles (1-39)
64 Table of factors associated with Meath's Anglo-Norman castles (40-78)
65 Meath's early roads and associated Anglo-Norman castles
66 Meath's early bridges, river crossings, and associated Anglo-Norman castles
67 Meath's ecclesiastical centres and associated Anglo-Norman castles
68 Hugh de Lacy's sub-infeudation of Meath
69 Early Irish Political Land Divisions in Midhe
70 Anglo-Norman barons, baronies and caputs in the Liberty of Meath, *c*.1172-1200
71 Baronies, caputs & castles in the Liberty of Meath
72 Genealogical table of the de Lacy's, 1066-1241
73 Bar-chart showing the results of 15 regional castle studies
74 Pie-chart showing the combined results of 15 regional castle studies
75 The extent of Roman occupation in Britain *c*.AD 40 and major Norman castles built in England by 1086

COLOUR PLATES

1   Nether Stowey Castle, Somerset
2   Dunster Castle, Somerset
3   Fenny Castle, Somerset
4   Cockroad Wood Castle, Somerset
5   Cary Castle, Somerset
6   Culverhay Castle, Somerset
7   Wimble Toot, Somerset
8   Burrow Mump, Somerset
9   Montacute Motte, Somerset
10 Caldicot Castle, Monmouthshire
11 Caerwent Motte, Monmouthshire
12 Raglan Castle, Monmouthshire
13 Grosmont Castle, Monmouthshire
14 Abergavenny Castle, Monmouthshire

15 Wern-y-Cwrt Castle Mound, Monmouthshire
16 Skenfrith Castle, Monmouthshire
17 Chanstone Tumps, Monmouthshire
18 The Moat, Treveddw, Monmouthshire
19 Longtown Castle, Monmouthshire
20 Mill Wood Castle Mound, Monmouthshire
21 Coed-y-Mount, Penrhos, Monmouthshire
22 Drumcondra Motte and Bailey, Co. Meath
23 Nobber Motte and Bailey, Co. Meath
24 Drogheda Motte and Bailey, Co. Meath
25 Trim Castle, Co. Meath
26 Clonard Motte, Co. Meath
27 Baronies, castles and boroughs in Meath
28 Chronological map of Meath's datable Anglo-Norman castles
29 View from Ardmulchan Motte, Co. Meath, looking west down the
    River Boyne
30 The donjon at Colchester

Acknowledgements

I should like to thank the following people for their help, advice, support and encouragement whilst writing this book. From the *University of Bristol*, Dr Mark Horton, Dr Michael Costen, Prof Ronald Hutton, Prof Mick Aston and Phillip Rowe. From the *University of Exeter*, Dr Oliver Creighton, Dr Bob Higham and Jon Freeman. From the *University of Wales, Lampeter*, Prof David Austin. From *University College Dublin*, Dr Tadhg O'Keeffe. From the *University of Gloucestershire*, Dr Paul Courtney. From the *University of Nottingham*, Dr Philip Dixon. From the *University of East Anglia, Norwich*, Dr Robert Liddiard. From the *University of Durham*, Prof Matthew Johnson; and from the *University of Oxford*, Trevor Rowley.

I owe a debt of gratitude for many of my Somerset references to David Bromwich of the *Somerset Local Studies Library*; for my Welsh references to Susan Hughes and Neil Maylan of *GGAT*; and for my Irish references to David Sweetman and Celine Walsh of *Dúcas*. I would also like to thank the staff of the various records offices visited whilst undertaking the research for this book, for their patience, assistance and helpful suggestions. Special thanks are also due to Dr Duncan Anderson, Andrew Orgill and Matthew Bennett of *The Royal Military Academy, Sandhurst*, and Maggie Magnusson of *The Royal Engineers Library, Chatham*, without whom it would have been virtually impossible to write chapter two.

I should also like to thank Katherine Dray, Charlie and Nancy Hollinrake, Bruce Eaton, Frank and Caroline Thorne, Arthur Hollinrake, Michael and Jenny Dray, Keith Faxon, Bob Croft, Chris Webster, Richard Brunning, Steve Membury, Vince Russet, Bob Sydes, Peter Leach, Paul Remfry, Neil Johnstone, George Eogan, Martin Fletcher, Ian and Rachael Elliott, Mark Jolliff and Neil Eddiford, as, in one way or another, all have made worthy contributions to this work.

Introduction

This book is primarily concerned with the strategies, tactics and stratagems that formed the basis of Norman castle warfare – a subject that up until now has received surprisingly little academic attention. The castle was the Normans' principal weapon of war, the tool that made their conquests possible and the key to their overwhelming success. In isolation the castle was simply a 'properly fortified residence', a place that offered refuge in times of adversity, a form of defence; but in concert with others, as integral components in a carefully planned campaign strategy, castles became unsurpassed instruments of war, items of military hardware with huge offensive capabilities. Between 1066 and 1186 the Normans, utilising strategic castle warfare, successfully conquered England, most of Wales and a large part of Ireland.

Utilising the tools and techniques available to the landscape archaeologist, in conjunction with knowledge contained in historic military manuals, and information from archaeological, historical, architectural, topographical, geological and documentary sources, this book explores the positioning of castles in the landscapes of Somerset, Monmouthshire and Co. Meath (1) between 1066 and 1186 in order to provide answers to the following four questions:

1. Did factors of a tactical and strategic nature provide the main incentives for the Norman castle building programme?

2. Which tactical and strategic considerations influenced castle siting, and how important were they in terms of the final locations chosen for castle erection?

3. Which strategies or stratagems did the Normans employ in regards to castle warfare, and were these schemes adapted from region to region, and over time?

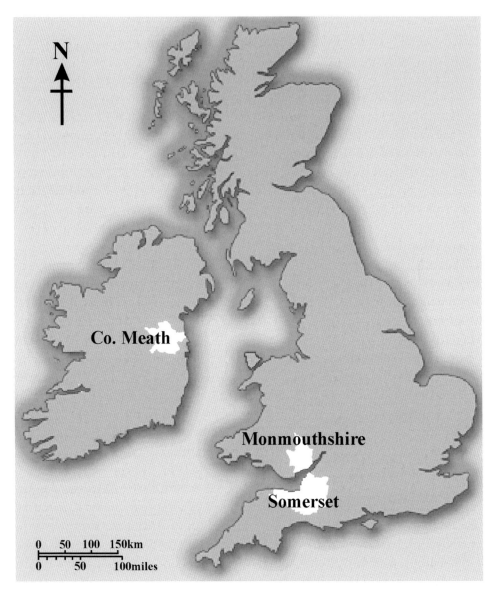

1 The locations of Somerset, Monmouthshire and Co. Meath

4. How successful were the Norman strategies of castle building in terms of establishing control in three very different environments?

Somerset, Monmouthshire and Co. Meath were selected as ideal counties for study as, from a practical viewpoint, they each contain well-preserved Norman castle sites, in relatively undisturbed surroundings, with suitable surviving documentary evidence, and when combined serve to highlight the chronological progression of Norman influence; whilst historically, from a military perspective, each was strategically and tactically important. Somerset was important since it had formerly been one of King Harold's major landholdings, forming the heart of Saxon Wessex; Monmouthshire was important as it was the first Welsh territory invaded by the Normans, forming their bridging point into Wales; and Co. Meath was important as it was near Dublin, and Dublin was important for several reasons. Tactically, without holding Dublin, the Normans could never hope to effectively hold Leinster. Strategically, Dublin was of great importance because of its geographical position vis-à-vis Ulster, Man, Wales, and England. Economically, Dublin was an internationally famous trading centre; and from a religious viewpoint, Dublin was of increasing ecclesiastical importance as a metropolitan see.

The date of 1066 for the start of the study is self-evident, marking the beginning of the Norman Conquest of England, but the closing date of 1186 merits explanation. In 1186 Hugh de Lacy, whilst supervising the construction of a castle at Durrow, Co. Offaly, was murdered – beheaded by an Irish axe. Hugh de Lacy was arguably the last of the great Anglo-Norman leaders, and in his lifetime gained renown as a great warrior, competent campaigner, proficient strategist, and effective statesman and politician. With his death the last real hope for complete Anglo-Norman domination in Ireland died also, and as 'there was no place further for the old warriors to go … they settled down to the thankless task of garrison duty along a frontier which no longer meant opportunity, but toil. Their frontier had come to an end' (Nelson, 1966, 150). The year 1186 thus marks the end of a major period of Norman expansionism and conquest.

Traditionally, the study of castles has been dominated by militaristic themes. Architectural historians have examined castles as functional structural entities, concentrating upon their fabric, design and construction, in order to assess their defensive military potential. The key element in their argument that the architectural evolution of the castle was the product of a continual struggle between increasingly sophisticated techniques of attack and progressively more scientific methods of defence, whilst military historians have examined their martial significance, operational capabilities and role in medieval warfare. During the closing decades of the twentieth century, there was a reaction against the traditional military approach, principally focused upon the later medieval period, but increasingly applied to the eleventh and twelfth centuries. As castellologists expanded their repertoires to include an ever-widening array of sites, source materials, methodologies and up-to-the-minute technologies, new questions began to be asked of castles, and consequently new agendas for research developed. Subsequently, in addition to the military role of castles, castle studies now frequently consider such aspects as lordly display, peaceable power, aesthetics, iconography and symbolism; and castles are often studied in their wider administrative, social, economic and political contexts.

Despite many years of military castle studies and the recent shift in emphasis, the strategies and tactics associated with castle usage remain virtually unexplored. These themes have often been mentioned in passing, but only a handful of scholars have attempted to confront them directly, and in general their work has been largely ignored. It is anticipated that this book will go someway towards addressing this problem, as it looks in detail at numerous sites selected for castle erection, explores the reasoning behind the various locations chosen, and works towards a greater appreciation of how castles were perceived and utilised by the Normans during their various campaigns, ultimately demonstrating the remarkable military prowess of the Normans themselves.

In essence then, this book is not particularly concerned with castles themselves, but rather with the positioning of castles in the immediate and wider landscape, and with the thinking underlying the various sites selected. This focus has guided the organisation of the book. In chapter one, in order to place the 'strategic approach' to castles into context, a brief history of castle studies is presented. The strategic approach to castles is then outlined and contemporary Norman sources are examined, with the aim of establishing the background to the Norman use of castles. In chapter two, historic military manuals are scrutinised to establish a framework against which the positions of castles in the landscape can be tested and understood. Chapters three, four and five explore the positions of castles in the landscapes of the chosen study areas. The strategies, tactics and stratagems that underpinned the choice of castle site are identified and explained and the results are tied into the historic narratives for the regions. Many of the principal Norman strategists involved in the decisions surrounding the erection of castles are also identified and discussed. The conclusion reached, in chapter six, is that, in the vast majority of cases, tactical and strategic considerations chiefly dictated where castles were constructed, and that, very often, these considerations also provided the main impetus for castle construction. It is further argued that the strategies, tactics and stratagems employed by the Normans made them a 'force-majeur par excellence', and that in order to fully appreciate this conclusion it is necessary to see the Normans as they saw themselves – as part of a wider European phenomenon, which took its inspiration from the Roman Empire.

As this book concentrates upon the strategies and tactics that formed the basis of Norman castle warfare, both the time span covered and the locations for study have been unashamedly chosen for their military potential. There would be little point in focusing initially, for example, upon the counties of Dorset, Worcestershire and Staffordshire, as these areas contain relatively few castles and seem to have offered little in the way of resistance to the Norman conquerors. Somerset, Monmouthshire and Co. Meath, on the other hand, contain large numbers of castles and appear to have presented fierce military opposition to Norman occupation. Similarly, a study of the castles built in England during the reign of Henry II (1154-89), during relatively peaceful times, would likely prove unfruitful, as such castles were almost certainly constructed to serve a variety of functions and their military capabilities may have been very low down on the list of priorities. Castles built in the wake of the Conquest, and for that matter subsequent conquests were, on the other hand, undoubtedly constructed to perform a variety of military functions, and as such are ideal candidates for a study of this kind. Therefore, both the time frame covered and the counties examined are in some respects extraordinary: the counties are among those which offered maximum resistance to Norman occupation during a time of prolonged conquest and conflict. A study of the castles constructed during this period in these counties does however produce significant results. Results which may, in time, influence the study of castles in other less exceptional regions, erected during less confrontational periods.

Finally, it is worth mentioning that this book avoids dogmatic arguments over what constitutes a 'castle', taking for its basic definition, 'the castle as a properly fortified military residence'. The term 'lordly', which is often used in many definitions to describe a castle, has been purposely omitted, as many of the castles reviewed in this book can hardly be described as residences befitting a lord. A large proportion of 'castles', especially in the frontier regions of Wales and Ireland, were simply roughly constructed earth and timber outposts, designed to hold nothing more than a few troops, alongside their mounts and provisions.

Architecturalists, landscapists, phenomenologists, strategists and Norman castles

For most of the twentieth century, castle studies were largely dominated by the theme of warfare. Those who studied castles, studied – at a macroscopic level – their military significance, operational potential and role in contemporary warfare, and – at a microscopic level – the ways in which a castle functioned as an item of military hardware. Towards the end of the century however there was a gradual shift in emphasis, and the traditional, somewhat formulaic, military approach to castle studies was increasingly rejected in favour of other avenues of research. As a result, the start of the twenty-first century has witnessed a substantial backlash against what has been termed 'military determinism' (Coulson, 2003, 1), and the military view of castles is currently argued to be in headlong retreat (Johnson, 2002, 6), with the militarists who supported such notions standing accused of casting long shadows over twentieth-century studies, retarding ambitions towards a more holistic understanding of castles (Creighton, 2002, 6). As this book focuses upon the strategies, tactics and stratagems that underpinned Norman castle warfare, and as these themes are categorically military in nature, it is important to understand why the militaristic approach to castles has become so unpopular. In this regard, a brief examination of the historiography of castle studies in Britain is instructive; and in addition demonstrates where the strategic approach to castles, presented in this book, fits into the castle studies agenda.

CASTLE STUDIES IN BRITAIN

Surprisingly, the study of castles is almost as old as the castles themselves. The focus for the earliest work was the enumeration of England's many castles. Recording began in the early thirteenth century with the *Mappa Mundi* of

Gervase of Canterbury, and continued in 1487 with William of Worcester, and in 1533 with John Leland, in their *Itineraries*. From the sixteenth century onwards, antiquarians took a keen interest in castles as reflections of aristocratic culture, and in 1789, James Moore published a directory for antiquarian tourists entitled *A List of Principal Castles and Monasteries in Great Britain*, which contained some 530 castle entries. During the early part of the nineteenth century, the study of ecclesiastical architecture advanced apace and from these roots grew a more mature approach to the study of secular architecture, leading to the publication of two highly influential works on castles. In 1884, George Thomas Clark published what can be considered the first academic study of castles in Britain, entitled *Medieval Military Architecture in England*; and in 1912, A. Hamilton Thompson published *Military Architecture in England during the Middle Ages*. Archaeologists also began to take a keen interest in castles at this time, and by the late nineteenth century Captain Morgan was excavating at Bishopston in Glamorgan, and General Pitt Rivers was excavating at Folkestone in Kent. The single most important publication during this period however was *Early Norman Castles of the British Isles*, published in 1912 by Ella Armitage. In her book Armitage successfully established the chronology of England's castles and ratified their Norman origins.

The works of Clark, Hamilton Thompson and Armitage, written in late Victorian Britain at a time when strategic, imperial and soldierly ideals prevailed, unsurprisingly, all contain a common ideology, that castles were predominantly military in nature (Coulson, 2003, 5). Armitage, gravitating towards historical accounts of the Norman Conquest such as the *Anglo-Saxon Chronicle* and the *Gesta Guillelmi*, championed a notion made popular by E.A. Freeman in his *The History of the Norman Conquest of England* (1867-1879), that castles were tools of English subjugation, whilst Clark and Hamilton Thompson saw castles primarily as military buildings, and their architectural development as a series of responses to the demands of war. The argument maintained was that castles of the eleventh and twelfth centuries were primarily military edifices, which eventually devolved into the fortified mansions of the fifteenth century, due to a steady decline in the need for martial structures with the demise of feudalism. Thus – argue modern castellologists – 'the castle's image as the fortification of a brutal age was set in place and attempts to understand and define its role and function became bound by the straitjacket of military architecture' (Liddiard, 2003, 6).

The militaristic approach to castles remained the dominant theme for most of the twentieth century, and was further popularised in the works of R. Allen Brown (1954 onwards) who successfully 'joined lifestyle to militarism with rare historical authority' (Coulson, 2003, 5). During the closing decades of the twentieth century however there was a reaction against the traditional military approach, the challenge coming initially from archaeology. In 1967, following a survey of mottes in Normandy which failed to date any to before 1066, Davidson contested Armitage's claim that the origin of England's castles lay with the Normans (Davidson, 1969). Davidson's work, although inconclusive, fired archaeological interest in earthwork castles, and Higham and Barker's book *Timber Castles* (1992) placed them firmly on the castle studies agenda. Around this time architectural studies also witnessed a move away from 'military functionalism' towards 'iconographic symbolism', with Coulson (1979 onwards) placing increasing emphasis upon the defensive shortcomings of many castles in an attempt to transport castle building into the realms of aristocratic chivalric culture, where status and social competition became the more dominant characteristics. Working along similar lines, Dixon (1990; [& with Marshall] 1993) and Heslop (1991) explored the social functions of castles, highlighting the sophistication of domestic planning to the detriment of military design. A debate widened in 1990, with the publication of Pound's book *The Medieval Castle,* which concentrated upon the social, political and economic roles of castles.

In 1984, Austin argued that castles needed to be studied within a wider historical framework, and his work on Barnard Castle (1982) was instrumental in demonstrating the importance of the castle's landscape setting. In 1990, Taylor, Everson and Wilson-North, following Austin's lead, recorded a series of 'pleasure-gardens' associated with Bodiam Castle, and thereby raised awareness of 'designed castle landscapes' (2). The success of these two projects gave rise to the landscape approach to castles, which, in turn, led to an explosion in castle landscape studies. As a result, there has been a move away from seeing castle landscapes as purely functional environments, and landscape archaeologists and historians are currently endeavouring to discover how castles may have functioned in relation to their surroundings (Creighton 1998 onwards; Hughes 1998; Liddiard 2000i & 2003; Taylor, 2000).

The most recent approach applied to the study of castles though is the *phenomenological approach.* Castellologists are becoming increasingly concerned with the ways in which castle landscapes were perceived and experienced by past societies, and with the impact of the castle 'monument' upon the human senses. For instance, O'Keeffe has suggested that the Greek Cross plan utilised in the construction of the donjon at Trim 'was more concerned with complex Christian symbolism and display than with defensibility' (2000, 37) (3). A suggestion complemented by the work of Marten-Holden, who argues that castle environs often contained landscape components that embodied biblical iconography – which would have been understood regardless of linguistic and cultural differences – as a means to symbolically exert Norman dominion (2001, 51-2).

2 Bodiam Castle, East Sussex, sits within a large lake, which, due to its shallow depth, is unlikely to have served in a defensive capacity. Instead there is evidence to suggest that the watery landscape and built architecture acted together to produce a visually impressive journey into the castle. *Photograph: M. Aston*

The idea that the iconic role of the castle as a symbol of power and influence often coexisted with, and sometimes transcended, its military importance was suggested by Johnson in 1996. This notion was quickly taken-up by Lewis *et al.* who proposed that the castle was a highly visible physical manifestation of seigneurial authority (1997, 231). Creighton subsequently added to this argument by demonstrating that the landscape around the castle was often remodelled to emphasise its iconic status, by presenting the seigneurial site from the most favourable angle, against a backcloth of landscape features with elite connotations (Creighton, 2002, 65). More recently, Johnson has argued that an entirely new approach to castles is required, an approach that views castles in relation to the identities of the people who used and lived in them (2002, i). Such an approach has been adopted by Wheatley, who has attempted to reveal the castle's place at the heart of medieval culture, by examining a range of medieval sources usually neglected in castle studies. Wheatley suggests that the castle was central in every aspect of medieval consciousness, from private religious contemplation to the creation of national mythologies (2004).

Today then, architecturalists, landscapists and phenomenologists tend to interpret castles and their landscapes in terms of lordly display, peaceable power, aesthetics, iconography and symbolism, whilst simultaneously emphasising the castle's wider administrative, social, economic and political functions. The *militaristic approach* to castles, as far as the vast majority of castellologists are concerned, is now long out of date and of limited use. This fact is suitably evidenced in Creighton and Higham's recent publication *Medieval Castles* (2003), where, despite over 100 years of military castle studies, 'Castles at War' forms one of the shortest chapters, whilst 'Castles: Status and Society' forms one of the longest. This publication is also useful for demonstrating another important factor. In the entire book (albeit very short) only three lines are given over to the tactical and strategic use and positioning of castles (ibid., 26). This is hardly surprising however, as the tactics and strategies associated with castles have been largely ignored as a subject for serious academic debate over the years, and current approaches to the study of castles are attempting to address an entirely different set of issues.

One of the first to adopt a strategic approach to castles was W. H. St John Hope, Director of the *Royal Archaeological Institute*. In his book *The Strategical Aspects of English Castles*, published in 1910, he succinctly covered many of the tactical and strategic principles relating to castle usage, and further argued that castles must 'be looked upon as forming part of ... [a] great offensive and defensive scheme' (292). A year later Alfred Harvey's *Castles and Walled Towns of England* was published; Harvey also believed that castles were not isolated fortresses, but were arranged on a definite scientific plan. Both works were quickly swept aside however, with the publication of Ella Armitage's book in 1912.

'Another brave effort was that of Professor John Beeler of the University of North Carolina' (King, 1983, xiii). Beeler, in three published works (1956, 1966 & 1971), was the first to properly analyse many of the tactical and strategic principles of castle warfare, but there were problems with his methodologies and conclusions ultimately leading to heavy criticisms of his work. Pounds states that Beeler 'ascribes to the Conqueror a topographical knowledge which few of us possess'; 'that the dates of foundation of all castles built before the end of the twelfth century were conflated, so that they appear contemporary, and, by implication, are ascribed to the early years of the Conquest'; and that 'the rationalisation by which the siting of the humblest ringwork is explained verges on the ludicrous' (1990, 54). In addition, Creighton opines that Beeler was wholly mistaken in interpreting 'the map of English castles as the product of the same type of strategic master planning that influenced the distribution of Roman forts and frontier works' (2002, 6). Finally, Bernard Bachrach adopted a more considered, but perhaps over-cautious, approach to the subject of strategy in *The Angevin Strategy of Castle-Building in the Reign of Fulk Nerra, 987-1040*; published in 1983. His approach no doubt tempered by the shifting emphasis in castle studies at that time.

3 It has been suggested that the Greek Cross plan of the donjon at Trim Castle, Co. Meath, had serious limitations from a defensive standpoint. Its unusual design provided no less than 12 potential points of attack, suggesting that it was more concerned with complex Christian symbolism and display than with defensibility

Apart from the few studies mentioned above then, it is fair to state that in general castle studies have continually neglected to tackle the important relationship between strategy and tactics and castle. As castellologists, by and large, fail to appreciate the assertion that in most instances *it was not what was built, but where it was built that was the key to Norman success*; structure in most cases being less important than location. Moreover, in the small number of books where the topic of location is discussed, most scholars maintain the belief that there was no 'abstract military thinking' and hence no real 'strategy' involved behind the siting of castles: the main reason advocated for the choice of site being simply one of convenience (McNeill, 1992, 33). This problem may perhaps be solved by adopting a new approach to the study of castles. An approach which takes into account, examines, and lays stress upon the importance of the military strategies and tactics associated with castles - the *strategic approach*.

THE STRATEGIC APPROACH TO CASTLES

The claim that the strategies and tactics associated with castle warfare have yet to be widely examined or properly investigated may seem surprising to some, as it is commonly believed that castles were tactically or strategically positioned in the landscape. Indeed, school textbooks on medieval history frequently and unequivocally state that castles were strategically located in the countryside in relation to rivers and roads. The basic concept of the tactically or strategically positioned castle has filtered down over time into popular culture from suggestions made in many of the traditional, militarily focused, studies of castles (e.g. Braun, 1936; Renn, 1968; Brown, 1976 & 1980i). In general however these studies lack the hard facts, or suitably convincing examples, necessary to support such theories – which has unquestionably led to their downfall of late (Coulson, 2003, 1; Johnson, 2002, 6; Creighton, 2002, 6).

In order to explain clearly and effectively the strategic approach to the study of castles, it is first necessary to clarify a couple of terms. The terms 'strategy' and 'tactics' are both in general use today, and are often used interchangeably. This however is a common mistake. The *Websters New World Dictionary* (1998) describes strategy as: (a) The science of planning and directing large-scale military operations, (b) A plan or action based on this; whilst tactics is described as: (a) The science of arranging and manoeuvring military and naval forces in action or before the enemy, esp. (as distinguished from Strategy) with reference to short-range objectives; (b) Actions in accord with this science. From these definitions it is apparent that the two 'sciences' are interrelated, but that there is a vital difference between them. Tactics relates specifically to 'short term objectives', whilst strategy 'is concerned with the overall conduct of military operations against the enemy'. The best definition comes from Clausewitz (1780-1831), one of the greatest western military thinkers of all time, who distinguishes between tactics – 'the art of winning battles' – and strategy – 'the art of using battles in order to gain the objectives of the campaign' (Creveld, 2000, 116).

Militarily, the terms strategy and tactics are also frequently used to refer directly to positions in the landscape. In any given expanse of land, there are two types of location that are important from the military's perspective: 'tactically significant locations' and 'strategically significant locations'. Tactically significant locations are points in the landscape that are topographically or geologically strong, where, due to the nature of the terrain, a weaker force could hold its own against a potentially stronger aggressor – such as a high, naturally defended, rocky outcrop. Strategically significant locations are points in the landscape which, due to their geographical positions, afford control of 'key strategic elements' – such as mountain passes, defiles, rivers, fords and road networks (British Army *Field Service*

Pocket Book, 1914). The modern British army refers to such locations as 'pivotal' or 'nodal' points. Relating this to the act of castle building, tactical considerations can be best understood in relation to decisions made at a local level, concerned with the positioning of a castle in the immediate vicinity, connected primarily with matters of defence. Whereas, strategic considerations relate to decisions made at a regional or possibly even national level, concerned with the positioning of castles at carefully selected points across an entire landscape, where, due to their geographical locations, the castles afford control of key strategic elements.

With the above points in mind, the basic tenet of the strategic approach to castles is the belief that, in the vast majority of cases, tactical and strategic considerations above all else dictated where castles were constructed; and that, very often, these considerations also provided the main impetus for castle construction. This obviously implies that there was a certain degree of planning involved in the locations selected for castle construction. In previous strategic approaches taken to castle studies 'castles have been seen as part of an integrated scheme, planned and controlled from somewhere close to the king' (Pounds, 1990, 54). This is not what is being argued in this instance however, as it is felt that such an overall plan was unnecessary, and the Normans could not have known the geography of each region invaded well enough to carry out such a plan. Rather, what is being suggested here is that the Norman castle-building programme developed in an ad hoc fashion over the course of various conquests, but that the programme was ultimately successful because it was based upon a sound understanding of – and adherence to – the strategic and tactical principles of warfare.

The model proposed is that the Normans, and later Anglo-Normans, upon entering a region, would assess the lie of the land, in terms of its strategically and tactically significant locations, and would then select the best site, or sites, upon which to erect their castles to afford them control of those locations: and further, that the vast majority of castles were constructed at carefully chosen positions in the landscape in order to affect Norman control over key strategic elements, leading ultimately to Norman victory. This action, of carefully choosing sites upon which to erect castles, is in itself a form of strategy, and can be sensibly termed *The Stratagem of Optimum Site Selection*. The dictionary definition of 'stratagem' being 'a plan or scheme for deceiving an enemy or gaining an advantage' (*Chambers Etymological English Dictionary*, 1900).

THE STRATAGEM OF OPTIMUM SITE SELECTION

The concept of 'the stratagem of optimum site selection' clearly deserves a fuller explanation, and the best way to achieve this is to look at *why* the Normans constructed castles, pointing out in the examples given where such stratagems could have been, and often probably were, implemented. This will also help to clarify the strategist's approach to castle studies, by highlighting where strategic and tactical considerations could have influenced the Norman castle building programme.

In what can be termed the *Initial Conquest Period* – that is during the initial military invasion and conquest of a region – the Normans would have needed to gain effective control of, and mastery over, terrain, territory, lines of transport, communication and supply, and their potential adversaries the native population; and to those ends they constructed castles (4).

Terrain in this instance refers to small localised areas of land. In order to capture and secure terrain the Normans utilised castles as items of military hardware. In this capacity, the castle functioned primarily as a base from which to plan and launch attacks, as a place to muster troops, as a depot for supplies, and as a safe retreat in times of crisis. The term 'castle' derives from the Latin 'castellum', meaning 'little fort', a highly apt description here for the castle's functional role – but the castle was also a powerful psychological device. For troops venturing into hostile territory, the familiar context of the castle's defences would have provided a welcome sense of security. With the enemy and wild beasts separated from the troops by a ditch, rampart and palisade, the men could eat, wash, care for their equipment and mounts, and converse in a relaxed atmosphere (King, 1983, xxvi). This same sense of security would also allow them to sleep soundly at night, and so be fit for action or battle the following day. In addition, although castle building took a huge investment of effort, once constructed the castle became a labour-saving device, as it could be guarded with a minimum of men, allowing the remainder of the troops to rest and recuperate in relative safety (Luttwak, 1981, 56-7). A castle used in this way enabled a smaller force to hold its own against a potentially stronger aggressor, thereby allowing commanders to hold terrain in perhaps otherwise untenable locations. The stratagem of optimum site selection almost certainly came into play here when selecting and co-opting tactically significant, naturally defensible, sites which were readily adaptable to fortification, and which effected access to potable water supplies, construction materials, the surrounding countryside, and routes of communication and supply.

Territory in this instance refers to larger areas of land, such as counties. In order to capture and secure territory the Normans positioned castles at carefully selected, strategically significant, 'optimum sites' in the landscape. This afforded them control over the region's physical geography, naturally occurring resources and key strategic elements (such as rivers and roads). In this scenario the features of the landscape did not necessarily govern the locations chosen for castle

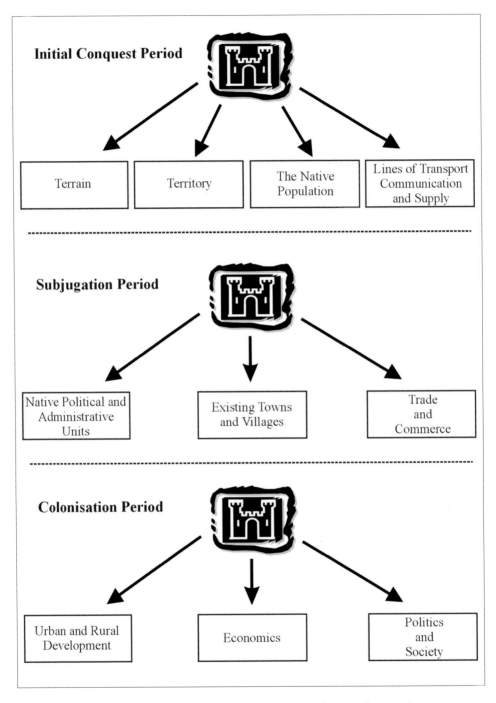

Initial Conquest Period

| Terrain | Territory | The Native Population | Lines of Transport Communication and Supply |

Subjugation Period

| Native Political and Administrative Units | Existing Towns and Villages | Trade and Commerce |

Colonisation Period

| Urban and Rural Development | Economics | Politics and Society |

4 Diagram showing the various factors controlled by castles at each stage of a campaign erection (i.e. 'physical determinism'), as conversely, through the process of the human selection of 'optimum sites', castles often dominated landscape features (Halsall, 2000). The erection of the fortifications often bestowed an additional bonus, as the naturally occurring physical obstacles of a region were further endowed with military strength. Thus, mountain ranges, ranges of hills, ridgeways and river courses all became physical barriers to movement with the addition of castles (Howard & Paret, 1984; Duffy, 1996).

Lines of transport, communication and supply are of utmost importance in every military campaign, and as such are considered separately here – although in reality they fall into the 'key strategic elements' category. In order to gain effective control of roads, navigable waterways and other lines of transport, communication and supply within a territory, the Normans positioned castles at carefully selected, strategically significant, 'optimum sites' in the landscape, close to, or overlooking such resources. This enabled the Normans to monitor and control all movement along the routes, effectively placing them firmly under their jurisdiction, whilst conversely guaranteeing their own lines of transport, communication and supply – the castles effectively forming useful 'way-stations' (King, 1983, xx-xxiii; Duffy, 1996, 22; Creighton, 2000, 105).

In the territories that they invaded, the Normans used castles to subdue and control the native populations in any number of ways. Two examples are given here. Firstly, to the network of castles initially constructed to win territory and lines of transport, communication and supply, the Normans added additional castles. This enlarged 'castle network' gave them spatial control, resulting in the suppression of the native population's freedom of movement (Orpen, 1906 & 1907; Graham, 1972, 1975 & 1980; McNeill, 2000, 67-8). The castles were again constructed at carefully selected, strategically significant, 'optimum sites' in the landscape, chosen for their ability to enable individual castles, or, better still, several castles acting in concert, to interpose a strategic barrier in the path of a potential aggressor. Secondly, in contrast to 'the active use of military force', castles may also have been utilised as 'images of force', for the purposes of diplomatic coercion. The Normans, through the erection of castles at carefully selected 'symbolically significant' sites, or through the construction of large, visually impressive castles, inflicted a form of psychological warfare upon the native populations, in an attempt to symbolically suppress them (King, 1983, xix).

Later, during what can be termed the *Subjugation Period* – in which the invader attempts to consolidate and secure his position, whilst forcibly suppressing and subjugating the invaded – the Normans would have needed to gain effective control of, and mastery over, pre-Norman political and administrative units (such as hundreds and estates), existing towns and villages, and trade and commerce; and to those ends they constructed castles (4).

5 The castle and borough founded at Stogursey, Somerset, quickly became the new 'central place' in the landscape, eclipsing the importance of the former royal estate at nearby Cannington. *S&N Buck, 1733*

In order to gain control of pre-Norman political and administrative units, the Normans, in some instances, appear to have divided up old estates and formed new ones from the constituent parts. At a central location inside each newly created estate, a castle was constructed. The site for the castle was no doubt chosen for its ability to allow the castle to develop as the caput of the newly created Norman lordship. A good example of this occurs in Somerset, where the castle and borough founded at Stogursey quickly replaced the importance and role of the former royal estate at nearby Cannington (Aston, 1986, 64) (5). The castle essentially became the new 'central place' in the landscape, the focus around which the entire local community was forced to revolve. In this way, old central places rapidly became redundant, the Normans effectively creating a new and highly symbolic 'social landscape'. Again, such tactics bear all the hallmarks of careful strategic planning.

Towns are an important consideration in any military campaign. As towns are heavily populated, they pose a potential threat to an invader, whilst their rich resources and provisions can be used to supply an army. The Normans gained control of towns in one of two ways. They either erected castles at carefully selected, tactically significant, 'optimum sites' inside existing town boundaries – as at Lincoln, York and Winchester – or they erected castles at carefully selected, strategically significant, 'optimum sites' in the countryside surrounding a town – good examples survive in Somerset, around Bath and Ilchester. The castles, in both instances, were constructed at locations that enabled the castle garrisons to easily observe, and thus govern, the actions and movements of the towns' inhabitants (Harvey, 1925; Pounds, 1990, 207-21; Creighton & Higham, 2003, 58-9). Villages posed a comparable threat, and were generally dealt with in a similar fashion; castles were erected close to, abutting, or even partly over them. At Montacute, Somerset, the castle overlooks the village from a distance of 91.44m (300ft) away (6). At Sheriff Hutton, North Yorkshire, the earlier castle abuts the east end of the village. At Rampton and Eaton Socon, Cambridgeshire, parts of the villages were obliterated during castle construction. Castles constructed in association with villages often became the new focal point in the settlement hierarchy, as the original village was frequently relegated in status to that of a suburb – a process that Lilley has termed 'suburbanization' (2002).

The two essential requirements of any evolving civilisation are said to be a sound material base and adequate security (Luttwak, 1981, 1). The challenge that the Normans faced in the territories that they occupied was to gain control of existing trade and commerce, and to encourage new trade, whilst continuing to protect themselves with adequate security; but without letting this security adversely affect the economy. This, it seems, was accomplished in two ways. Firstly, it is known that many of the existing castles became bastions for commercial enterprise, with fairs and markets often being forced to relocate to an area within the bounds of the castle – allowing the castle's owner to control and tax such enterprise (Austin, 1982, 293-300; Dyer, 1998, 80-3). Secondly, new castles were erected in areas of rich agricultural land, at carefully selected strategically significant 'optimum sites', where castle garrisons could oversee, and thereby control, the production and movement of produce and goods. Many such castles were constructed close to the river and road networks used in the transportation process. Castles thus enabled the Normans to capitalise upon the economic wealth present within their newly won territories, and such sites often developed into 'New Towns' (Beresford, 1967).

By the time of what can be termed the *Colonisation Period* – in which the invader settles down, assumes control, and establishes a new home for himself – the Normans, through their castle building programme, had already effectively

6 As this old photograph shows, the village of Montacute, Somerset, is completely dominated by the motte and bailey castle that sits atop the conical hill in the distance

gained control of, and mastery over, urban and rural development, economics, politics and society (4).

From the late eleventh century onwards, urban development and urban castles rapidly became symbiotically related. Purpose built 'New Towns' or 'Boroughs' were constructed adjacent to the existing castles, and large numbers of the population moved into them (Pounds, 1990, 216-21; Rowley, 1999, 94-7). Good examples of castles and new towns that functioned as complementary units can be seen at Kidwelly in Carmarthenshire, Plympton in Devon, Tickhill in South Yorkshire, and Warkworth in Northumberland (7). Some towns, such as Bridgnorth in Shropshire, Richmond in North Yorkshire and Trowbridge in Wiltshire, grew up inside castle precincts, while others, such as Corfe in Dorset, developed around the existing market place (Creighton & Higham, 2003, 60). The urban centres offered a greater degree of personal freedom for the individual, along with the prospect of economic enterprise, whilst conversely providing an income for the lord through burgage rents and market tolls. The borough, or new town, relied on the might of the lordly castle which overshadowed it for its protection and survival, whilst rural development came to depend heavily upon the castles already located amongst the small dispersed rural settlements. Such castles effectively became the 'machinery of manorial complexes', protecting, monitoring, and governing the welfare, enterprise, and subsequent growth of the local farming communities.

Castles, now firmly established as permanent centres of governance, also became centres for the regulation of economic factors. From the safety of his castle, the Norman lord oversaw the production, distribution and consumption of wealth, and could influence the fortunes of the local economy, which would, in turn, affect the national economy (Britnell, 1978; Coulson, 2003; Liddiard, 2003).

The castle, by design the most striking feature in the medieval landscape, eventually became the focal point around which the whole of society was forced to revolve. The population, through fear, necessity or ambition, came to rely heavily upon the feudal lord in his castle, especially when it came to matters of protection, political governance, employment, the continuation of trade, commercial enterprise and administration.

It has often been argued that the control of roads, tracks, passes, rivers or fords, via castles, was, in reality, fairly ineffective, as the highly mobile armies of the Middle Ages could easily circumnavigate a castle's position (King, 1983, xxi; Pounds, 1990, 54; Creighton & Higham, 2003, 26). Those with a tendency to evaluate defensive systems in absolute terms fail, however, to fully appreciate the military *raison d'être* of strategically positioned castles. If a defence can be penetrated it is said to be 'useless', and only an impenetrable defence is conceded

7 The medieval 'New Town' of Warkworth, Northumberland, is located entirely within a loop of the River Coquet, the castle blocking the only dry approach. In a mutually beneficial relationship, the castle afforded protection to the town, whilst, through rents and tolls, the town provided an income for the lord. *Photograph: Crown Copyright, NMR, English Heritage*

to be of value. Such an appraisal is highly misleading, as its equivalent for offence would be to regard as useless any offensive system that could not prevail against all forms of resistance, under all circumstances (Luttwak, 1976, 61). Defensive systems should instead be evaluated in relative terms.

The vast majority of Norman castles were erected in 'occupied territory'. The threat, therefore, was predominantly 'internal'. With castles dominating the landscape, and castle garrisons monitoring the systems of transport, communication and supply, it would have been virtually impossible to raise an army against the Normans from within. If, on the other hand, an invading army managed to by-pass a chain or network of castles, once past, they could be cut-off by the castle garrisons and their messengers would not be able to get back or their supplies forward. The foremost strategic function of a castle was, however, to hold territory. In a report to Edward III on the defence of the Channel Islands, that dates from around 1330, John des Roches' states that 'The castles (Mont Orgueil and Castle Cornet) must never be unprepared, for should the isles be taken by overwhelming numbers, you can always get back your land by means of your castles' (King, 1983, xxii). The true strategic value of castles lay in the hold that they exerted over the landscape, and 'no area could be permanently occupied as long as its castles held out' (Beeler, 1971, 148).

Strategic and tactical considerations were undeniably of vital importance in the military campaigns of the Normans, especially when it is remembered that they were conquerors who were seeking to gain control of territories that they had taken by force. Logically, these same considerations would, in the first instance, have compelled the Normans to build castles and, in the second instance, guided their castle-building programme – especially in terms of the sites selected. The above examples appear to support this argument, as they suggest that the Normans carefully singled out the best sites upon which to erect their castles (strategy of optimum site selection) with tactical or strategic objectives in mind. Tactically sited, a castle was highly defensible. Strategically sited, castles could dominate terrain and afford their builders control of political and administrative units (such as hundreds and estates) and towns and villages. Whilst in concert with others, castles could dominate territory and lines of transport, communication and supply, and, in addition, suppress the native population's freedom of movement. Moreover, as long as their castles held out, the Normans were secure in the territories that they had occupied. Thus, through diligent planning and castle building, the Normans were able to gain the upper hand militarily, which lead ultimately to their victory.

In order to validate the *strategic approach* to castle studies then, it is obviously essential to prove that the suggestions, theories and ideas embodied in the above examples are, in fact, historical realities. To that end, in this book, an in-depth examination of the strategies and tactics that underpinned Norman castle warfare will be carried out, and examples that provide tangible proof of their existence and usage in the field will be given.

THE NORMANS AND THEIR CASTLES

To gain an appreciation of the place, nature and true value of the castle in the Norman period, it is necessary to examine both the context in which castles were constructed, and the society that constructed them. For, as has been so correctly stated, if we are to ever understand the true significance of castles, 'castles must not be studied in an historical vacuum' (Coulson, 2003, Intro.) or in isolation from those who built them (Johnson, 2002).

For centuries all those that have studied, or encountered their achievements, or the fragmentary remains of their culture, have held the Normans in the highest regard. They earned the respect of their contemporaries through their conquests and their martial prowess, and came to be admired by generations of historians for the ways in which they adopted, and often improved upon, the cultures and civilisations of the peoples they came to dominate. Historically, during the tenth century, they succeeded in acquiring the civilisation of the Franks, without losing any of their martial virtues, and knights from Normandy were abroad conquering lands in Italy – capturing Aversa in 1030, and Apulia and Calabria in 1059 – and most of Sicily by 1072. They launched expeditions against the mighty

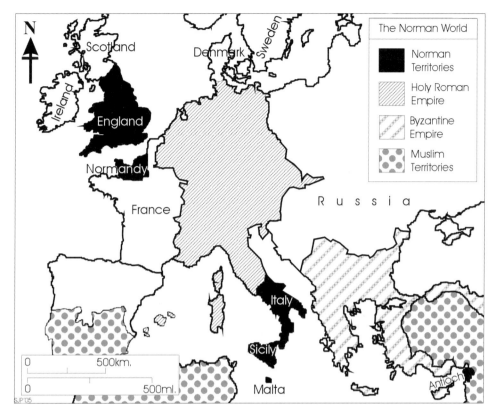

The Norman World

- Norman Territories
- Holy Roman Empire
- Byzantine Empire
- Muslim Territories

8 The Norman Conquests of the eleventh century

Byzantine Empire on the mainland of Greece, between 1082 and 1084, and played a major role in the first crusade – annexing the principality of Antioch in 1098 (*8*). By the second half of the eleventh century, the Normans were at the forefront of European civilisation, famous for their monasteries, their schools and their architecture whilst still unsurpassed in the arts of war. The achievement that most people associate with the Normans though is the Conquest of England, beginning with the Battle of Hastings in 1066. The Conquest was quick, complete and permanent, and as a result the Normans became some of the richest people in Europe and their Duke was made a King.

When the Normans first arrived in England few of them could have had an intimate knowledge of the country that they had invaded, and although many of William's men had already successfully campaigned under his command, all were probably well aware that the Conquest was somewhat of a gamble. The success of the whole campaign hinged upon the winning of time, so that a strategy of settlement might develop. To that end, one of William's earliest tasks in England was to provide a secure political and military base. Domesday Book, a land register compiled for administrative purposes in the aftermath of the Conquest, provides a detailed picture of most of England in 1066 and 1085. From it, for the first time, the size of England's population can be estimated. It stood at around two million. As many as one tenth of these people lived in towns, but the majority lived in the rural landscape, with 13,418 named *vills* and 268,984 recorded individuals (Welch, 1994, 120). William's army, on the other hand, numbered somewhere in the region of 7000 men, many of whom were mercenaries, to be paid off and sent home at the earliest opportunity. If William was not planning to rely solely upon strength of numbers to conquer England, subjugate the populace, and take permanent control, then it follows that he had to have devised a strategy for the rapid appropriation of territory, a means of securing quickly and permanently the many areas of land captured. William's strategy was simple, but brilliant. He instigated the development and use of the most formidable tool of conquest, the castle. The Normans introduced into England a new type of fortification, which they called *castella*, and these structures firmly anchored their Conquest to English soil. By 1086, there were at least 50 castles in England for which documentation survives, and many more were constructed without record.

The Normans were by no means the first people to build castles, as castles first appeared on the European mainland in the late ninth and early tenth centuries following the collapse of the empire of Charlemagne, and the resulting collapse of the authority of central government in western Europe. But the Normans were the first to appreciate their full potential, and constructed them in enormous numbers in England to secure their grip on the land, and ensure the continued subjection of the people they had conquered.

The most acclaimed statement on Norman castle building for the period following the Conquest was written *c*.1125 by Orderic Vitalis; a Benedictine monk from the abbey of St-Evroult, southern Normandy. In his *Historia Ecclesiastica* Orderic states, 'to meet the danger the king [William] rode to all parts of the kingdom and fortified strategic sites against enemy attacks, and the English, though brave and warlike, have very few of those fortifications which the French call castles [*castella*] in their land. It was this which made their resistance to the conquerors so feeble' (Chibnall, 1969, 218-19). Liddiard has however recently cautioned against the use of this statement as a prop to support the *militaristic approach* to castles. He believes that Orderic's work may have drawn upon the lost conclusion of William of Poitiers' *Gesta Guillelmi*, and the comment should therefore 'be seen within the context of a piece of writing with the chief aim being the eulogising of William the Conqueror, and [is] not necessarily an accurate picture of events … [or] a commentary on nation-wide castle building in the period 1066-1070' (2000i, 4). Most historians conversely believe that Orderic's work comprises the most accurate account of Norman history however; whilst Orderic himself is viewed as the most remarkable of the chroniclers (Chibnall, 2003, 119-32; Albu, 2001, 180-213). Bates states, 'The range of his interests and the vividness with which he presented his material are truly remarkable ... [as] is his desire to tell an accurate and unbiased story' (2001, 29).

Orderic, when writing, may have drawn upon William of Poitiers' work, but this is not necessarily a bad thing. William of Poiters, a knight turned cleric who became one of Duke William's chaplains, was well informed, well connected, and very well educated, and his *Gesta Guillelmi ducis Normannorum et regis Anglorum* (History of William the Conqueror) is a first-hand account of events in England between 1066 and 1071, as seen through Norman eyes. If Orderic's *Historia Ecclesiastica* does indeed preserve material from this manuscript, that would otherwise have been lost, we should firstly applaud him for his foresight, and secondly remember that his work, although perhaps partially copied, still contains a wealth of information on the Norman world.

It is evident from his writing that Orderic was acutely aware of the impact of the castle on daily life, and he describes the use, role and changing fortunes of many such fortifications. He discusses castles as instruments of public order, as refuges for brigands, as homes, and as administrative centres. Most importantly though, Orderic wrote most extensively on the use of the castle in war. He emphasises the castle's importance in both attack and defence, and he makes it clear that castle building was perceived as a normal process in conquest and the suppression of rebellion.

It is unnecessary to rely exclusively upon Orderic's work to establish the castle's primarily military role however, as other contemporary sources also place emphasis on the castle's martial characteristics. The *Anglo-Saxon Chronicle* entry for 1066, states 'Bishop Odo and Earl William stayed behind and built castles far and wide throughout this country, and distressed the wretched folk, and always after that it grew much worse'; whilst an entry in the *Laud Chronicle* for 1086, states 'he caused castles to be built, which were a sore burden to the poor, a hard man was the king'. It is in the work of William of Poiters himself that the most informative statement on the Norman use of castles is to be found though. William of Poiters states 'the King pursued his march into diverse parts of the kingdom, everywhere making dispositions as he pleased ... he placed capable castellans with ample forces of horse and foot in his castles, men brought over from France in whose loyalty no less than competence he could trust. He gave them rich fiefs in return for which they willingly endured hardship and danger' (Brown, 1984, 39). In other words, in response to a significant and very real threat, the Normans, at strategic locations across the kingdom, erected castles and furnished them with well-equipped and highly mobile garrisons, who were placed under the command of trusted and capable war veterans.

That the Normans built castles as part of their Conquest is widely accepted. What is often forgotten however, is the nature of conquest itself. Conquest is the act of acquiring land, people or goods through *force of arms*, and is usually a dangerous, brutal and bloody undertaking. As Pounds states:

> It is important to realise that the England of the years following the Conquest was not a peaceful realm, where the rule of law was enforced and the King's writ ran everywhere. It was, by contrast, violent, bloody and disorderly … we must think … of fearful men seeking to control a rebellious land under the threat of hostile invasion, men ruthless and rapacious, driven by repressions and barbarous cruelties, conquerors in many ways inferior to the conquered. (1990, 10)

During the Harrying of the North, for instance, the Normans carried out a scorched earth policy, and William slaughtered anyone who stood in his path, regardless of age or sex. Crops and livestock were burnt and villages destroyed. Contemporary accounts estimating that between 10,000 and 20,000 people starved to death as a direct result of the ensuing famine (Cruickshank, 2001, 18). As the Conqueror himself said, 'I have persecuted [England's] … native inhabitants beyond all reason. Whether gentle or simple, I have cruelly oppressed them; many I unjustly disinherited; innumerable multitudes … perished through me by famine or the sword' (Chibnall, 1969, 286). These were then 'barbaric times', in which military considerations were of paramount importance, and during which the castle undoubtedly played a key role as a decisive tool for both oppression and defence. In light of the above, it can be argued that castles are best understood as primarily martial structures, which were utilised in large numbers by the Normans during their conquests, in order to afford them a means of protection, to subjugate their enemies, gain control of resources and ensure that any land captured could be held indefinitely. In the words of Brown, 'the castle's role in war was the most obvious, the most romantic and basically the most important' (1976, 172).

2

Military considerations

Military action is important to the nation – it is the ground of death and life, the path of survival and destruction, so it is imperative to examine it.

Sun Tzu, *The Art of War*, fifth century BC
(Cleary, 1998, 41)

In order to state with any degree of certainty that this or that castle was tactically or strategically positioned in the landscape it is necessary to establish a set of criteria, against which the positions of castles can be tested and understood. In previous castle studies, the rationale behind the choice of castle site was judged to be either unrecoverable, due to a distinct lack of sources, or military, a classification usually based upon twentieth-century tactical principles. Twentieth-century tactical principles, in isolation, cannot be relied upon to produce a valid and acceptable framework for study however, as they are basically far too modern in origin. Rather, it is necessary to look deeper into the past and draw upon the expertise of some of history's greatest military thinkers. Historic military manuals, texts and treatises all contain numerous strategic and tactical principles, which are known to have formerly affected decisions taken in regard to the siting of fortifications in the landscape. A study of these age-old principles affords the production of a workable, practical framework.

The most logical starting point in the search for relevant strategic and tactical principles, which have previously guided engineers to suitable sites for fortifications, would be to examine any surviving Norman military treatises that document the act of castle building. Unfortunately, despite the fact that Norman chroniclers produced vast amounts of literature upon their culture and achievements, it appears that no such military treatises were ever penned. Almost every nation martial enough to have warranted study by military historians produced military manuals; especially those associated with the term 'Empire'. These manuals document the military thinking, technical abilities, popular strategies, tactical ideologies and theories of the day. For instance, the 'Warring States' period in ancient China (400-200 BC) produced Sun Tzu's *The Art of War*, the Greek 'Empire' spawned Xenophon's *Cyropaedia* (430-355 BC), the Roman Empire generated Frontinus' *Strategemata* (late first century AD), whilst the Byzantine Empire inspired Emperor Maurice's *Strategikon* (AD 582-602). Either the Norman 'Empire' failed to produce any such texts or, if such texts were produced, they have not survived the ravages of time.

To those unfamiliar with military history and theory, it would appear that the lack of Norman military treatises would pose an insurmountable obstacle to progress – the Norman Empire being an enigma in *not* having any military manuals to claim as its own. Fortunately, however, as 'the laws of strategy are eternal', they have changed very little down through the ages. Although the technology of warfare has progressively evolved throughout history, its underlying principles remain largely unchanged and, as such, much of the experience of the past is still relevant today. Indeed, a comparison of numerous military manuals quickly demonstrates that there is hardly any perceptible change in the tactics and strategies presented, until the adoption of powered flight by the military around 1916. Subsequently, all of the surviving historic military treatises can be said to contain sets of 'enduring laws', which are relevant in discussions on warfare, no matter what the period in question. Therefore, although the Normans themselves never produced any kind of military manual, their engineers, when selecting sites in the landscape for the erection of their castles, must have adhered to lines of reasoning similar to those presented in the various military manuals dating from other periods. Assuming of course that their castles were intended to fulfil military functions.

In this chapter, a selection of military manuals from a wide range of historic periods will be examined in an effort to establish the strategic and tactical criteria applicable to the siting of military fortifications in the landscape. Principles, in fact, that any military engineer would consider when selecting a site upon which to erect a fortification. As these criteria tend to remain eerily consistent throughout the ages they provide the perfect framework for assessing the locations selected for Norman castles. It is worth mentioning here that no study of this sort has previously been attempted, because until very recently the perception of the castle as a military edifice remained largely unchallenged, so such a study was unwarranted.

THE SOURCES

In order to establish an accurate and comprehensive set of criteria, upon which to base the framework for study, a wide range of specialist military texts were consulted. The vast majority of these texts were examined in the library of The College of Royal Engineers, Chatham, whilst copies of others were obtained from the library of The Royal Military Academy, Sandhurst. A short summary of the career of each author consulted is given below, along with any relevant dates, the title of the author's work, and a bibliographical reference to a translation (if applicable). The summaries have been included to enable the reader establish a picture of the time in which each text was written and thereby place each work into its proper historical context.

China

Sun Tzu (first half of the fifth century BC)
The Art of War (translated by Cleary, 1998)

Sun Tzu was a mysterious warrior-philosopher who wrote *The Art of War* during the so-called 'Warring States' period in ancient China, which lasted from the fifth to the third century BC. This was a time of protracted disintegration of the Chou (Zhou) dynasty, which had been founded over 500 years earlier by the political sages who wrote the *I Ching*. 'The collapse of the ancient order was marked by destabilisation of interstate relationships and interminable warfare among aspirants to hegemony in the midst of ever-shifting alliance and opposition' (Cleary, 1998, 27). Sun Tzu's work was and remains highly influential, being translated many times over. The translation by Cleary is based upon a standard collection of commentaries by 11 interpreters, some of whom will be mentioned independently. These include Cao Cao (155-200 BC), Li Quan (Tang Dynasty, AD 618-906), Jia Lin (Tang Dynasty, AD 618-906), Du You (AD 735-812), Du Mu (AD 803-852), Zhang Yu (Sung Dynasty, AD 960-1278), Ho Yanxi (Sung Dynasty), Mei Yaochen (AD 1002-1060), and Wang Xi (Sung Dynasty, early twelfth century AD).

The Roman Empire

Sextus Julius Frontinus (late first century AD)
Strategemata (translated by Bennett & McElwain, 1925)

Frontinus was probably born in AD 35, and was almost certainly educated at the Alexandrian School of Mathematics. He was three times elected consul, first in AD 73 or 74, again in AD 98 and a third time in AD 100. After his first incumbency of this office, he was dispatched to Britain to act as provincial governor where he succeeded in subduing the Silures, a powerful and warlike tribe from Wales. He returned to Rome in AD 78, and probably wrote his treatise on the art of war at this time. He is best known for his *De Aquis*, a work on the aqueducts of Rome – holding the office of 'Water Commissioner' himself for a time.

Hyginus Gromaticus (second century AD)
De Munitionibus Castrorum (translated into French by Lenoir, 1979)

'Hyginus' is a Latinised version of a Greek name, and 'Gromaticus' means 'the surveyor'. Three authors are known under this name: Hyginus 'the first' wrote *De Limitibus* and *De Condicionibus Agrorum*, at the time of Trajan; Hyginus 'the second' wrote *De Constituendis*; and Hyginus 'the third' was the author of *De Munitionibus Castrorum*. The third Hyginus hardly ever uses the third person, so the work appears to be a compilation, and although no sources are ever mentioned, it may derive from *Polybus*.

Flavius Renatus Vegetius (late fourth century AD)
Epitoma rei Militaris (translated by Clark & Phillips, 1985) and *De re Militari* (edited by Lester, 1988)

Vegetius was a high ranking officer of state, serving under the Christian Emperor Theodosius I 'the Great' (AD 379-395) at the end of the fourth century AD. He was probably born in the eastern part of the empire, or in one of the border provinces (Pannonia of Illyria) and, as he himself states, 'journeyed widely throughout the empire' (Shrader, 1979, 280). He held office as *comes sacrarum largitionum*, or imperial finance minister, his duties rapidly acquainting him with various military matters, including recruiting, equipment and training. *Epitoma rei Militaris* became one of the most influential treatise in the western world from Roman times to the nineteenth century.

France and Sweden

Count Maurice de Saxe (1696-1750)
Reveries of Memoirs upon the Art of War (first published in 1732; published in English in 1787)

Saxe was a French Commander-in-Chief during the War of Austrian Succession. In 1732, allegedly over the course of 13 feverish nights, he wrote his book *Reveries of Memoirs upon the Art of War*. The book quickly gained renown in military circles, and in many ways epitomises eighteenth-century warfare.

Sébastien le Prestre de Vauban (1633-1707)
The Attack and Defence of Places (first published in 1737; in Duffy, 1996)

Vauban was a French soldier, a military engineer and an expert on fortification and siegecraft. He spent his life alternately building fortifications for Louis XIV, or conducting sieges in the king's name. His book (in two volumes) was a model of its kind and a starting point for the 'enlightenment of military thought'.

Philippe Maigret (*c.*1680-1740)
A Treatise on the Safety and Maintenance of States, by the Means of Fortresses (first published in 1727; in Duffy, 1996)

Maigret was the principal engineer to Charles XII of Sweden on his fatal Norwegian campaign in 1718. Consequently, Maigret ended his military career in the comparatively lowly position of resident engineer at Péronne. However, he is credited with drawing up one of the most complete and convincing statements on the purposes of fortification.

The Prussian Empire

Carl von Clausewitz (1780-1831)
On War (first published in 1832; translated by Howard & Paret, 1984)

Clausewitz is credited as being one of the greatest western military thinkers of all time. His early military career was somewhat unfortunate however, as he was taken prisoner by the French for his part in the disastrous campaign of 1806. Following his incarceration he was appointed to the General Staff in Berlin, where he helped Scharnhorst, his revered master, rebuild the Prussian army. During this period he developed his talents as a theoretician and by 1811 he was instructing the Crown Prince (later, Friedrich Wilhelm IV) on war. In 1812, he found himself fighting for Napoleon in Russia. During the campaigns of 1813-5 he was active as a staff officer, and in 1817 he assumed administrative control of the Berlin Staff College, or *Kreigsakademie*. Rising to the rank of general, it was there that he produced his great work *On War*.

Captain Reinhold Wagner (*c*.1830-90)
Principles of Fortification (first published in 1870; revised, enlarged and republished 1872; translated by Shaw & Pilkington, 1876)

Wagner rose to the rank of Captain in the Prussian Engineers. His book, *Principles of Fortification*, contains information on tactical fortification as taught in the German Military Schools after the experiences of war in 1870-71. The philosophical spirit in which the book is written, the careful manner in which strategy and tactics are considered in relation to fortification, and the way in which the various relationships existing between defensive works and the troops who use them is covered, gives it a particularly high value.

England

Manual of Field Fortification – Military Sketching and Reconnaissance (MFF) (British Army Publications, 1871)

Field Service Pocket Book (*FSPB*) (His Majesty's Stationary Office, 1914)

These training manuals were produced by, and for, the British Army. Both were designed to act as 'handy and concise books of reference for use on active service, at manoeuvres, or on instructional exercise' (from the introductions of both manuals). the *Field Service Pocket Book* is still actively studied, and its contents utilised, by soldiers in the modern British Army.

MILITARY MANUALS, TEXTS AND TREATISES

On the strategic and tactical importance of terrain
All of the works consulted, without exception, agreed upon one vitally important issue – that the possession of certain types or areas of terrain are essential if the war is to be won. Zhang Yu states that 'advantage in a military operation is [gained by] getting help from the land' (Cleary, 1998, 133), and Wang Xi echoes this statement with the words 'you cannot overlook the question of the advantages of terrain' (ibid., 147). Vegetius, on the same topic, writes that 'the nature of the ground is often more of consequence than courage' (Clark & Phillips, 1985, 112). The most complete statement on the subject comes, however, from Wagner, who writes, 'the importance of a place, whether it be for a particular theatre of war, or for the whole country, may be so great that possibly the result of the

campaign, or even that of the whole war, may depend on its possession' (Shaw & Pilkington, 1872, 5).

As mentioned in chapter one, in any given expanse of land there are two types of location that are important from the military's perspective, 'tactically significant locations' and 'strategically significant locations'. Dealing firstly with tactically significant locations, 'a defensive position will normally include a number of localities of special tactical importance. The efforts of the defender must be directed in the first instance to occupying and securing these points, so that they may form pivots upon which to hinge the defence of the remainder of the position. The defences at these localities should be arranged so that they give each other mutual support' (*FSPB*, 1914, 88). Furthermore, 'in the presence of an enemy, tactical considerations, e.g. favourable ground for defence in case of attack, concealment, facilities for protection, and economy in outposts are of the first importance' (ibid., 43). Tactically significant locations are topographically or geologically strong points in the landscape, such as elevated, naturally defended, rocky outcrops, where, due to the nature of the terrain, a weaker force can hold its own against a potentially stronger aggressor.

Clausewitz, on strategically significant locations, writes 'rivers which traverse the country, mountain ranges, and other natural obstacles will serve [well] as … [strategic] defensive lines' (Howard & Paret, 1984, 402). Wagner takes this idea a step further, stating that 'those places which are [the] most important strategically, because of their inherent advantages [must be] secured as "fortified places" … The permanent fortifications [at these] special points may be either fortresses or forts … Securing the possession of such points [is] indispensable for carrying on the war' (Shaw & Pilkington, 1872, 6). Strategically significant locations are points in the landscape which, due to their geographical positions, afford control of 'key strategic elements' – such as mountain passes, defiles, rivers, fords and road networks. The ancient Chinese termed such locations 'grounds of contention':

A ground of inevitable contention is any natural barricade or strategic pass.

(Du Mu; Cleary, 1998, 149)

A ground of contention is ground from which a few could overcome the many. The weak could strike at the powerful.

(Cao Cao; ibid, 87)

It is not advantageous to attack an enemy on a ground of contention; what is advantageous is to get there first.

(Cao Cao; ibid., 151)

The modern British Army tends to refer to these locations as pivotal or nodal points, and 'the result of the campaign, or even that of the whole war, may depend on … [their] possession' (Wagner; Shaw & Pilkington, 1872, 5). As 'the army that finds its ground flourishes, and the army that loses its ground perishes. Here the ground means a place of strategic importance' (Li Quan; Cleary, 1998, 90).

In the eleventh century, the Normans, through conquest, gained lands in Italy, Sicily, Malta, the British Isles, Turkey and Syria (principality of Antioch) (8), adding, in the twelfth century, lands in Ireland and a large section of the North African coast; all the while holding Normandy despite the heated political climate. Given the success of their military campaigns, it is logical to assume that the Normans fully understood the importance of gaining control of the above types or areas of terrain and key military positions: the possession of which was essential if the war was to be won and occupied lands held. The Normans, in order to hold and defend these critical areas and positions, presumably erected castles on them.

On the importance of 'Defended Places'

The value of 'defended places' is made clear by Wagner, who states, 'however small the [strategically significant] number of places may be, the possession of which … [is] essential from the … point of view for carrying on a war successfully; to hold them by troops alone would not be admissible, because it would entail too much division and frittering away of the army' (Shaw & Pilkington, 1872, 3). Strategically significant locations must be secured with the minimum number of troops, so as to leave as many men as possible available for active operations in the field. 'The means by which this can be affected is via the construction of fortifications' (ibid.). The Normans, it seems, were well aware of this point, and constructed their fortifications to great effect: 'to meet the danger the king [William] rode to all parts of the kingdom and fortified strategic sites against enemy attacks, and the English, though brave and warlike, have very few of those fortifications which the French call castles [castella] in their land. It was this which made their resistance to the conquerors so feeble' (Orderic Vitalis; Chibnall, 1969, 218-19).

Once fortifications have been constructed, many advantages are gained. The fortifications, in addition to securing the strategically significant positions, serve 'as entrenched camps, or war-harbours, for the safe sheltering and formation of active forces ... as arsenals, manufactories of war materials, or war dockyards ... as magazines and depots, or marine depots, for the safe storage of war materials ... as points governing the use of communications ... as barriers ... [and] as bridge-heads, as well as securing ... passage in the presence of an enemies' army' (Wagner; Shaw & Pilkington, 1872, 3). Moreover, they 'cover a country, and subject an enemy to the necessity of attacking them, before he can penetrate further' (Saxe, 1787, 84). Sun Tzu writes that 'the rule of military operations is not to count on opponents not coming, but to rely on having ways of dealing with them; not to count on opponents not attacking, but to rely on having what cannot be attacked. The *I Ching* says, 'if you take on too much without a solid foundation you will eventually be drained leaving you with embarrassment and bad luck' (Cleary, 1998, 23). There can be little doubt that with a chain of fortresses constructed at strategically significant locations across a landscape, in combination with the additional benefits that each fortress confers, any army would have 'strong enough foundations' from which to confront their enemy.

Finally here, Vegetius reminds us of the disadvantages of not having such fortifications:

> This valuable art is now entirely lost, for it is long since any of our camps have been fortified either with trenches or palisades. By this neglect our forces have been often surprised, day and night, by the enemy's cavalry and have suffered severe losses. The importance of this custom appears not only from the danger to which our troops are perpetually exposed who camp without such precautions. But also, from the distressful situation of an army, which after receiving a check in the field, finds itself without a retreat to which to retire, and consequently at the mercy of the enemy.

(Clark & Phillips, 1985, 27-9)

On the siting of 'Defended Places' – generally
Tactical considerations
All of the manuals and treatises consulted contained a good deal of general advice on the selection of sites for the erection of fortifications. In terms of the most suitable tactical locations, the *Manual of Field Fortification* states, 'a good military position ... should command a view of the movements of an assailant ... [and] should not be commanded in front or on the flanks by any higher ground' (1871, 148-9). To which can be added, 'a fortress ... must offer a full view of the countryside' (Clausewitz; Howard & Paret,

1984, 398) (*colour plate 1*). Higher ground is preferable as 'a flat country will not furnish so many good positions as a hilly one' (MFF, 1871, 149). In situations where hills are lacking however, good positions may still be found, 'particularly where natural obstacles exist, such as villages, woods, marshes, hollow roads, and enclosures' (ibid.).

In the manuals, in discussions on the suitability of tactical locations for the erection of fortifications, rivers also feature. Vegetius states, 'all cities and castles must be warded, either by kind, or by the craft of man's hand, or by both ... By kind, the city may be set on a high hill, or on a slope, or in a place where can be seen the ebb and flow all about, or in a mire, or where a fresh river may run all about – all these are wards of a kind' (Clark & Phillips, 1985, 160) (*9*). But 'in a country where rivers are wanting, there are nevertheless other situations to be found, so strongly fortified by nature, that it is next to an impossibility to invest them; and which being only accessible in one place; may at a small expense be rendered in a manner impregnable, for in general, I look upon the works of mother nature to be infinitely stronger than those of art: what reason therefore can we plausibly assign for neglecting to make proper use of them?' (Saxe, 1787, 85).

In addition to stating where fortifications should be constructed, the military manuals also stress the locations and conditions that should be avoided. Hyginus states that 'unfavourable positions ... should be avoided at all costs ... [so that there is neither] a ravine, or valleys, by which one could approach the camp without being seen' (Lenoir, 1979, 22). Whilst Vegetius suggests that 'an army should not encamp in summer near bad water, or far from good, nor in winter in a situation without plenty of forage and wood. The camp should not be liable to sudden inundations. The avenues of approach should not be too steep and narrow lest, if vested, the troops should find it difficult to retreat; nor should it be commanded by any eminences from which it may be harmed by the enemies' weapons' (Clark & Phillips, 1985, 82).

The manuals also consider access to 'local amenities' – important to the well-being of one's own troops – and the selection of sites to aid with the general health of the army. The *Field Service Pocket Book* states that 'the site [for a camp] should be dry and on grass if possible ... avoid[ing] steep slopes, large woods with undergrowth, low meadows, the bottom of narrow valleys and newly turned soil; as all are apt to be unhealthy'. Further adding that, 'ravines and watercourses are dangerous sites' (1914, 44). During the seventeenth and eighteenth centuries, the healthiness of a site was one of the most important considerations for determining its suitability for a fortress. Pestilential and swampy sites were notorious for the rate at which they killed off their garrisons and the prospecting engineers tried to shun districts where they noticed that the inhabitants wore yellow or greyish complexions and died young, and where the livers of animals were pallid and

9 The ideal site for a medieval castle has been described as 'an isolated rocky hillock, 100-300m diameter, sited alongside a navigable river'. The site chosen for Chepstow Castle, on the lower reaches of the River Wye, Monmouthshire, matches this description perfectly. The castle was supplied with provisions from the port at Bristol

corrupt (Duffy, 1996, 30). Vegetius also makes this point, stating that 'a camp, especially in the neighbourhood of an enemy, must be chosen with great care. Its situation should be topographically strong, and there should be plenty of wood, forage and water. If the army is to continue in it any considerable time, attention must also be had to the sanitation of the place' (Clark & Phillips, 1985, 27-9).

It is known from the accounts of William of Poitiers that the Norman army, whilst encamped at Dover, succumbed to an outbreak of dysentery. If William the Conqueror's troops had paid more heed to the sanitation within their camp, they would have benefited greatly, as William of Poitiers states that a number of Normans actually died from the disease. Orderic Vitalis notes that the outbreak was so severe that many men suffered from its effects for the rest of their natural lives (Chibnall, 1969-80, ii, 180). For large armies billeted in confined quarters, disease was a constant threat. In addition to coping with the problems of human sanitation, there were hundreds of tons of horse manure to deal with, which posed a serious risk to health.

The most complete statement on the selection of sites for the construction of fortifications comes from the *Manual of Field Fortification*, which succinctly covers all of the above points:

> A camp should be well supplied with water within a convenient distance and secure from interruption by the enemy. It should also afford the means of fuel, so as to prevent the necessity of its being brought from a distance. The neighbourhood of a camp should furnish as many supplies as possible for the support of the troops. A camp should be situated upon dry, healthy ground, and should of course be accessible from the road. (1871, 152)

Strategic considerations

Several of the manuals and treatises consulted, contained advice on the strategic positioning of fortifications in the landscape. Clausewitz emerges as the leading authority on this subject: 'Having examined the roles of fortresses, let us now consider their location. At first glance, the matter looks extremely complicated, given the wide variety of determinants, every one of which is modified by its locality. But ... it will be clear that all requirements can be satisfied simultaneously if all the largest and wealthiest towns in the area of the operational theatre are fortified – those that lie on the main highways linking the two countries, and especially those located at ports and gulfs, on major rivers and in mountains. Major towns and major roads always go together, and both have a natural affinity for the great rivers and the seacoast. These four requirements will, therefore, coexist easily and cause no conflicts' (Howard & Paret, 1984, 400). Similarly, Wagner suggests that: 'the choice of place to be fortified must be made, like most other engineering questions, with reference to the 'best possible use of the ground' (*terrainbenutzung*). The most secure basis for the choice rests therefore on the geographical configuration of the country: The great centres of habitation, cities, and the systems of communication between them (*10*). Both are means by which war can be carried on, and their possession is consequently essential in a greater or lesser degree' (Shaw & Pilkington, 1872, 2).

On the siting of 'Defended Places' specifically

So far, this chapter has considered what can be termed 'general criteria' for the siting of fortifications in the landscape. The sources covering such diverse topics as the advantages or dangers inherent in certain types of terrain, the significance of centres of habitation, the importance of routes of communication and supply, the value of health and sanitation, and the necessity to ensure access to supplies of potable water, fuel and sustenance. However, the military manuals, texts and

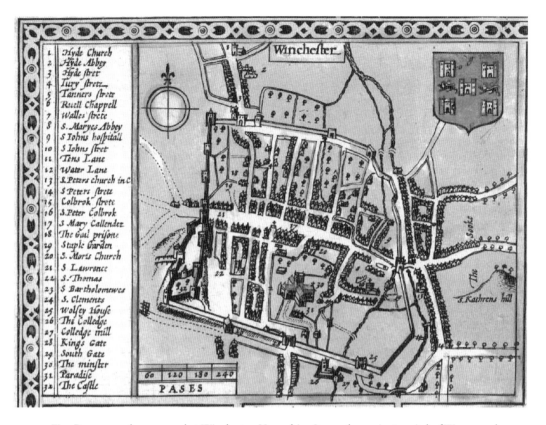

1	Hyde Church
2	Hyde Abbey
3	Hyde ftret
4	Iury ftret
5	Tanners ftret
6	Ruell Chappell
7	Walles ftrete
8	S. Maryes Abbey
9	S Iohns hofpitall
10	S Iohns ftret
11	Tens Lane
12	Water Lane
13	S.Peters church in C
14	S Peters ftret
15	Colbrok ftret
16	S.Peter Colbrok
17	S Mary Callender
18	The Gail prifone
19	Staple Garden
20	S. Morts Church
21	S Lawrence
22	S. Thomas
23	S Bartholomewes
24	S. Clementes
25	Wolfey Houfe
26	The Colledge
27	Colledge mill
28	Kings Gate
29	South Gate
30	The minfter
31	Paradife
32	The Caftle

10 Five Roman roads converged at Winchester, Hampshire. It was the ancient capital of Wessex, and, after London, the most important urban centre in southern England. Unsurprisingly, as John Speed's early seventeenth-century plan shows, the Normans erected a castle in the south-west corner of the Roman city walls

treatises also contain numerous examples of 'specific criteria', which provide a much fuller picture of what prospecting engineers were looking for when considering the suitability of a site for fortification. In many cases these 'specifics' relate directly to points already discussed, but offer a much deeper insight. They are therefore of great value and usefulness, and, as such, they are examined in detail here.

On higher ground

Ordinarily, an army likes high places and dislikes low ground, values light and despises darkness.

Sun Tzu; Cleary, 1998, 132

> In Cappadocia, Gnaeus Pompey chose a lofty sight for his camp. As a result the
> elevation so assisted the outset of his troops that he easily overcame Mithridates by
> the sheer weight of his assault [In 66 BC].

> Frontinus; Bennett & McElwain, 1925, 98-101

Sun Tzu states that 'the rule for military operations is not to face a high hill, and not to oppose those with their backs to a hill' (Cleary, 1988, 122). Sentiments echoed both by Du Mu, who writes 'when opponents are on high ground you shouldn't attack upward, and when they are charging downward you shouldn't oppose them', and Mei Yaochen, who writes 'it is convenient for your fighters if they are heading downhill' (ibid., 122 & 132). Frontinus records an event in 47 BC that highlights the advantages of higher ground: 'when Gaius Caesar was about to contend with Pharnaces, son of Mithridates, he drew up his line of battle on a hill. This move made victory easy for him. Since the darts hurled from higher ground against the barbarians charging from below, straight-away put them to flight' (Bennett & McElwain, 1925, 101). Vegetius covers a similar point when discussing camps: 'a camp, especially in the neighbourhood of the enemy, must be chosen with great care … the camp must not be commanded by any higher ground from whence it might be annoyed by the enemy' (Clark & Phillips, 1985, 29). Lieut. Henry Yule, in a book entitled *Fortifications for Officers of the Army and Students of Military History*, published in 1851, summarises the advantages of higher ground, 'the strength [of a military position on a hill] is attained in proportion as: 1st – The defenders position is protected from the observation and missiles of his assailant; 2nd – The assailants access to the position is difficult and obstructed; 3rd – The defenders position affords him every advantage in the observation of his assailant, and in the direction of his troops and weapons against him' (1851, 2).

The manuals also warn against allowing the enemy access to higher ground. Frontinus records that 'Lysimachus, one of the heirs to Alexander's power, having determined on one occasion to pitch his camp on a high hill, was conducted by the inadvertence of his men to a lower one. Fearing that the enemy would attack from above, he dug a triple line of trenches and encircled these with a rampart. Then running a single trench all around the tents, he thus fortified the entire camp. [Later] Having thus shut off the advance of the enemy, he filled in the ditches with earth and leaves and made his way across them to higher ground [323-281 BC]' (Bennett & McElwain, 1925, 40-3). Hyginus issues a similar warning:

> Unfavourable positions … should be avoided at all costs; lest any mountain should
> dominate the camp which the enemy could use to attack from on high, or see from

11 At 404m A.O.D., Twyn-Bar-Lwm is Monmouthshire's most elevated Norman castle. Due to its position, it was well protected, and on a clear day a beacon fire lit on Twyn-Bar-Lwm would be visible not only in the lowland Newport lordship, but could be seen from the English side of the Bristol Channel

a distance what is going on in the camp (Lenoir, 1979, 22). Thus, 'when selecting the site [for a camp] the necessity for occupying the chief points from which snipers can fire into the camp and for forming a defensive perimeter around it should be borne in mind.'

(FSPB, 1914, 44)

Higher ground is then the location of choice for the construction of military fortifications, as it affords natural protection, offers many advantages in conflict, increases the effectiveness of missile weapons, permits the ready observation of an advancing enemy, and allows for inter-visibility between fortifications. In addition, a fortification set on higher ground visually dominates the locale, which sends out a powerful psychological message to any would-be enemy (*11*). This was a stratagem not unknown to the Romans, as Hyginus states, 'As far as the choice of terrain is concerned, the first choice goes to a camp on a gentle slope towards a height; positioned so that the *portus decumanus* [gate] is placed at the highest point, so that the camp dominates the country' (Lenoir, 1979, 22).

Furthermore, 'high grounds are exhilarating, so the people are comfortable … Low ground is damp, which promotes illness, and makes it hard to fight' (Mei Yaochen; Cleary, 1988, 132).

On mountains and passes

Whenever you station an army to observe an opponent, cut off the mountains and stay by the valleys.

Sun Tzu; Cleary, 1998, 130

If … you hold an essential pass, you can make it impossible for opponents to get to you. As it is said: 'One cat at the hole, and ten-thousand mice dare not come out; one tiger in the valley, and ten-thousand deer cannot pass through'.

Du You; Cleary, 1998, 101

Mountain and valley passes have always played an important role in warfare. Frontinus makes their virtue very clear: 'Against a countless horde of Persians, three hundred Spartans seized and held the pass of Thermopylae which was capable of admitting only a like number of hand to hand opponents. In consequence, the Spartans became numerically equal to the barbarians, so far as the opportunity for fighting was concerned, and being superior to them in valour, slew large numbers of them. Nor would they have been overcome, had not the enemy been led around to the rear by the traitor Ephialtes the Trachinian, and thus been enabled to overwhelm them [in 480 BC]' (Bennett & McElwain, 1925, 104-5). Therefore, 'if the location and direction of a chain of mountains make it a suitable line of defence, it will be necessary to block its roads and passes with minor forts especially built for that purpose' (Clausewitz; Howard & Paret, 1984, 400). As, 'in mountainous areas … fortresses … can open or close whole networks of roads that converge upon them, and thereby dominate the whole area to which the roads give access. Thus, they serve as a veritable buttress for the whole defensive system' (ibid., 399). Furthermore, 'well sited fortresses [can] endow natural obstacles with additional strength. In mountain valleys a single fortress can hermetically seal the only path of access, and seal the pasturelands from enemy foragers (Vauban & Maigret; Duffy, 1996, 22).

Fortifications were also often built on the enemies' side of the mountains: 'For many powers, the maintenance of a fortress on the far, or enemy, side of a mountain chain was the only means of keeping a military presence in a distant

12 Situated above the Ebbw river valley, which forms a natural north–south pass, St Illtyd's Motte, Monmouthshire, acted in concert with Twyn-Bar-Lwm Castle (*11*) to protect the lowland lordship of Newport from invasion by the Welsh of the uplands

province … The defence of such isolated strategic footholds demanded a great deal of garrisons … [and] for that reason … one or more major strong-points … [were often planted on one's] own side of the watershed, to act as a rearward barrier and a base of operations' (Vauban & Maigret; Duffy, 1996, 23). Clausewitz cautions against this practice however, arguing that 'a fortress on the enemy's side of a mountain range is poorly placed because it is difficult to relieve. [Whereas] … if it is located on the near side, the enemy will be hard put to besiege it, for the mountains will obstruct his lines of communication' (Howard & Paret, 1984, 403).

The mountain or valley pass is the first example of a specific strategic location, or 'pivotal point', that can be included in the list of criteria for the siting of fortifications in the landscape. In other words, where there is a pass, we should also expect to find a castle. In a passive or defensive role, a castle constructed in or adjacent to a pass effectively granted its garrison control of the route-way. From the safety of the castle, the garrison, utilising missile fire, could easily deny an enemy passage through the pass; or, filled with the sense of security that the castle provided, the garrison could confidently sally forth to physically block an enemy's way. In an active or aggressive role, a castle constructed at the enemy's end of the pass enabled its garrison to observe the movements and actions of potential assailants, and, if necessary, launch attacks against them. The castle builders, in both instances, gained an extra defensive advantage, as the naturally occurring physical obstacles were further endowed with additional strength. Interesting also is the idea that two fortifications should be built: with one castle on the 'home side' and the other on the 'away side', the pair could act in concert for mutual support (*12*).

On supplies and supply routes

> If a position is to be occupied for any length of time it should, of course, afford the means of supplying water, fuel and provisions.

Manual of Field Fortification, 1871, 150

The need for adequate supplies in wartime is patently obvious. It is essential to ensure that your own army is well provided for, whilst conversely ensuring that your enemy receives no provisions whatsoever. One of the first rules of war is that your provisions should be taken from the enemy, either directly, or from his land or people. This is especially true in an invasion situation, as the 'transportation of provisions itself consumes twenty times the amount transported' and 'if the terrain is rugged, it takes more than that' (Cao Cao & Zhang Yu; Cleary, 1998, 62). Cutting off an enemy's supplies is absolutely essential in every military campaign, as it will weaken his army whilst strengthening your own. Wang Xi states that you should 'first occupy a position of advantage, and then cut off their supply routes by special strike forces, and they will do as you plan' (Cleary, 1998, 152). Zhang Yu takes a similar line, stating 'a skilful martialist ruins plans, spoils relations, cuts supplies, or blocks the way, and hence can overcome people without fighting' (ibid., 73). Cao Cao and Li Quan add, 'cut off their supply routes, guard their return routes, and attack their civilian leadership' (ibid., 105).

Enemy supply routes can be severed very effectively via the construction of fortifications adjacent to roads and rivers. The erection of such fortifications, on the one hand, guarantees that food, water, materials, and the munitions of war can be safely transported to your own troops, whilst, on the other hand, they serve to ensure that the enemy receives no supplies at all. 'If [however] there are many roads in an area, and there is free travel that cannot be cut off, this is what is called "trafficked ground"' (Zhang Yu; Cleary, 1998, 149). 'Trafficked ground should not be cut off, so that the roads may be used advantageously as supply routes' (Wang Xi; ibid., 151). The Chinese writers' references to 'trafficked ground' is especially important here, as they imply that the optimum locations available for taking control of existing road networks are to be found in areas where many roads converge.

On lines of communication

If there is a division among the ranks of the enemy, so that there is no coherent chain of command, then they will fall apart by themselves.

Du Mu; Cleary, 1998, 74

All ranks are responsible for doing everything in their power to keep the means of communication intact.

Field Service Pocket Book, 1914, 59

Good routes of communication are imperative if military operations are to succeed. Traditionally, fortifications have been used to great effect in maintaining or severing such routes. Clausewitz on this subject writes, '[With] fortresses block[ing] the roads, and also, in most cases, the rivers on which they are located. It is not so easy as one might think to find a serviceable detour to bypass the fortress … If the terrain is at all difficult, the slightest deviation from the road can often cause delays worth a whole days march. This can be of great importance if the road is used repeatedly. The extent to which a blockage of river traffic will affect operations is clear enough … A fortress itself must block one of the main roads and must effectively cover an expanse of 15 to 20 miles' (Howard & Paret, 1984, 395-7). 'A well-stocked stronghold … effectively shorten[ing] … [the] lines of communication' (Vauban & Maigret; Duffy, 1996, 22).

All of the manuals and treatises consulted contained advice on the selection of sites suitable for fortification, where the fortification was intended to safeguard or disrupt a communications route. Hyginus suggests that 'one must chiefly look out for a road to pass along the side of the camp' (Lenoir, 1979, 22). The *Field Service Pocket Book* concurs, stating that 'depots should be near good roads' (1914, 43). The Chinese writers suggest the use of 'intersecting ground'. 'Intersecting ground means the intersections of main arteries linking together numerous highway systems: occupy this ground, and the people will have to go with you. So if you get it you are secure, if you lose it you are in peril' (Ho Yanxi; Cleary, 1998, 149). The most complete statement on the subject comes, however, from Wagner, who states:

for freedom of communication … points in a system of communications are essential, the occupation of which would influence their use for considerable distances ... [and] the most important of these, are those which pass the greatest natural obstacles (rivers, swamps, mountains) ... towards which the greatest number of communications converge, as generally happens at important river crossings, whence as a rule, roads branch off into important towns. These latter are therefore also essential as junctions of communications, either for concentration of bodies of troops, or for bases of operations for armies, enabling them to act in several different directions. (Shaw & Pilkington, 1872, 2-3)

A fortification constructed adjacent to a single road or river was clearly useful, as it enabled its garrison to control a small stretch of the overall communications route. A fortification constructed at the point where a great number of communication routes converged was better still, as its garrison was able to act in several different directions simultaneously and thereby gain considerable influence over a number of communications routes. But a combination of the two, where castles acted in concert, was the most useful, as the garrisons gained total control of the communications routes; effectively meaning that an enemy had little chance of organising or mobilising an opposing force or of launching a surprise attack.

On rivers

Rivers are of the utmost importance in war, as they have a great influence upon military operations.

Manual of Field Fortification, 1871, 143

Fortifications constructed close to rivers offer many strategic advantages. Clausewitz makes this point when he states, 'Nowhere can a fortress serve so many purposes or play so many parts as when it is located on a great river. Here it can assure a safe crossing at any time, prevent the enemy from crossing within a radius of several miles, command river traffic, shelter ships, close roads and bridges, and make it possible to defend the river indirectly – this is, by holding a position on the enemy's bank (9). It is clear that this versatile influence greatly facilitates the defence of a river and must rank as one of the essential elements in warfare' (Howard & Paret, 1984, 399). Similarly, Vauban and Maigret suggest that 'a skilful defender could derive much profit by combining the peculiar properties of fortresses and river barriers. He could secure the best bridges and fords and intercept the roads which followed the bank, thereby endangering the flank and rear of the enemy who was rash enough to have passed the river at some other place' (Vauban & Maigret; Duffy, 1996, 25). Also, 'on rivers, or narrow straits, a fortress could deny a useful crossing to the enemy, and compel water-borne foreign trade to stop and pay dues' (ibid., 22).

Rivers can also aid in the defence of the fortification itself, as Saxe explains:

> we shall find it most prudent and advantageous to have them [fortresses] erected at the junction of two rivers, because in such situations the enemy will be obliged to divide his army into three distinct bodies, before he can be able to invest them, one of which may be repulsed and discomforted, before it can be succoured by the others: two sides of your fortress will likewise always remain open, till the blockade is complete, which cannot possibly be done in a single day; neither can the necessary communication between the divisions of his army be kept up, without the use of three bridges, which will be exposed to the hazard of those sudden storms and inundations which usually happen in campaign season. Moreover, in being thus master of the rivers, one thereby obtains command of the whole country: one may divert their course, if occasion shall require it; may be readily furnished with supplies of provisions; may have magazines formed, and ammunition, or other sorts of military stores transported to you with ease. (1787, 84)

Despite the apparent usefulness of rivers to military engineers, there are also inherent dangers associated with large bodies of water. As these dangers can prove costly or fatal if overlooked, they are considered by the manuals. Jia Lin says that, 'In a river basin your armies can be flooded out, and poison can be put into the streams'; to which Du Mu adds, 'that your boats should not be moored downstream, lest the enemy ride the current right over you' (Cleary, 1998, 131). 'Unfavourable positions … should [therefore] be avoided at all costs … [so] that there is not … a torrent nearby, the sudden swell of which could flood and annihilate the camp' (Hyginus; Lenoir, 1979, 22). Frontinus provides an example of such an event: 'Lucius Metellus, when fighting in Hither Spain, diverted the course of a river and directed it from a higher level against the camp of an enemy, which was located on low ground. Then when the enemy were in panic from the sudden flood he had them slain by men whom he had stationed in ambush for this very purpose [143-2 BC]' (Bennett & McElwain, 1925, 226-7). Clearly then, no fortification should be constructed within a river basin, or upon the very low ground adjacent to a river, lest it be flooded out – either intentionally, at the hands of an enemy, or through natural circumstance. In addition, a fortification should not be constructed in a downstream location, if the stream is intended to serve as a source of drinking water for the garrison, as an enemy could easily poison the watercourse. Tactically, the most suitable position for the construction of a fortification associated with a river was undoubtedly on an area of higher ground close to, and overlooking, the river, and upstream if possible.

Rivers form natural barriers, which, in combination with well-placed fortresses, can be used to great effect to hinder an enemy. If fortresses are poorly positioned, however, the river can have an adverse effect. 'A good military position should ... be perfectly free and uninterrupted by ravines, marshes or other impassable obstacles [such as rivers] which would prevent the free circulation of troops from one part of the position to the other ... because ... in that case the enemy might attack and beat one part of the defensive force before the other part could come to its assistance' (*MFF*, 1871, 148-50). Therefore, even though 'a fortress will be twice as useful if it lies on the coast, on a stream or great river, or in the mountains ... if a fortress cannot be located directly on a river, it is better not to place it in the immediate vicinity ... otherwise the river will cut through and interfere with its sphere of influence' (Clausewitz; Howard & Paret, 1984, 403).

With careful planning, the river and fortress combination clearly offers many benefits. Because of the inherent tactical advantages that rivers afford (i.e. they are difficult to cross) fortresses are able to repel enemy crossings with considerable ease – the river essentially forming a strategic barrier. The river provides a means of transport, communication and supply. Bridges, fords and other river crossings are secured, and control is gained over the roads which follow the river banks. Furthermore, all waterborne traffic can be monitored and, if necessary, intercepted.

On potable water supplies

> As the health of the force depends largely on the purity of the water provided, everything possible must be done to ensure an ample supply of pure drinking water.
>
> *Field Service Pocket Book*, 1914, 52

> When Marius was fighting against the Cimbrians and Teutons his engineers on one occasion had heedlessly chosen such a site for camp that the barbarians controlled the water supply. In response to the soldier's demands for water, Marius pointed his finger toward the enemy and said: 'there is where you must get it.' Thus inspired, the Romans straightaway drove the barbarians from the place [102 BC].
>
> Frontinus; Bennett & McElwain, 1925, 174-5

An old Tamil proverb states, If you have planted a tree you must water it too. In other words, if men are stationed in one location for any length of time, then

13 Strategically positioned between the Rivers Parrett and Brue, at the western end of the Polden Hills, Somerset, the Downend Motte and Bailey was supplied with its own source of potable water. A spring erupts at the foot of the motte. *Photograph: M. Aston*

they must be amply supplied with water. The *Field Service Pocket Book* states that 'a daily average of 1 gallon per man is sufficient for drinking and cooking purposes. A horse, bullock or mule drinks about 1½ gallons at a time. In standing camps, an average allowance of 5 gallons should be given for a man and 10 gallons for a horse.... Each mule or ox drinks 6 to 8 gallons. Each sheep or pig 6 to 8 pints. These are minimum quantities' (1914, 52). Relating this information to a castle garrison, if a castle is manned by 20 men, the size of an average garrison based upon the dimensions of many motte and baileys, and each man has a horse, then the castle must be supplied with approximately 300 gallons of water a day, which is a surprisingly large amount. It is often argued that potable water is more of a tactical consideration, but once the vast quantity of water involved is extrapolated, it is obvious that it must instead have formed one of the most important strategic considerations – 'he who controls the water wins the war'. Water is a resource which has been much underrated in the past when looking at the locations selected for castle erection. As Hyginus states, 'the camp ... should have, on one side of it, or the other, a river, or a spring' (Lenoir, 1979, 22) (*13*).

On woodland and marsh

> Large impenetrable forests and marshes should be avoided; for, although they make
> life difficult for any besieging enemy, they tend to interfere adversely with the
> fortresses sphere of influence.

> Clausewitz; Howard & Paret, 1984, 403

Woodland, despite being an invaluable commodity, providing timber for building
and wood for fuel, can conversely prove dangerous to any army that encamps,
or builds, too close to the trees. Hyginus states that 'unfavourable positions ...
should be avoided at all costs; [so that] there is not a nearby forest which could
hide the enemy' (Lenoir, 1979, 22). Furthermore, in addition to an approaching
enemy being obscured from vision, they could set the woods alight. Frontinus
records such an event: 'When the camp of the Volscians had been pitched near
bushes and woods, Camillus set fire to everything which could carry the flames,
once started, up to the very fortifications. In this way he deprived the enemy of
their camp [in 389 BC]' (Bennett & McElwain, 1925, 326-7).

Marshy and swampy areas frequently offer a means of protection (*14*), but there
are several major drawbacks in their usage as positions for fortifications. Swamp
fortresses enjoy the advantage that they can be attacked only at a few points and
the strength of the marsh fortress increases with every yard that the besieger
has to cross. However, a swamp fortress suffers from the disadvantage of being
unsuited to sorties, and is generally easier for the enemy to blockade. Whilst it
may be completely deprived of its watery protection by summer drought or
winter frost, and the worst feature of all is that such areas often harbour disease
(Vauban & Maigret; Duffy, 1996, 23).

On the military importance of towns and fortified places
Towns are the hubs of communications networks; Vauban and Maigret both
agreeing that 'major towns ... [are] nearly always important military objects, if only
because they ... [are] sited almost by definition on nodal points of communication'
(Vauban & Maigret; Duffy, 1996, 27). In addition, towns also contain supplies for
one's own troops: 'We suggest that fortresses constitute ... protection for large and
prosperous towns ... because large and prosperous towns, especially commercial
ones, are an army's natural sources of supply, which is therefore, immediately
affected by their possession or loss' (Clausewitz; Howard & Paret, 1984, 395).
Thus, 'it is well worth while to fortify rich cities ... since their wealth had to
be protected against the enemy, and because these places nearly always stood on
important avenues of access' (Vauban & Maigret; Duffy, 1996, 22).

14 Fenny Castle, between Glastonbury and Wells on the Somerset Levels, relied upon the surrounding marshland to bolster its defences

In friendly territory, 'the large towns of a district offer the greatest assistance to an army, both giving shelter to the troops, and safe storage for their provisions and war materials, partly by themselves, partly by the military establishments of all sorts found in them. Their possession is therefore more or less essential for the organisation of armies, as well as for their administration and maintenance' (Wagner; Shaw & Pilkington, 1872, 2). In enemy territory, towns must be invested with a fortress and closely guarded, lest the citizens rise up against the invaders. Towns are a major strategic consideration in any military campaign.

On the distances between fortifications

In their treatises, Saxe, Vauban, Maigret, Clausewitz and Wagner all speculate upon the proper positioning of fortresses in relation to one another. Their arguments are not discussed here however, as they are, for the most part, unhelpful, rambling and inconclusive discourses, that are overly concerned with 'patterns' of fortresses (e.g. 'should fortresses be distributed evenly, or in groups'; 'is a geometric pattern better than a line of fortresses'; 'should fortresses be placed in one or several rows'; or 'should they be arranged as on a checkerboard'). Importantly though, all of the sources consulted agreed that fortresses should not be positioned more than half a day's journey apart – by horse. The *Field Service Pocket Book* contains a table of 'rates of movement in the field' (1914, 37). For a mounted rider the distances given are: Walking – yards in a minute = 117; miles per hour – including short halts = 3½; minutes required to traverse 1 mile = 15. Trotting – yards in a minute = 235; miles per hour – including short halts = 7; minutes required to traverse 1 mile = 8. It therefore follows that the appropriate distance separating fortresses lays somewhere between 16 and 30 miles apart (based upon a ride lasting four hours).

It is often stated that the Normans owed a great deal of their success to their use of cavalry. Based upon the above figures, it is evident that a mounted garrison, stationed at a castle, could easily dominate a relatively large area of the adjacent landscape. If the castle was the instrument that enabled the Normans to consolidate their grip on England, the task was unquestionably aided by the use of the horse. The horse transformed the castle from a means of passive defence into an instrument for controlling the surrounding countryside.

On medieval artillery

In discussions on castle defence, much is often made of the ranges that medieval weaponry and artillery could shoot or hurl projectiles. These discussions become all the more relevant when considering whether or not a castle is located a safe distance away from nearby 'higher ground'; as an enemy can use higher ground to his advantage, showering projectiles down upon the castle. The distances that medieval weaponry and artillery could shoot or hurl projectiles are often wildly exaggerated however, and based upon these inflated figures, castles situated close to higher ground are often claimed to be indefensible. It is therefore desirable to establish a reasonable approximation of the range achievable by medieval weaponry and artillery. Before tackling this subject however, it is necessary to draw attention to three important points: the word 'artillery' was originally used to cover all types of war gear; the term 'fire' should never be used in relation to early projectile weapons, as 'fire' applies only to later gunpowder weapons – thus you 'fire a gun, but shoot an arrow'; it is traditional and correct to give the ranges of projectile weapons in yards.

Historically, the exact distances that medieval weaponry and artillery could shoot or hurl projectiles are unrecorded, but later medieval military manuals offer some clues, and modern reconstructions of medieval weaponry affords some approximations of possible ranges. Beginning with hand-held weapons, medieval warfare was largely dominated by the use of the shortbow, the longbow and the crossbow. The shortbow could achieve a range of approximately 200 yards (Oakeshott, 1960, 293-4), the longbow approximately 250 yards, and the crossbow, in the eleventh and twelfth centuries, approximately 100 yards – rising to 220 yards in the thirteenth century with improvements in design (Bradbury, 1997, 146-50).

Prior to the introduction of the cannon, artillery pieces could be divided into three basic categories: those that worked by tension, by torsion or by counterpoise. The most basic tension-based engine was the 'springal'. The springal relied for its propulsion on the tension of a bent beam of wood. There were two types of springal; in both the beam was winched back and then quickly released, but in one the tip of the beam struck the rear end of a missile set on a platform before it, the impact discharging the missile, whilst in the other a cup was fixed at the end of the beam to hold a projectile. Reconstructions have shown that these could shoot approximately 200 yards (Liddiard, 2000, 7). A more accurate tension-based engine was the 'ballista', which was essentially a giant crossbow, the propulsion being provided by a large horizontal bow. The ballista was used to pick off individual defenders on the ramparts, and had an effective range of approximately 165 yards (ibid., 6-7).

The most widely used torsion-based engine was the 'mangonel', which was basically the earliest form of catapult. The mangonel relied for its propulsion on the torsion of a tightly twisted rope. A skein was set horizontally and a stout beam inserted into the middle before twisting the skein and so forcing the beam up vertically against a padded crossbar. The end of the beam was furnished with a cup, and the whole forced down by a winch. The mangonel could achieve distances of approximately 180 yards (Gravett, 2000, 49). However, the most feared siege engine before the advent of cannon was the trebuchet, which relied on counterpoise for propulsion. There were two types of trebuchet, the earliest form was the traction trebuchet, and the later the counterweight trebuchet. The traction trebuchet consisted of a long beam (or set of beams bound together) pivoted between a pair of uprights. Ropes were attached to one end of the beam and a sling to the other. A stone was placed in the sling and a group of men hauled on the ropes and so pivoted the beam. At the critical moment the sling opened and released its missile. The counterweight trebuchet, which appeared in the Mediterranean in the late twelfth century, worked on the same principal except that a box filled with earth, sand, stones or lead was substituted for the muscle power of the men.

Reconstructions have shown that a traction trebuchet could hurl a 15lb missile over 190 yards with the accuracy of a modern mortar (Liddiard, 2000, 7), whilst the larger counterweight trebuchet could hurl stone balls weighing about 100-200lb about 300 yards (Gravett, 2000, 51). There is some debate over the date of the introduction of the trebuchet into western Europe. Gravett suggests that it appeared in the west in the early twelfth century (2000, 49), but Liddiard has demonstrated that dates anywhere between the ninth and the thirteenth centuries are commonly given (2000, 7). The most detailed surveys show however, that while there is clear evidence for trebuchets being used in the thirteenth century, there is little firm evidence to confirm when they first made their appearance in European siege warfare (Hill, 1973, 99-144; Gillmoor, 1981, 1-8).

The average maximum effective range (or mean distance) of all these weapons then, is around 200 yards. Thus, in later chapters, if it is argued that a castle is ideally 'tactically located', one of the considerations that will have taken into account is the fact that the castle is not overlooked by higher ground within 200 yards. Conversely, if it is argued that a castle is compromised militarily by virtue of the fact that it is overlooked by higher ground, this refers to a situation where an enemy would have gained a significant advantage had they placed their siege weapons within 200 yards of the castle.

THE CRITERIA ESTABLISHED

Part three of the *Manual of Field Fortification* deals specifically with the issue of military reconnaissance. The sub-headings of the section clearly illustrate the factors that any engineer, from any age, involved in the construction of fortifications, would have been forced to consider. These are 'Topographical Reconnaissances', 'Reconnaissance of a Road', 'of a River', 'of a Wood', 'of a Position' and 'of a Camping Ground'. The section also covers such diverse topics as the nature of defiles, supplies, water, towns and villages, the population, the enemy, bridges, fords and marshes, and the extent to which rivers freeze – the majority of which have been outlined above. In chapter one, there was a discussion on *why* the Normans constructed castles; if the points raised during that discussion are combined with the above criteria – which in effect details *where* castles were (or should have been) constructed – the considerations applied to the satisfactory construction of a fortress, or castle, may be summarised as follows:

Strategic considerations
'A reason, or reasons, for a fortress, or castle, to exist', which may include one or more of the following:

a. to control and protect a border, or border area;
b. to command lines of communication and supply, particularly river crossings, roads, defiles or passes;
c. to dominate a locality or region of perceived value – such as a commercial centre, rich agricultural land, or a resource-producing area;
d. to provide a secure base from which field armies may operate, or a place of refuge in times of adversity.

Tactical considerations

a. Defensibility: this is enhanced by the presence of natural obstacles, such as steep slopes, cliffs, rivers, marshes or shorelines. Where such features are not available, they may be provided by the construction of ditches or moats.

b. Security: the site should not be overlooked, particularly by higher ground, or be within the range of currently available missile weapons and artillery, and ideally should provide good visibility, hence a common preference for dominating areas of higher ground.

c. Accessibility: while it is essential to exclude hostile forces, it is also important to ensure relatively easy access for friendly troops and supplies, and, in case of emergency, an escape route. Ready access to potable water is also vitally important.

d. Practicality: there are a number of practical considerations that any military engineer needs to take into account when constructing fortifications. These include ready access to suitable construction materials, firm foundations upon which to build, a reliable water supply and the selection of a well-drained, 'healthy', site.

The fundamental requirements (including strategic purpose) and practical essentials of fortress, or castle, construction are all, to a greater or lesser extent, constrained by local and/or regional geological factors and topographical features (after Halsall, 2000, 3–5).

The above considerations therefore, constitute the strategic and tactical principles that can be looked for, or contemplated, when seeking to determine whether or not a castle has been situated in the landscape with military objectives in mind. In the past, similar considerations have been applied haphazardly to the study of castles, but these considerations were generally drawn from unsuitable modern military sources, instead of from the works of some of history's greatest military strategists and tacticians. Having thus established a practical workable framework, against which the positions of castles in the landscape can be tested and understood, these considerations can now be systematically applied to the castles in the chosen study areas.

3

Early castles in Somerset

Neither rashly nor unjustly, but after taking council and guided by equity I have crossed the sea to enter this land, of which my lord and kinsman King Edward made me his heir, on account of the great honours and numerous benefits which I and my ancestors conferred on him and his brothers and their men; also because, of all those belonging to his line, he believed me to be the most worthy and the most able to help him while he lived or to govern the kingdom after his death.

Duke William of Normandy, in a letter written
to Harold Godwinson, 13 October 1066
(William of Poitiers; Chibnall & Davis, 1998, 121)

TOWARDS THE CONSOLIDATION OF NORMAN CONTROL

Following Norman victory at Hastings on 14 October 1066, and a circuitous march through the counties of Surrey, Hampshire and Berkshire that resulted in the fall of London, William was crowned king of England in Westminster Abbey on Christmas Day 1066. After his coronation William remained in England until March 1067, during which time, according to William of Poitiers, he received English submissions, made laws – including confirming to London the laws which it had enjoyed under Edward the Confessor – meted out justice and ensured that a firm discipline was maintained within the ranks of his large army. He forbade his men to drink in taverns, in order to prevent the kind of troubles that would follow, whilst ordering them to keep within the law, and to refrain from killing and rape; setting up severe punishments for those who disobeyed. There can be little doubt that during this time his thoughts must also have

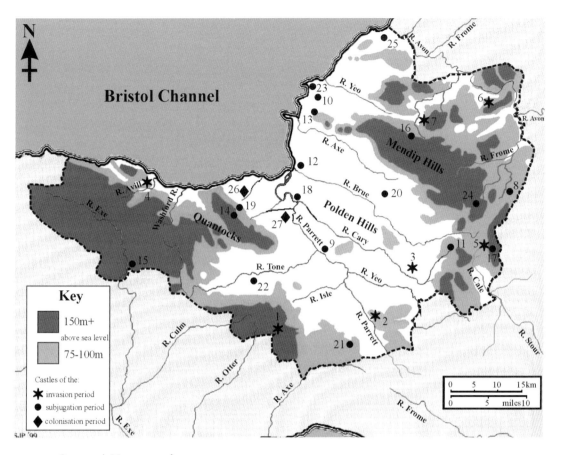

15 Somerset's Norman castles

turned to the rest of the country, and what was to be done there in order to consolidate his grip on the entire kingdom.

It is often stated that when William left for Normandy – to embark upon his triumphal procession – he placed England into the care of his most trusted lieutenants. The closest of these were his two half-brothers, Bishop Odo of Bayeux and Robert the Count of Mortain, and beyond them, Roger of Montgomery and William fitz Osbern. William delegated control of the south-east of the country to Bishop Odo, who was duly installed in Dover Castle and made earl of Kent, and power over all of the land to the north of the Thames was given to William fitz Osbern, the new earl of Hereford, who was installed in a newly constructed castle at Winchester (*10*). The sources remain silent about the fate of the south-west of England at this time. Following this, the next topic generally discussed in the multitude of histories that cover the Norman Conquest, is the uprising in Herefordshire. During the uprising, in the summer of 1067, the men of Kent, having found themselves an unlikely ally in Count Eustace of Boulogne, laid siege to Dover castle. Count Eustace apparently supported their cause because he felt that he had been ill-rewarded for his services at Hastings. There is then a jump in all of the sources, both contemporary and modern, into early 1068. William, shortly after his return from Normandy, marched into the south-west of England, into the furthest reaches of Wessex, to lay siege to the city of Exeter, where Harold's mother had taken up refuge.

Currently then, our knowledge of the initial phase of the Norman Conquest is, at best, fragmentary. There is a finite amount of contemporary source material documenting the period, whilst later accounts and narratives are of limited use, as they tend to rely too heavily upon the information contained in William of Poitiers' incomplete *Gesta Guillelmi*, and upon other contemporary, but largely inadequate, Norman sources. Thus, the written word can only go so far in telling the story of the Norman Conquest of England. A story which, at present, is missing an entire chapter; namely The Norman Campaign in the West Country. Fortunately, however, there is another avenue open for study. An examination of the surviving physical remains of the Conquest (i.e. Norman castles), via archaeology, can greatly enrich our understanding of the Norman invasion and Conquest of England.

SOMERSET'S NORMAN CASTLES

Between 1067 and 1202, the Normans built 27 castles in Somerset. Figure *15* shows the locations of those castles and the period in which each was founded. The numbers allocated to the castles on figure *15* appear again in the first column of figure *16*, which lists the castle's name, the type of castle first constructed at the site, the likely owner or builder of the castle, the probable date for the first phase of castle construction and any later or associated features. The identities of the castle builders and the dates of initial castle foundation derive from entries in Domesday Book, Pipe and Court Rolls, the works of contemporary writers such as William of Poiters, Orderic Vitalis and William of Malmesbury, and from data contained in various archaeological excavation reports.

No.	Name	Earliest phase	Probable builder	Probable date	Later or associated features
I	Castle Neroche	Large enclosure castle	Robert, Count of Mortain	1067–1069	Motte and bailey, shell keep
2	Montacute Castle	Very large motte and bailey	Robert, Count of Mortain	1067–1069	Banks, berms and rubble

3	Wimble Toot	Small motte	Two porters of Montacute	1067–1069	Possible tower
4	Dunster Castle (Torre)	Motte and bailey castle	William de Mohun	1067–1086	Developed stone castle
5	Cockroad Wood Castle	Ringwork	Walter of Douai	Pre-1086	Motte and two baileys
6	Culverhay Castle	Ringwork and small bailey	Nigel de Gourney	Pre-1086	Small circular stone keep
7	Stowey Castle	Ringwork	Uncertain	Pre-1086	Possible stone buildings
8	Hales Castle	Ringwork & unfinished bailey	Uncertain	Pre-1086?	Possible drawbridge entrance
9	Burrow Mump	Hillock scarped to form a motte	Uncertain	Pre-1086?	Possible Norman keep
10	Castle Batch	Ringwork	Walter of Douai	Pre-1086	Possible bailey
11	Cary Castle	Ringwork	Walter of Douai	Pre-1086	Norman keep and bailey
12	Edithmead	Motte and bailey	Walter of Douai	Pre-1086	None
13	Locking Head Castle	Small motte and bailey	William of Falaise	Pre-1086	Possible Norman building
14	Over Stowey Castle	Large flat mound (motte)	Alfred d'Epaignes	Pre-1086	Possible outworks
15	Bury Castle	Small motte and strong bailey	William de Say	1086–1100	Counter-scarp bank
16	Richmont Castle	Two wards and a stone keep	Robert of Bampton	1086–1100	Semi-circular stone towers
17	Ballands Castle	Motte and bailey(s)	Uncertain	1100	Ditch and outworks
18	Downend Earthworks	Motte and baileys	de Columbers (?)	1100	Planned settlement and port
19	Nether Stowey Castle	Motte and baileys	Robert and Isabel de Chandos	1100	Rectangular stone keep
20	Fenny Castle	Motte and bailey	Uncertain	1100	Summit wall
21	Croft Castle	Motte and possible bailey	Richard & Baldwin Redvers	1100–1150	Possible out-works
22	Taunton Castle	Enclosure castle	William Gifford	1107–1129	Developed stone castle
23	Swallow Cliff Mound	Motte	Uncertain	1100–1140	Possible bailey
24	Breach Wood Castle	Motte and possible bailey	Uncertain	1100–1140	None
25	Portbury Mound	Motte	Fitzharding	1134–1154	Possible bailey and outworks
26	Stogursey Castle	Motte and baileys	William de Curci	Pre-1166	Developed stone castle
27	Bridgwater Castle	Stone keep and bailey castle	William de Briwerre	1202	Developed stone castle

16 Table of details for Somerset's Norman castles

Having established dates for the first phase of castle construction at each site throughout the county, it is possible to create phased distribution maps. Figure *17* shows Somerset's earliest Norman castles (pre-1086). This map clearly highlights the areas in the county first infiltrated by the Normans, as well as giving an insight into the various locations selected for initial castle construction. It is worth mentioning at this stage that throughout the text, for the sake of clarity, castles will generally be referred to by their name and number: the numbers correspond to those shown on the relevant maps and tables.

On castle morphology

The earliest Norman castles in England were not mottes, but enclosures built up against earlier defences. These *Enclosure Castles* were designed to provide space for large garrisons of 'invasion troops'. The Normans would utilise an existing fortification and construct within it an earthen enclosure castle of their own. Examples of this early type of refortification can be seen inside the remains of the Roman forts at Pevensey and Folkestone, within the Roman and Saxon defences at London and Winchester, and possibly within the Iron Age and Saxon defences at Hastings and Dover (Higham & Barker, 1992, 58). Later *Enclosure Castles* were free-standing (i.e. not utilising existing defensive structures), good examples of which can be seen at Deddington (Oxfordshire) and Rochester (Kent).

Following on from, and in a few places contemporaneous with, early *Enclosure Castles* were *Castle Ringworks* and *Ringwork and Bailey Castles*. The ringwork – a defensive bank and ditch that was circular or oval in plan – was utilised in two ways. In the *Ringwork and Bailey Castle*, the ringwork took the place of a motte and stood within, or adjacent to, a bailey, and surrounded the hall or other central buildings, offering those within a means of protection, whilst the *Castle Ringwork*, which comprised a small defensive earthen ditch, rampart and palisade, was probably utilised as a defensive structure in its own right. These were perfect for use during the initial conquest period as temporary campaign fortifications, as they would have been quick and easy to construct. Good examples of *Ringwork and Bailey Castles* can be seen at Warrington (Lancashire) and Cefn Bryntalch, Llandyssil (Powys), whilst good examples of *Castle Ringworks* can be seen at Sweyn's Camp (Kent), Y-Gaer, St Nicholas (Glamorgan) and Sulgrave (Northamptonshire).

In general then, the stages of development for the various types of Norman castle in England are, in the 'initial conquest period', *Enclosure Castles* – constructed within existing defensive structures in order to provide enough space for large garrisons of invasion troops – closely followed by *Castle Ringworks* – designed for use as temporary campaign fortifications. Later, during the *Subjugation Period* – with the addition of a bailey to the ringwork – the *Ringwork and Bailey Castle* evolved,

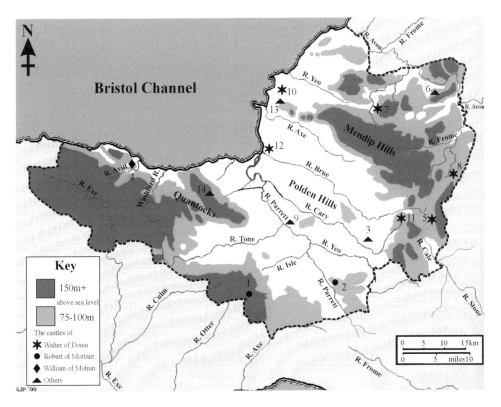

17 Somerset's earliest Norman castles (pre-1086)

alongside the *Motte and Bailey Castle* – both designed to keep the household's knights together around the Tenant-in-Chief, who was safely housed within a central strong-point. This led, in the 'colonisation period', to the development of the *Keep and Bailey Castle* – where the wooden tower on the motte was replaced by a stone one (a shell-keep or donjon), or, where no motte existed, by a very large stone keep or donjon constructed at ground level; in both instances, the baileys were surrounded by a defensive stone curtain-wall or timber palisade.

Looking to Somerset, it is immediately apparent that all of the various types of Norman castle are present within the boundaries of the county (*16*). Firstly – in the initial conquest period – an *Enclosure Castle* appears to have been constructed at Neroche (*16*, 1), within an existing Iron Age hillfort, to provide space for a large garrison of invasion troops; whilst contemporaneously in other parts of the county *Castle Ringworks*, such as those at Cockroad Wood (*16*, 5) and Stowey (*16*, 7), were thrown up to act as temporary campaign fortifications. Then later, with the county somewhat more secure – during the *Subjugation Period* – the Normans built *Ringwork and Bailey Castles,* such as Hales (*16*, 8), Culverhay (*16*, 6) and

Cary (*16*, 11), alongside *Motte and Bailey Castles*, like those found at Edithmead (*16*, 12) and Locking Head (*16*, 13). These were eventually followed – during the colonisation period – by the construction of 'Feudal Strongholds'. A *Keep and Bailey Castle* was erected at Bridgwater (*16*, 27), whilst at Stogursey (*16*, 26) the wooden tower on the motte was replaced by a shell-keep; in both cases the baileys were defended by stone curtain-walls. This suggests that the Normans, in order to conquer, hold and subdue Somerset, had to implement a full programme of castle building within the county.

THE NORMAN INVASION OF SOMERSET

Based upon a study of the historical evidence, it has been stated that 'we do not know how and when the first Normans entered Somerset' (Costen, 1992, 158). A study of the archaeological evidence, in the form of the county's castles, allows this statement to be challenged. When William left England for Normandy in March 1067 – delegating control of the south-east of the country to Bishop Odo and the lands to the north of the Thames to William fitz Osbern – it seems that it was to his half-brother, Robert of Mortain, that he entrusted the lands of the south-west.

The distribution of Somerset's earliest castles (*17*), the dates of their foundation and the identities of the castle builders (*16*) suggest that the Normans carried out a planned offensive in Somerset, in the form of a three-pronged invasion, shortly after William's departure for Normandy, and that three Norman lords were involved in this campaign. The lords were Robert of Mortain, Walter of Douai and William of Mohun, and the locations of the castles they founded indicate three main entry points into the county: from the north-east near Bath, from the south-east, and from the west, probably via the Bristol Channel (*18*). A planned offensive was in all probability deemed necessary, as the Normans undoubtedly expected to meet with strong resistance in the region; bearing in mind that King Harold himself had formerly been 'Earl of Wessex'. Little wonder then that William sent his own half-brother to capture and subdue Saxon Somerset.

From the north-east came Walter of Douai and his forces. Walter may have marched his troops overland from the east, possibly treading the same roads across the Wiltshire uplands that the Saxons had taken in 577, when the armies of the West Saxons marched to the Battle of Dyrham (*Deorham*), slew three British kings and captured the cities of Gloucester, Cirencester and Bath (Garmonsway, 1990, 18-19), or he may have sailed up the Bristol Channel, and from there up the River Avon. What is certain however is that by 1086 the north and east of the county, including the coastline, was ringed by castles of his making (*17*). Walter

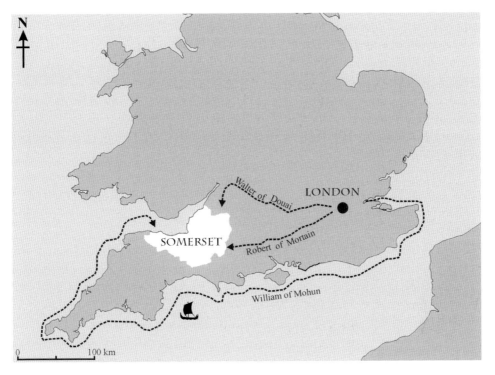

18 Based upon the locations of the castles they founded, this map shows the probable routes that the Norman lords took to reach Somerset

founded the castles of Edithmead [12] (a motte and bailey), Batch [10] (a ringwork that later developed into a ringwork and bailey), Cary [11] (a ringwork that later developed into a ringwork and bailey) and Cockroad Wood [5] (a ringwork that later developed into a motte with two baileys) and was probably also responsible for founding Stowey [7] (a ringwork that later developed into a motte and bailey) and Hales [8] (a ringwork and bailey). The castle ringworks primarily acted as temporary campaign fortifications for Walter and his men, who, once established, set about developing their motte and bailey, and ringwork and bailey castles.

From the south-east came Robert of Mortain and his forces. It is tempting and not improbable to suggest that Robert marched his troops straight down an old well-used route-way dating back into prehistory, known today as the A303. Three Norman castles near Penselwood lie on its course, as does the motte and bailey at Montacute [2] and the early enclosure castle at Neroche [1]. In recent years, when the Wincanton by-pass was constructed, archaeological research was carried out into the history of the A303 route-way. The research highlighted the fact that the road is quite literally littered with important archaeological remains from all periods (Hollinrake, 1991). The three Norman castles constructed near

Penselwood – Cockroad Wood [5], Ballands [17] and Stourton [Wiltshire] – occupy an area of both military and historical importance. Militarily, the area is strategically important as the greensand escarpment in Selwood Forest is the only place where a large army can easily descend from the uplands of Wiltshire, and it is where the Dorset, Wiltshire and Somerset borders meet. Traditionally, the West Saxon army is reputed to have fought the Battle of Pen (*Peonna*) here in 658, and the Egbricht stone is located here, marking the place where King Alfred supposedly rallied the armies of Dorset, Wiltshire and Somerset before marching on to the Battle of Edington, fought against the Danes in 878 (Garmonsway, 1990, 32-3 & 74-7). A co-ordinated march, by Robert and his forces, down such an important route-way as this, could have been used to display the Normans military might and their rights of conquest, or if stealth were required, the Forest of Selwood, which lined the route, would have provided excellent cover.

Robert and his men, upon their arrival in Somerset, began the construction of two castles. The first, an early style enclosure castle erected inside the defences of an existing Iron Age hillfort at Neroche (*20, 1*) (*19*), was built to provide space for Robert's large garrison of 'invasion troops'. The second, a motte and bailey at Montacute (*20, 2*), appears to have been constructed to act as a base for Robert himself. Thus, by 1068, Robert held two large castles on the southern border of Somerset.

Lastly, from the west came William of Mohun and his forces. It is likely that William and his troops came to Somerset by sea, sailing up the Bristol Channel. William had been granted estates in both east and west Somerset, but his estates in the west were by far the most important. Due to their size and coastal location, William's estates in west Somerset incorporated many positions of great strategic military value. Indeed, the locations of both William and Walter's estates (*20*) appear to indicate that William the Conqueror still saw the sons of the defeated King Harold as a continued threat along the coast. The county was obviously vulnerable to sea-borne attack, and it seems that it was this that William in the west and Walter in the north were set to defend against. The locations of their estates and the positions of their castles suggest a role similar to the coastal defences of Alfred and Edward the Elder, namely the first line of defence against sea-borne invasion (Dunning, 1995, 7). To this end, William of Mohun constructed a mighty motte and bailey at Dunster (*20, 4*), on a rocky cliff above an inlet of the sea (*colour plate 2*).

Robert's campaign in the south-west

Robert of Mortain, half brother of William the Conqueror, was second only to Roger of Montgomery amongst the lay magnates in terms of landed wealth in

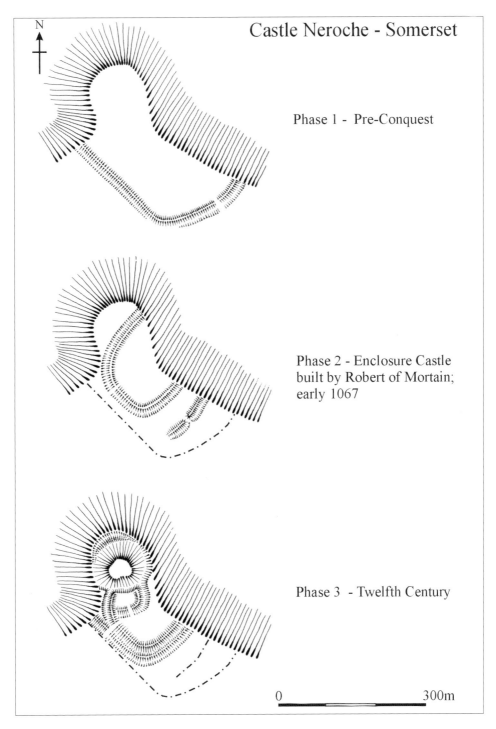

Castle Neroche - Somerset

Phase 1 - Pre-Conquest

Phase 2 - Enclosure Castle
built by Robert of Mortain;
early 1067

Phase 3 - Twelfth Century

0   300m

19 Plan of Castle Neroche, Somerset, showing the three main construction phases. *After: Higham & Barker, 1992, 49*

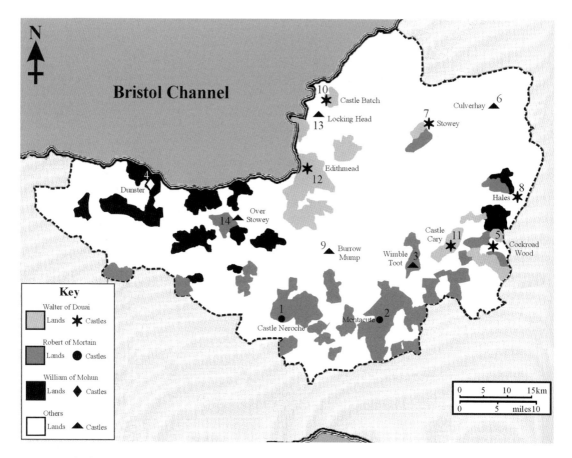

20 The landholdings of Somerset's principal Norman lords and the locations of the earliest castles

post-conquest England. Yet strangely he remained the least known of William's leading vassals. As Count of Mortain he held a frontier lordship of great strategic importance in the south-west of the duchy of Normandy, bordering on Brittany, Maine and Bellême. In England he held estates in twenty counties. He totally dominated feudal society in the south-west, especially in Cornwall; he held the important rape of Pevensey; he had a number of strategically placed manors round London; his lands in Northamptonshire and Yorkshire were extensive. By his death in 1095 he had established a large 'empire' stretching from northern England to Maine: his legacy, though short lived, was enormous. Yet this man, seemingly so important, appears to have been largely ignored by his contemporaries and modern historians alike.

Golding, 1991, 119

History records that the Normans prided themselves on their military prowess, and Robert of Mortain was a champion of this virtue. Orderic Vitalis calls him one of the most important Norman magnates (Chibnall, 1969-80, ii, 141). The *Brevis Relatio* records that Robert provided 120 ships for his brother's invasion fleet, more than any other individual (Van Houts, 1987, 169). William of Poitiers notes his presence at the Duke's pre-invasion councils (Chibnall & Davis, 1998, 149) and on the Bayeux Tapestry he is shown having dinner with his brothers after the Pevensey landing. He held a leading position on the field at Hastings; a charter in favour of Mont St Michel stating that he carried the standard of St Michael during the battle (Golding, 1991, 121). Robert was through-and-through a great military commander, one whose judgement could be trusted implicitly when it came to dealing with the affairs of war. Unsurprisingly then, it was he who was sent into the west to deal with the rebellious West Saxons.

As mentioned above, Robert and his forces advanced westwards from London shortly after William's departure for Normandy, presumably arriving in Somerset in April 1067. Upon their arrival they began to construct castles to secure and advance their positions: the Normans seeing castles 'not just as places for civilians to hide in, nor as simple barracks for the soldiery, but as integral units … and … solid bases for a very mobile form of warfare' (Brice, 1984, 74-5). It seems unlikely that the Normans moved much beyond the boundaries of the county at this time however, as Devon and Cornwall appear to have actively resisted their advance: Gytha, Harold's mother, and Godwin, Edmund and Magnus, his bastard sons, had found refuge in Exeter amongst thegns still loyal to the English cause. For a short time then, Somerset became 'frontier territory', with the heights of Exmoor and the Brendon and Blackdown hills interposing a physical barrier between both Saxon resistance and Norman advance, and the shires of Wessex that had fallen and those that still stood firm. Once safely encamped in Somerset, the Normans no doubt dispatched scouts and raiding parties into Devon to test the strength of the opposition there; falling back to the safety of their castles if the enemy or the local Somerset militia gained the upper hand. Robert at this time alternated between the border castle at Neroche, where he organised the troops and the military operations, and the castle at Montacute, which for a short while became his second home, the castle from which he administered his estates in the south-west (Golding, 1991, 121). This situation appears to have persisted into early 1068, Robert probably spending Christmas at Montacute.

William returned to England in December 1067, and after receiving news from Robert regarding the situation in the south-west, immediately called for the submission of Exeter. 'Exeter replied as York may have answered King

Harold two years earlier: it would pay its accustomed tribute and perform its due services, but it would not swear fealty or receive the king within its walls' (Barlow, 1999, 72). This reply must have greatly enraged William and in January 1068, in a totally unprecedented move, he mobilised his army in the thick of winter and marched into the west to join his half-brother: together they marched on Exeter. Exeter's gates and walls were manned by her citizens, and William, having taken hostages en-route, had one blinded before them in an attempt to affect a swift surrender. The ruse failed, so the Norman forces surrounded the city and lay siege to it for 18 days. Exeter eventually surrendered when it became obvious that further resistance was futile. William then entered the city and ordered the construction of the so-called 'Rougemont Castle' within Exeter's walls. Unfortunately for William, Harold's sons had managed to escape during the siege, but Gytha remained a 'guest' of the city. After the fall of Exeter, Devon and Cornwall quickly submitted, and Gloucester and Bristol soon followed suit. However, the siege and its aftermath marked a turning point in the relationship between the English and the Normans. William's policy of coexistence turned into one of domination.

With Exeter safely in Norman hands, William and Robert marched on into Cornwall – presumably to obtain more English submissions – installing a Breton named Brian as the new earl of Cornwall before returning to Winchester for Easter (23 March 1068). After Easter Matilda was brought to England from Normandy, to be crowned queen at Westminster on Whit Sunday (11 May 1068), the witness list confirming that among the many important guests present were Robert the Count of Mortain, as well as the lesser known English thegn Tovi, the Sheriff of Somerset.

Following Matilda's coronation, Robert does not appear to have returned to the West Country. During the Harrying of the North, Orderic states that he was left in Lindsey with Robert the Count of Eu, to deal with the Danish threat (Chibnall, 1969-80, ii, 230) and after the suppression of the English rebellions in 1069 it seems likely that he returned to Normandy. His whereabouts in the 1070s are unknown. He may have been in England between the summer of 1080 and 1082 but his first certain appearance in England after that date was in 1086 (Golding, 1991, 124).

Robert may have left the West Country in early 1068, but Saxon resistance in the region remained strong. Harold's sons, who had escaped during the siege of Exeter, fled to Ireland where they succeeded in raising a force to support their cause. They returned to England on two separate occasions. In 1068, they raided North Somerset and attacked Bristol, which fought them off only to see them continue their raids down the entire length of Somerset's coastline. Then a year later, in 1069, they brought a fleet of 64 ships to England and landed them at the mouth of the River Taw, North Devon, before moving on Exeter and causing devastation all around the city. They were eventually driven off in two attacks led by Brian, earl of Cornwall and escaped in two small ships back to Ireland, William of Jumièges recording that 1,700 had been killed in their venture (Van Houts, 1992-5). The failure of her grandsons was sufficient to cause Gytha, Harold's mother, to leave Exeter and travel to Flanders, where she went into exile and later died.

Saxon resistance to the Norman Conquest persisted just as strongly in south Somerset and North Dorset. In 1069, the men of Somerset and Dorset rose up and attacked Robert's stronghold at Montacute. The rebellion was crushed by Bishop Geoffrey of Coutances, 'with the help … of the English forces of the shires and cities which were already conquered … The ferocity with which the attack on Montacute was suppressed and the devastation in the surrounding area which followed the English defeat possibly explaining why so many of the manors in south Somerset are recorded in the Domesday Survey as having decreased in value' (Trask, 1898, 30).

This brief study of Robert of Mortain's campaign in the West Country has highlighted the important role that Somerset played in the Norman war of conquest. Somerset inadvertently became a bridgehead for the Norman advance into Devon and Cornwall. Halted in Somerset, the Normans took full advantage of the local topography by constructing a strategically and tactically strong castle at Neroche, which commanded all of the approaches to the south-west peninsula (Davidson, 1972, 16-24). Safely entrenched in this position, and secure in the knowledge that their enemies could not be supplied with additional men or resources, the Normans were able to bring about the swift downfall of Devon and Cornwall. The strategies and tactics associated with castle building appear to have led directly to Norman victory in the region. Before moving on to examine this topic in detail however, one question remains: Why was so little written of Robert's campaign in the south-west?

It is clear from contemporary documentation that Robert played a comparatively minor role in English politics and government. This has led Golding to suggest that Robert was not regarded as sufficiently intelligent to take part in royal councils or to take an active role in politics (1991, 122). Indeed, William of Malmesbury in his *Gesta Regum* states that 'Herluin of Conteville, a man of moderate wealth, had two sons. Robert was of stupid dull disposition (*crassi et hebetis ingenii*) while Odo was of quicker talents'. It must be remembered however that Robert was considered sufficiently responsible to hold a position of considerable importance as lord of the frontier lands of Mortain; a task entrusted to him by Duke William, which could not have been performed by a complete incompetent. In an account given in the *Vita* of Vital of Savigny, Robert is further accused of abusing and beating his wife and terrorising his chaplain (Sauvage, 1882, 362-4), which suggests that he was a headstrong individual given to rages and bouts of exaggerated remorse. Robert may have been a competent military commander, but he was apparently not a born councillor, and his stubborn, hard-headed and violent disposition seems to have ensured that his actions went largely unrecorded, because he was a wholly unpopular character.

HISTORIC SOMERSET

Situated on the southern shore of the Bristol Channel, the historic county of Somerset, some 70 miles (112km) east–west and 50 miles (80km) north–south, is enclosed by a rough semi-circle of hills. In the far west are the heights of Exmoor and the Brendons. In the south-west, marking the boundary with Devon, are the Blackdowns. In the south, there is a vast ridge of limestone, which continues south-east as a series of abrupt hills. In the east are the foothills of Salisbury Plain, and in the north the lower reaches of the Cotswolds. Within this semi-circle, running north-west to south-east, are three further parallel ridges of hills: the Mendips in the north, the Quantocks in the west and the Poldens in between. Between these ridges, across the county's rich heartland, the Somerset Levels, run the valleys of the Axe, Tone, Isle, Brue, Cary, Yeo and Parrett Rivers.

It is clear from the distribution and boundaries of the estates granted to the first Norman lords of Somerset (*20*) that the Normans recognised the county as an entity in its own right – the land grants respecting the long established county boundaries. This fact is relatively unsurprising, considering that Somerset was one of six West Saxon shires in existence by the early ninth century, but this does mean that it is perfectly acceptable to write about 'the castles of Somerset', as the Normans obviously recognised the county as such.

Geology and castle locations

It has been suggested that in certain circumstances underlying geology may have had a direct effect upon the locations selected for castle erection and upon the types of castle constructed (Halsall, 2000; Spurgeon, 1987; Neaverson, 1947). Somerset's underlying geology is very diverse, but a variety of castle types occur randomly across this geological spectrum. This suggests that no specific type of underlying geology gave rise to a particular form of castle, and that underlying geology was not a significant factor in the siting of castles in the Somerset landscape.

NORMAN CASTLE BUILDING STRATEGIES IN SOMERSET

Castles and rivers

Rivers are of the utmost importance in war, as they have a great influence upon military operations.

Manual of Field Fortification, 1871, 143

Rivers, to date, remain a largely untapped source of information for archaeological studies. This is surprising considering that until fairly recently rivers formed the backbone of the transportation system in England. Two early maps of Britain, the *c.*1250 Matthew Paris map and the *c.*1360 'Gough' map, both emphasise the importance of rivers for trade and communication within the country. Unlike their modern counterparts, which depict rivers as a series of fine lines, both maps show rivers as broad snakes leading to the sea, indicative of the great distances that navigable waterways once penetrated into the middle of the English landmass.

It is well documented that the Vikings used rivers to raid inland, their longships, with clinkered hulls of oak strakes and a single keel for unprecedented stability, were shallow enough in draught for river passage. Yet of the Normans, the descendants of Rollo and his Vikings, we know little of their use of ships or boats. It is widely accepted that the Normans had maritime expertise, Normandy having a long coastline with many inhabitants who made their living from the sea. But by 1066, Normandy had yet to engage in naval warfare and had no naval traditions, apart from its Viking past.

Fortunately, the Bayeux Tapestry provides an incomparable pictorial record of the construction, provisioning and launching of William's armada. The Tapestry depicts shallow-draft, Viking-style longships, with masts, sails, rigging, oar-holes, tillers and anchors. Contemporary accounts call William's own ship a '*snecca*': the poetic keening for a longship derived from the Old Norse word for 'serpent'. The Normans, like their Viking ancestors, had the capacity to strike upriver far inland. The invasion fleet would also have comprised other types of ship, including large cargo-style vessels for the safe transportation of the many war-horses needed for the Conquest. The true size of William's fleet is unknown, as there are no reliable figures: Wace suggests 696 vessels, but this estimate seems rather low. In addition to large cargo ships and warships, the waterways of northern Europe teemed with smaller boats, for fishing, travel and other local purposes, and the Normans almost certainly made use of such vessels.

When discussing the probable invasion routes taken by the Normans into Somerset, it was suggested that William of Mohun, Walter of Douai and their troops might have sailed up the Bristol Channel, disembarking when they reached points where they could safely establish themselves and begin to erect their castles. The fact that the Normans had various shallow-draft vessels at their disposal makes this argument highly plausible, and further suggests that rivers played a vitally important, yet hitherto unexplored role in the Norman Conquest of England.

In Somerset, every castle is located on or very close to a river (*15*). Out of the county's 27 castles, 13 are situated on or less than a quarter of a mile away from a navigable stretch of river, 13 are located within 2.50 miles (4.02km), and 1 is within 3.50 miles (5.63km) (*21*). Due to a fall in the water table since the Middle Ages, in combination with the deliberate draining of the Somerset Levels, and the natural silting up of many of the old watercourses due to neglect, certain sections of these rivers are no longer navigable. For castles that currently sit upon non-navigable sections, the location of the nearest navigable portion of the river during the Norman period has been deduced from data sets, hydrographic and navigational charts, provided by the United Kingdom Hydrographic Office, Taunton. With so many Somerset castles so close to navigable stretches of water, it is clear that rivers were a locus in the eleventh-century landscape, and a justifiable focus for Norman activity.

No.	Name	Nearest navigable river	Proximity
1	Castle Neroche	River Isle	2.00 miles
2	Montacute Castle	River Parrett	2.25 miles
3	Wimble Toot	River Cary	< 0.25 miles
4	Dunster Castle (Torre)	River Avill (also on the coast)	< 0.25 miles
5	Cockroad Wood Castle	River Brue / River Cale	1.00 / < 0.25 miles
6	Culverhay Castle	River Avon	1.50 miles
7	Stowey Castle	River Chew	1.50 miles
8	Hales Castle	River Frome	1.50 miles
9	Burrow Mump	River Parrett	< 0.25 miles
10	Castle Batch	River Yeo	2.00 miles
11	Cary Castle	River Brue	1.00 mile
12	Edithmead	River Brue	1.50 miles
13	Locking Head Castle	River Lox Yeo	2.25 miles
14	Over Stowey Castle	Tributary of the River Parrett	< 0.25 miles

15	Bury Castle	R. Exe	< 0.25 miles
16	Richmont Castle	R. Chew	1.00 mile
17	Ballands Castle	R. Stour / R. Cale	1.25 / < 0.25 miles
18	Downend Earthworks	R. Parrett	< 0.25 miles
19	Nether Stowey Castle	Tributary of the R. Parrett	< 0.25 miles
20	Fenny Castle	R. Sheppy	< 0.25 miles
21	Croft Castle	R. Parrett / R. Axe	2.50 / 2.50 miles
22	Taunton Castle	R. Tone	< 0.25 miles
23	Swallow Cliff Mound	On the coast	N/A
24	Breach Wood Castle	R. Frome	0.75 miles
25	Portbury Mound	R. Avon	1.50 miles
26	Stogursey Castle	R. Parrett / ?Stogursey Brook	3.50 / < 0.25 miles
27	Bridgwater Castle	R. Parrett	< 0.25 miles

21 Table showing the distance between castle and nearest navigable river in Somerset. Thirteen of the county's castles are situated on or less than a quarter of a mile away from a navigable stretch of river, and 13 are located within 2.5 miles

The majority of Somerset's castles were skilfully positioned on areas of higher ground, close to and overlooking rivers, in many cases upstream. In tactical terms, these, as previously mentioned, are prime locations for such fortifications. The castle is safe from flooding, and the garrison, freed from the threat of stagnant or poisoned water, has access to a ready supply of fresh potable water. Geologists usefully divide rivers into three zones – youth, maturity and old age – each zone having distinctive features and characteristics. In Somerset, castles were erected in all three zones. Castles overlook river sources (e.g. Cary (*21*, 11) & Cockroad Wood (*21*, 5)), castles are situated midway along river courses in the river valleys (e.g. Taunton (*21*, 22) & Burrow Mump (*21*, 9)), and castles are located at river mouths (e.g. Dunster (*21*, 4) & Downend (*21*, 18)). The Normans constructed a strategic network of castles in the county, which afforded them control over the waterways and waterborne traffic, as well as providing them with a means of transport, communication and supply. River crossings were also secured, enabling the interception and control of traffic on the roads that either crossed, or followed, the riverbanks.

Most accounts of the Conquest record the Norman advance as a purely land-based affair, the Normans presumably moving across the country by way of the old Roman roads. It is just as likely however, that much of their movement around the country was by water. William the Conqueror, for instance, crossed the Channel at least 17 times in the 21 years of his reign. For the Normans, rivers were a lifeline to the outside world, a watery road which led straight to their Normandy homeland, along which goods, news or loved ones could travel. It is not hard to imagine the Normans utilising shallow-draft watercraft to carry troops, messages and supplies up shallow rivers far inland, just as their Viking forefathers had done 200 years earlier.

A study of the relationship between rivers and castles can also, on occasion, help to explain the logic behind a seemingly random choice of castle site. Croft Castle (*21*, 21), near Crewkerne, was positioned exactly midway between the navigable stretches of the rivers Parrett and Axe. Fenny Castle (*21*, 20) (*colour plate 3*), near Wells, on the Somerset Levels, was located on the River Sheppy, within a mile of the rivers Brue and Axe. In the medieval period, the Brue flowed north through the Panborough Gap to join the Axe, along with the Whitelake and Heartlake rivers; whilst Cockroad Wood Castle (*21*, 5) (*colour plate 4*), near Wincanton, lay less than a quarter of a mile away from the River Cale, and 1 mile away from the River Brue (*15*). The locations of these castles strongly suggest that they lay upon portage-routes. Portage-routes ran overland between rivers, and were used to transport cargoes back and forth. Croft Castle was probably built to guard an important portage-route between the River Parrett in Somerset and the River Axe in Dorset. Theoretically, one could sail across the Channel from Normandy, up the Axe, exit the river, carry goods, or march men overland past Croft Castle, and then, by way of the Parrett, reach the Bristol Channel. Fenny Castle appears to have acted in a similar capacity, controlling portage-routes leading from the Sheppy, Brue and Axe rivers to Glastonbury and Wells. And from the Brue, by way of the Cockroad Wood portage-route, one could join the River Cale, then the River Stour, and travel as far east as Christchurch Harbour or, via the Wiltshire Avon, north to Salisbury and the Plains.

Castle Cary Castle and the River Cary

Having considered the overall distribution of castles in relation to Somerset's rivers, a couple of specific sites can now be discussed. A castle at Cary (*colour plate 5*) is first mentioned in 1138 when attacked and taken by King Stephen (Potter, 1955), and this has led many to assign a twelfth-century date to the site (Meade, 1856, 1877-8; King, 1983, ii, 442; Fry, 1996, 134). However, the finding of a succession of ditches, and of tenth- to eleventh-century pottery, during recent archaeological excavations on the site (Leach & Ellis, 2004) appear to indicate an earlier date of foundation. According to Domesday Book the first Norman lord to hold *Cari* was Walter of Douai (Williams & Martin, 2002, 261), and it can be argued that the holding dated back to the Conquest. Walter of Douai

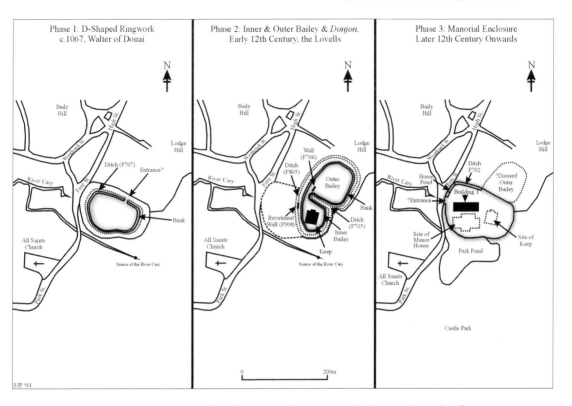

22 Plan showing the development of Castle Cary Castle, Somerset, based upon the results of recent excavations

was the most prolific of the Norman castle builders in Somerset. His sphere of influence was in the north and east of the county, where he was responsible for the construction of three, or possibly even five, early castles (*17*). The topography of the site at Cary and the location of the recently recorded ditch and other early features suggest that initial Norman occupation on the site was in the form of a D-shaped ringwork; a type that compares favourably with the other castles known to have been constructed by Walter. The castle was situated upon the lower north-west-facing slope of Lodge Hill, and the ringwork is seen as occupying a natural spur extending south-west from the foot of the hill overlooking the source of the River Cary (*22*).

Tactically, the Cary site was ideal. It was naturally defensible, it occupied an area of higher ground that provided good all round visibility, it afforded an elevated escape route along a ridge to the north-east, and it enabled ready access to a potable water supply. It has been suggested that the higher ground to the south-east of the site could have compromised its tactical viability (NMR no.200127), but this ground is approximately 400m away, placing the ringwork well outside of the range of weapons of the period.

87

Tactical considerations alone were seldom sufficiently influential to dictate that a fortification should be erected however. The decision to build invariably derived from the wider strategic importance of the location. The decision to construct a ringwork at Cary likely came from two such strategic considerations. Firstly, it was important to guard and control the county's borders and Cary is situated only 6 miles (9.65km) from the Wiltshire border and 6½ miles (10.46km) from the Dorset border. The ringwork, acting in concert with Walter of Douai's other castles in the region, could have formed part of a chain of linked sites around the north of the county. Secondly, in order to ensure the success of their campaign in Somerset, the Normans had to gain control of the county's systems of transport, communication and supply. The Cary ringwork was positioned to completely dominate the source of the River Cary; it was only 1 mile (1.6km) from a navigable stretch of the River Brue and 2½ miles (4.02km) from the source of the River Cale. But more significantly, 7 miles (11km) downstream from the ringwork, at the point where the River Cary became navigable, was the small motte of Wimble Toot (*21*, 3), and 19 miles (30km) further downstream again, at the point where the Cary ends, was the motte and bailey of Downend (*21*, 18). Thus, working in concert with other castles in Somerset, the Cary ringwork could have formed part of a strategic network that was designed to afford the Normans control of the county's river systems.

Downend Castle and the River Parrett

At the western end of the Polden ridge, between the mouths of the rivers Parrett and Brue, lies the small and rather unimportant looking motte and bailey of Downend (*13*). The motte, which was formed by cutting a trench across the terminus of the ridge and scarping what remained into an elliptical mound, rises 5m above the surrounding, low-lying, levels. The associated earthworks, three large banks, which form the defences for one or possibly two baileys, lie in an adjacent roughly circular field named 'Bally Field' (Bailey Field), to the north. At the foot of the motte, on the southern side, a spring used to erupt, but this has now been capped. The site was the subject of a small-scale excavation in 1908 (Chater & Major, 1910) and pottery from the excavation has subsequently been matched to similar Norman wares found at Castle Neroche, suggesting a *c*.1100 date for the construction of the castle.

To grasp the strategic significance of Downend, it is essential to understand the importance of the River Parrett. The Parrett has its source in Dorset, entering Somerset near North Perrott. From there, it flows east of Crewkerne, in a northerly direction, and on past South Petherton, Kingsbury Episcopi and the ruins of Muchelney Abbey, to Langport. It then runs in a north–westerly course to Burrow Bridge and Bridgwater, and then on, by a very winding channel, to

Combwich, entering the Bristol Channel at Burnham. The Parrett is a large tidal river, and in Somerset only it and its tributaries are open to the influx of the tide. This tidal influence can be felt as far inland as Langport on the Parrett, and Creech St Michael on the Tone; its navigability making it second in importance only to the River Avon. Until fairly recently the Parrett was navigable for larger vessels as far as the port of Bridgwater, whilst by its branches, the rivers Brue, Tone and Yeo, barges could journey to Glastonbury, Taunton, Langport and Ilchester. The Parrett, now a forgotten highway, was once vital for transport, trade and communication within the county: a recent study highlighting its strategic importance in the campaign of King Alfred in AD 878, and its influence upon the siting of early monasteries and royal estates during the Anglo-Saxon period (Hollinrake, in Blair, forthcoming).

The navigability of the River Parrett was unquestionably the reason for the erection of a castle at Downend. The Normans recognised early on in their campaign the strategic significance of the gap between the western end of the Polden Hills and the River Parrett: 'the junction of the north-south routes with the sea and river traffic, and the east-west Polden ridgeway' (Aston & Leech, 1977, 39). Tactically the site was also ideal, situated between the confluence of two rivers, the Parrett and Brue, and additionally defended north and west by a stream, it was highly defensible, and it was supplied with its own source of fresh water (the spring).

Unsurprisingly, with such a well-positioned castle, once military tensions lessened, the agriculturally rich environs were soon being exploited for their economic potential, and a 'New Town' with thriving river port developed. By 1266, a borough had been established at Downend, but the town may have been in existence as early as 1159, Philip de Columbers owing 10 shillings for *burgriht* (the right to hold a *burh*) (Aston & Leech, 1977, 39). The de Columbers family were the most likely founders of the *c.*1100 motte and bailey.

CASTLES AND ROADS

One must chiefly look out for a road to pass along the side of the camp.

Hyginus; Lenoir, 1979, 22

Roman roads

Anglo-Saxon charters contain evidence that suggests that England's Roman roads were still very much in use when the Normans invaded. The fact that the earliest castles in England follow a pattern similar to the spread of the Roman Conquest of Britain in the first century AD may be testament to the Norman use of those roads. The Normans constructed castles along the south coast from Exeter to Dover. A scatter of fortifications were built in the Midlands stretching up as far as Lincoln and York. There was another concentration in the West Midlands, and in the Welsh Marches, where Chester formed the north-western point of attack and, at the estuary of the River Wye, Chepstow the southernmost. The north-western chain of defences roughly coincided with the line of Icknield Street, which the Romans originally intended as the north-western boundary of their occupied territory in Britain (Rowley, 1999, 88-9).

A study of the Anglo-Saxon charters reveals that the Fosseway was recognised and in use in Somerset, and across north-west Wiltshire, and there are hints that other parts of the Roman road system around Swindon and Salisbury were still operational. The Normans may have made use of the Roman roads in Somerset, but, significantly, these roads do not appear to have exerted much influence over the siting of their castles (*23*). The correlation between castles and Roman roads in Somerset is nowhere near as good as it is between castles and rivers. This is to be expected though, as on the Levels transport was predominately by water. There are nevertheless a few exceptions.

It was mentioned above that Downend (*21*, 18) was sited to take advantage of the junction of the north–south routes with the sea and river traffic, and the east–west Polden ridgeway. It is likely that the east–west route was actually a Roman road. Greenhill states, that 'many years ago a Roman road could be traced, starting at the mound, running through the adjoining orchard, and along the ridge of the hill; and it seemed not unlikely that the road between Street and Glastonbury was connected to it' (*PSANHS*, 1886, vol.23, 35).

Breach Wood Castle (*21*, 24), near Wanstrow, was situated close to a Roman road which appears to have run all the way from Salisbury to Shepton Mallet, whilst nearby Hales Castle (*21*, 8), close to Longleat Park, was situated on the route of a Roman road which may have run all the way from Poole Harbour to Bath, and on into Gloucestershire. The siting of these two castles can almost certainly be attributed to the continuing use of Roman roads in the Norman period, as can the ringwork at Culverhay (*21*, 6) (*colour plate 6*), near Bath, which sat close to a major road junction, between the Roman road from Poole Harbour and the Fosseway.

Croft Castle (*21*, 21), near Crewkerne, was strategically placed upon one of the highest hills in the area (Castle Hill at 140m above ordnance datum [A.O.D.]) overlooking the Fosseway, which lay 2¾ miles (4.42km) to the north-west. It was mentioned above that Croft Castle lay exactly midway between the navigable portions of the rivers Parrett and Axe, on what may have been a portage-route. If one were looking for an easy way to transport cargoes, men and supplies

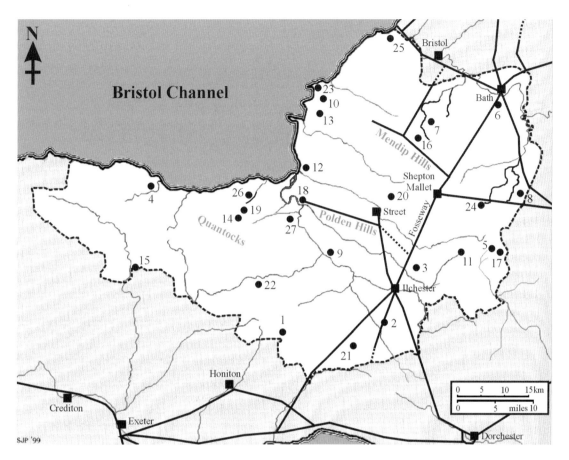

23 Somerset's Roman roads and Norman castles. The Normans may have made use of the county's Roman roads but, as the map shows, the roads do not appear to have had much influence upon the locations selected for castle erection

between the two rivers, then the Fosseway would have provided the ideal route. It crosses both rivers, the distance between the crossing points being as little as 12 miles (19.31km). The fact that Croft Castle was skilfully positioned to overlook the Fosseway, as well as lying equidistant between the two rivers, lends further credence to the argument that there may have been a portage-route in operation in the area.

Costen writes of Montacute Castle (*21*, *2*), 'that it was close to the Fosseway, running down to Exeter. In addition it was only a few miles south of Ilchester and within easy striking distance of the routes through Sherborne to Crewkerne and from Ilchester south to Dorchester' (1992, 160). The castle at Montacute is also situated close to both the A303 (a prehistoric route-way) and another minor road that is almost certainly of Roman origin. On modern maps this minor road forms part of the 'Leland Trail', and is labelled 'Monarchs Way'. It heads south from Ilchester, passing through Sock Dennis and Cole Cross to Kissmedown Lane, where it climbs to a height of 81m A.O.D., passing close to the Roman villa site at Ball's Water. The road then descends, continuing southwards through Montacute, and climbs again to pass close to the Iron Age hillfort at Ham Hill, running on towards Odcombe; at which point it is known as 'Street Lane', a good indication of its Roman origin. From there, it continues southwards towards Haselbury Plucknett and the River Parrett. This road has previously been overlooked, and was only recognised during an intensive study of the Montacute area (Prior, 2000), and it may well be that other castles in the West Country lie on similar roads of Roman origin that have yet to be rediscovered.

One of the most important towns in Roman Somerset was Ilchester. Ilchester was located at a major crossing of the River Yeo, at the junction of five Roman roads, and 'despite its relatively modest status today, Ilchester lay towards the centre of that part of the Durotrigian *civitas* within Somerset and has some claim to administrative importance rivalling the *civitas* capital at Dorchester' (Leach, 2001, 52). The Normans could not possibly have overlooked Ilchester's importance and strategic significance, and it follows that at some point there must have been a Norman castle in, or near, the town. It was traditionally believed that a castle stood where Ilchester Gaol was later erected: on the southern bank of the Yeo, just inside the north gate of the town, at Castle Farm (Sandford, in Page, 1911, *VCH*, vol.2). Unsurprisingly, Cox, an Ordnance Survey Field Investigator, was unable to find any satisfactory evidence of this castle (NMR no.196543), but his search was almost certainly carried out in the wrong place. It is well known that not a single early castle was built inside a Somerset town, the search should instead have occurred outside the town, adjacent to the roads themselves.

About 3¼ miles (5.23km) north-east of Ilchester, as the crow flies, is a mound named Wimble Toot (*21*, *3*) (*colour plate 7*). In the past, this earthwork has been listed as a tumulus, a round barrow, a bowl barrow and, as its name suggests, a windmill mound (Somerset Heritage Record PRN.53520). A thorough examination of the mound has revealed that it is in fact the remains of a small motte, some 2.74m in height with a diameter of 27.47m, with a well-preserved ditch around most of its eastern side. The motte lies in the ancient parish of Steart, or *Esturt* in Domesday Book, the name deriving either from the Old English word *steort*, meaning 'a tongue or neck of land', or from a vagrant form of the Old English word *stræt*, meaning 'a [Roman] street'. Steart and neighbouring Babcary are both situated upon an area of raised land, which stretches south-west to north-east, that is surrounded by marshy ground, with Steart clearly sitting upon a 'neck of land' (*24*). Wimble Toot is located upon the highest point of this pronounced headland, overlooking the Cary Valley to the north, a tributary of the Cary to the south, and the Fosseway ('a Roman street') to the east. An ideal location for a castle erected to monitor movement along the Fosseway, and along the River Cary and its adjoining tributary. The Normans, it seems, decided not to construct a castle within Ilchester itself, opting instead for a tactically superior site, of greater strategic value, that enabled them to command more of the area's militarily important features. Domesday Book states that 'two porters from Montacute hold Steart for the Count of Mortain' (Williams & Martin, 2002, 251). Robert, the competent military commander and strategist, was unquestionably the man behind the choice of castle site.

It would be pointless having a castle to the north of Ilchester, without another to act in concert with it to the south. About 1¼ miles (2.01km) south of Ilchester, midway between the Fosseway and the Roman road from Dorchester, on the Leland Trail, lies the small settlement of Sock Dennis (*24*). Sock Dennis, like Wimble Toot, is situated upon the highest point of a pronounced headland, surrounded by marshy ground, overlooking Roman roads to the east and west, and Ilchester and the River Yeo to the north. At Sock Dennis, there is a sub-rectangular moat with a raised platform in the south-east corner, along with the remains of partly destroyed fishponds and a second platform to the north (Somerset Heritage Record PRN.53043). In 1205, King John stayed at Sock Dennis, and it is likely, due to its strategic military location, that the origins of the manor lay in the early Norman period.

With the exception of the seven castles mentioned above, the network of Roman roads appears to have had less of an impact upon the locations chosen for Somerset's castles than would have been thought likely. The Normans may have utilised the surviving Roman roads, but these roads do not appear to have exerted much influence over the siting of their castles. This may be due to the fact that Somerset's rivers were thought to be of far greater importance, but another factor may also have been at work, Saxon *herepaðs*.

Saxon herepaðs

Roman roads were not the only roads in existence when the Normans arrived in England. The Anglo-Saxons had also established a system of roads, known as *herepaðs*. The *herepað* is often described as an 'Army Road', but there is little to suggest that such roads were military roads built for the purposes of war. Since *herepaðs* carried traffic over relatively long distances, it is perhaps wiser to think of them as routes upon which one might chance across the war-band of a king or nobleman. Costen breaks the *herepað* system down into three groups. *Long-distance routes* stretched between the major political, religious and trading centres. These would have been frequented by high-status individuals, such as the King and other noblemen, travelling between estates or centres of ecclesiastical

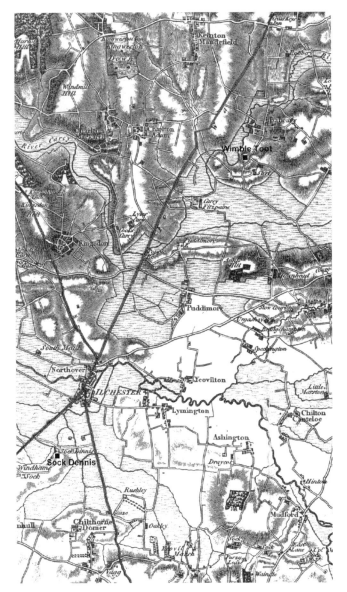

24 O.S. map of 1811 showing Ilchester and the locations of Wimble Toot, Sock Dennis and the associated Roman roads

power, who would have been joined on route by merchants carrying currency and goods of high commercial value, who would have been anxious to pass swiftly through the countryside. *Middle-distance routes* stretched between central places, facilitating political exchanges and the redistribution of high-value goods and the exchange of surpluses. *Short-local routes* linked smaller dependent and tributary estates, providing them with a means of internal communication and a way of moving goods around within the central place's territory, enabling the influence of the central place, as a site of justice and as a religious centre, to be exercised (Costen, 1994, 105).

The evidence for the existence of *herepaðs* comes from Anglo-Saxon charters, where they are described in terms of boundaries delimiting the edges of estates. 'In Somerset references to *herepað, lanu, pað, stræt and weg* occur 117 times. In Wiltshire, the figure is 178 times and in Dorset 64 times' (ibid.). There are two major problems associated with the study of *herepaðs* however. Firstly, although counties such as Somerset are rich in charters, to date little academic use has been made of the information they contain, and even less work has been carried out transcribing the relevant information on *herepaðs* onto maps. Secondly, the charters only ever refer to the short sections of *herepaðs* pertaining to the boundaries of estates. Presently then, the information available on the routes of *herepaðs* is somewhat limited, and until a large number of bounds are plotted nationally, many of the long distance *herepað* routes remain highly conjectural.

Anglo-Saxon charters show that by the tenth century *herepaðs* to Bath were vitally important. 'Roads are mentioned in the charters for Weston and North Stoke, on the western side of Bath, to the north of the River Avon and Stanton Prior, Marksbury, Priston, Corston and Evesty all use roads as parts of boundaries. Nearly all these roads run to Bath, showing how much it dominated the communications and trade of the north-eastern part of Somerset' (Costen, 1992, 139). The Normans appear to have placed castles at strategic locations alongside, or at the ends of these *herepaðs*, in order to exert their influence over the city (*25*). Each *herepað* leaving Bath on its southern side can be observed heading towards a Norman castle: namely Hales (*21*, 8), Breach Wood (*21*, 24), Richmont (*21*, 16) Stowey (*21*, 7) and Culverhay (*21*, 6); and it is possible that an early castle was also in existence at Newton St Loe (ST 693 640). Whilst to the north of Bath, *herepaðs* run towards Bristol (castle established *c*.1088), Lasborough Castle (Glos. – ST 824 941) and Castle Combe (Wilts. – ST 837 777) and it is possible that an early castle was also in existence at Kelston Tump, Roundhill (ST 711 677). Additionally, Bath, situated upon the lowest reaches of the Cotswolds, is surrounded north and north-east by a very high range of hills, and the Normans no doubt relied upon this natural topography to further bolster their strategic castle system: 'as natural obstacles often serve well as strategic defensive lines' (Clausewitz, in Howard & Paret, 1984, 402).

By the time of the Norman invasion, the city of Bath was dominating communications and trade in the north-eastern part of Somerset, and had grown quite large. It is well known that the Normans perceived towns and cities as centres of resistance and in Somerset they avoided building castles in them until at least 1107; Taunton castle (*21*, 22), founded sometime between 1107 and 1129, was the first. Bath posed a major threat to Norman power in the region, and to combat that threat the Normans constructed castles at strategically significant locations in the surrounding countryside, adjacent to the *herepaðs*. This would have afforded them a large degree of control over the affairs of the city, whilst avoiding the necessity of building castles within. The proliferation of castles in the region suggests an area of military tension, where the castles acted as a group rather than as individual units. In the words of Vauban and Maigret, 'within enemy territory, towns must be closely guarded, lest the citizens rise up against the invaders; they are therefore a major strategic consideration in any military campaign' (in Duffy, 1996, 22).

Other examples exist in Somerset of castles in close association with *herepaðs*, which again suggest that Anglo-Saxon roads sometimes influenced castle siting. For instance, the castle at Neroche (*21*, 1) is situated alongside the *Broadway Herepað*. A *herepað* that appears to run from Sherborne to the Fosseway, which formed the westerly boundary of an estate at Rimpton, passes suggestively close to Montacute (*21*, 2). Whilst another *herepað*, noted in the same charter, runs from Ilchester to Milborne Port and thence eastwards towards Wilton, passing close to the site at Sock Dennis. In Somerset, there is enough evidence to suggest that a correlation existed between Anglo-Saxon *herepaðs* and the locations chosen for Norman castles, but not enough evidence to state with any degree of certainty how significant this correlation was. In order to do this it is necessary to await the transcription of more *herepað* routes onto maps in the future.

SAXON HUNDREDS, BURHS, TOWNS AND NORMAN CASTLES

In the eighth and ninth centuries, Somerset had no towns. Activities such as manufacturing and trade, that would later become urban, took place at royal centres, where stood the king's hall and associated service buildings. This situation persisted until the late ninth century when, in the reign of Alfred (871-99), the Danes began attacking and raiding along the English coast. As a child, Alfred had been taken to Rome, and on his travels, he would have encountered fortified continental towns. These towns appear to have provided Alfred with a model and, in an effort to counter the Danish attacks, he set about creating a chain of 'burhs' or strongholds across southern England. These burhs were earth and timber forts designed for communal defence, and an administrative text connected with their construction, known as the *Burghal Hidage*, indicates that at no point in the country was a *vill* more than 20 miles (32.18km) from a fortified centre. Somerset has five burhs named in the *Burghal Hidage* document: Axbridge, Bath, Langport, Lyng and Watchet, all of which were linked to royal estates. By the early eleventh century, defences had been built at South Cadbury,

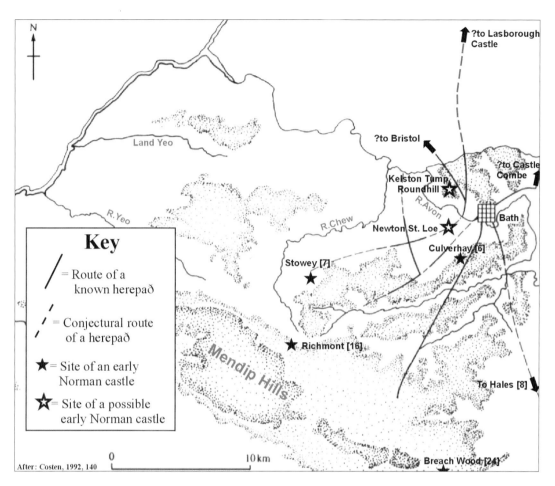

Key

/ = Route of a known herepað

/ = Conjectural route of a herepað

★ = Site of an early Norman castle

☆ = Site of a possible early Norman castle

0   10 km

After: Costen, 1992, 140

25 The Normans appear to have placed castles in strategic locations alongside, or at the ends of the *herepaðs* radiating out from Bath, in order to exert their influence over the city

and probably also at Bristol, Ilchester and Taunton; at least some of these burhs were planned as fortified towns, rather than as simple refuges (Cambell *et al.*, 1982, 152-3).

With the establishment of the burhs, and the security that they provided, it was not long before other sites began to be exploited as towns, and during the tenth century more urban centres developed in Somerset than anywhere else in the southwest. By 1086, in addition to Bath and Axbridge, Bruton, Ilchester, Langport, Milborne Port, Milverton and Taunton all had burgesses, Crewkerne, South Cadbury, South Petherton and Watchet all had royal mints, and Frome and Ilminster had markets, and nowhere in the well-developed eastern part of the county was more than 10 miles (16km) from a 'town' of some sort.

From the ninth century onwards the basic administration and organisation of the Anglo-Saxon countryside was conducted through the arrangement of hundreds (*26*), and the meeting of courts for those hundreds on a regular basis. In Somerset, there is noticeable correlation between 'towns' in the Anglo-Saxon period and hundredal arrangements. Each hundred seems to have had a 'central place' fulfilling its administrative, economic, social, judicial, religious and trading requirements; and many of these towns are hundred centres on hundredal manors (Aston, 1986, 61).

The Anglo-Saxon system of hundreds, each complete with governing 'central place', was the territorial system that the Normans would have encountered covering almost all of southern England upon their arrival in 1066. As Costen states, 'the royal foundations of the tenth century provided the skeleton around which the flesh was later wrapped' (1992, 143). Interestingly however, Somerset's central places, which were obviously of great significance to the West Saxons, seem to have had only a minor impact upon the siting of the county's Norman castles (*27*). This is unusual, considering that many of these central places were burhs, and burhs were usually located to take advantage of naturally occurring defensive features such as rivers and hills. The only places where the old can clearly be seen to meet the new are Taunton, Crewkerne and Athelney, suggesting that it was deliberate Norman policy to avoid the existing Saxon centres of governance.

Taunton Castle (*21, 22*) was most likely constructed between 1107 and 1129, by William Gifford, to replace the royal – and later episcopal – centre at the heart of the vast Taunton estate. Croft Castle (*21, 21*), Crewkerne, was established some time between 1100 and 1150, by father and son Richard and Baldwin de Redvers, Earls of Devon. Thus, both castles are of a relatively late date, established long after the West Saxons had been subdued. Burrow Mump (*21, 9*) (*colour plate 8*), on the other hand, whilst possibly of relatively early date (?pre-1086), cannot be directly associated with the burh at Athelney as it is situated too far beyond its outer perimeter to be of much effective use; although it may have acted in a similar capacity to Wimble Toot and Sock Dennis at Ilchester. Traditionally, it has been argued that Somerset's 'castles were imposed upon the countryside in order to … provide a counterweight to the towns which were potentially dangerous to the Normans, since they were often defensible and difficult to capture' (Costen, 1992, 161). There is, however, another equally plausible scenario. The Normans, rather than imposing their castles upon the countryside because they were unable to capture any of Somerset's towns, may instead have chosen to site their castles away from existing Saxon central places as part of a carefully conceived stratagem.

It has been convincingly argued by Aston that the redistribution of lands at the time of the Norman Conquest resulted in the redefining of old Saxon estates and holdings into new Norman baronies, and that the caputs of the

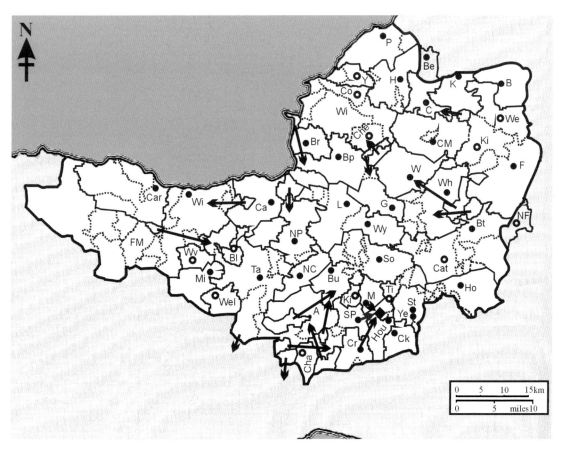

26 Somerset's hundredal arrangements. *After: Aston, 1986, 55*

old Saxon estates were replaced by new Norman centres. Also, that from 1066 onwards, castles were a direct manifestation of the rearrangement of estates, emphasising that new administrative Norman centres were being created in the landscape, replacing the earlier Saxon central places (Aston, 1986, 64). These arguments are clearly supported by the evidence in Somerset. If the bounds of the landholdings of Somerset's first Norman lords (*20*) are compared to the bounds of the county's original Saxon hundreds (*26*), it is apparent that many of the old Saxon estates were rearranged to form the new Norman baronies; whilst the Saxon caputs of burhs and towns were usurped by a new mechanism for governance, the Norman castle (*27*). Watchet appears to have been supplanted by Over Stowey (*21*, 14), Cadbury appears to have been supplanted by Cary (*21*, 11), Ilchester appears to have been supplanted by Montacute (*21*, 2), and Axbridge appears to have been supplanted by Edithmead (*21*, 12). Given the fact that the

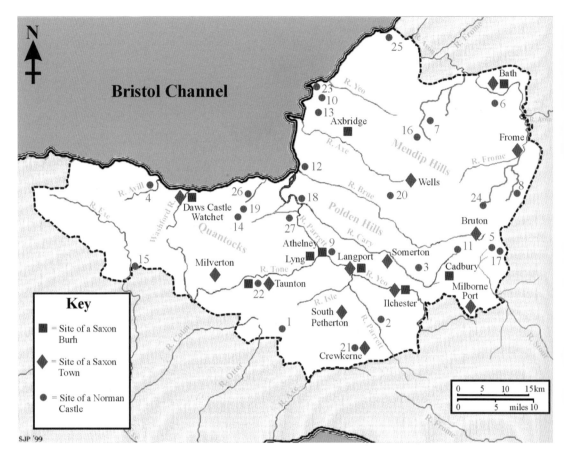

27 Somerset's Anglo-Saxon burhs and towns seem to have had very little impact upon the siting of the county's Norman castles. Only at Taunton, Crewkerne and Athelney do castles sit close to the old central places

Normans intentionally redistributed Saxon estates and purposefully transferred power away from important Saxon central places, their stratagem becomes clear: the wholesale destruction of the Saxon hundred system. With the destruction of the Saxon 'political landscape' the Normans were free to institute a political landscape of their own, the 'landscape of feudalism', which, according to many Anglo-Saxon scholars, spelt the end for the traditional Anglo-Saxon way of life.

MONTACUTE CASTLE: A SYMBOL OF NORMAN DOMINION?

Castles are such conspicuous and characteristic monuments of aristocratic activity, in war and peace, that their impact on the rest of society can easily be neglected.

Since they were both instrument and symbol of lordship to the ruling classes who possessed them, castles were conversely reminders of inferior status to the commons.

Brown, 1980i, 101

A castle at Montacute (*21, 2*) (*colour plate 9*) is first mentioned in 1069, when it was attacked by the men of Somerset and Dorset (Orderic Vitalis; Chibnall, 1969, 193). According to Domesday Book the first Norman lord to hold Montacute was Robert, Count of Mortain; William the Conqueror's half-brother. Domesday Book states 'The Count holds Bishopstone himself, in lordship. His castle, called Montacute, is there' (Williams & Martin, 2002, 253). It is likely that the castle was constructed between 1067 and 1069; Domesday Book, by the inclusion of the word 'himself', implies that Robert made considerable use of the castle, probably as a permanent residence.

Strategically, the castle at Montacute is reasonably well positioned. It is situated upon the edge of a vast ridge of limestone that scribes a line between the uplands of Dorset and the lowlands of Somerset. It is situated only 5 miles from the Dorset border, to the south, and 19 miles from the meeting point of the Somerset, Wiltshire and Dorset borders, to the north-east: an important military location, as the greensand escarpment in Selwood Forest is the only place where a large army can easily descend from the uplands of Wiltshire. The castle is also close to the Fosseway running down to Exeter and, as it is only a few miles south of Ilchester, it was within easy striking distance of the routes through Sherborne to Crewkerne and from Ilchester south to Dorchester (Costen, 1992, 160). In addition, the castle overlooks the modern A303 road, which is known to have been an important route-way from prehistory onwards (Hollinrake, 1991). It is also directly adjacent to another minor road that is almost certainly of Roman origin, which heads south from Ilchester into Dorset (Prior, 2000).

In terms of its tactical location however the castle at Montacute was very poorly positioned indeed. The castle is hemmed in from south-east to south-west by a curving area of high ground. To the west it is overlooked by the heights of Hedgecock Hill. The castle's bailey extends all the way to the foot of the hill in the south-east, affording it very little protection. There is no easy escape route, and the nearest potable water supply is 120m south-east of the bailey. Fletcher, discussing the castle at Montacute, states that 'its position, apparently partially obscured by Ham Hill, suggests that it had both a limited impact and significance as a prominent feature in the landscape' (2000, 1). This is puzzling, considering that the castle is situated only 500m away from one of the largest Iron Age hillforts in England: Ham Hill. Ham Hill was continually occupied from the Mesolithic period until the end of the Roman period due to its strategic importance and natural defensibility, the Romans building first a fort and later a villa in its interior. The ideal position for a castle in this locale was therefore, unquestionably, upon Ham Hill. Strange then that the Normans chose to ignore the strategically significant, tactically superior, hillfort as a site upon which to erect their castle, opting instead for a location that was far less suited to their purpose.

The origins of the settlement at Montacute supposedly lay in the estate known as *Logworesbeorh*, *Lodegaresberghe* or *Logderesdone*, in the seventh century (Abrams, 1996, 160). The name may derive from the personal name '*Logor*', whom William of Malmesbury links to one of the 12 original monks of Glastonbury when St Patrick arrived (Dunning, 1974, 212), and the Old English word '*beorg*' meaning 'a hill'. The persistent genitival endings of *Logwores* and *Lodgares* certainly point to a personal name, though this is not otherwise recorded. However, the spellings are all thirteenth century and no great reliance can be placed on them. William of Malmesbury may well have seen the originals, but the discussion of St Patrick and his monks is simply not credible. No documents relating to this estate survive from the tenth or first half of the eleventh centuries, but the *Cronica* states that William the Conqueror himself seized *Lodgaresburgh* from Glastonbury Abbey (Carley, 1985, 154). The evidence that Glastonbury Abbey ever held this estate is questionable though, as the documentary evidence is conflicting and cannot be properly substantiated, and other independent evidence survives which seems to indicate that during Cnut's reign Montacute was in the hands of Tovi, the Sheriff of Somerset (Abrams, 1996, 160). In Domesday Book the estate is called *Bishopstone* and Robert of Mortain is recorded as holding nine hides there in 1086, which Athelney Abbey held in 1066: Robert obtaining this land in exchange for the manor of Purse Caundle (*Candel*), Dorset. Nothing survives to suggest how the estate might have come to belong to Athelney Abbey. What can be agreed upon nevertheless, is that either William or Robert considered the estate to be of some importance, and took steps in the period immediately following William's coronation to obtain it. The question that needs to be addressed here is why?

The Saxon word '*beorg*' is generally taken to mean 'a hill', it can equally apply to artificial works however, and is often confused with '*byrig*' or '*burh*'. The name may therefore suggest some form of pre-Norman defensive works. Significantly, the surviving earthworks of the motte and bailey appear to support this argument. 'St Michael's Hill … has recognisably been carved into a motte or castle mound with a bailey on its ESE side and a wide terrace on the remaining sides, but whether this terrace constituted a lower bailey is not certain … a bank around the base of the motte on the W side appears to be continued as a perimeter feature by terrace works within the bailey; these are incompatible with the bailey ... could suggest an original ?ring-work, possibly pre-Norman' (Somerset Heritage Record PRN.54297). Furthermore, John Leland, Henry VIII's Antiquarian, who travelled through the region between 1535 and 1543, recorded the tradition of a Saxon stronghold here. Possibly the reason why Ham Hill was ignored as an ideal castle location, and the reason why either William or Robert was so quick to secure the estate after the coronation, was that St Michael's Hill itself was a place of significance to the West Saxons. This notion is further supported by the fact that the hill was considered important enough to be given an individual Saxon name (*Logworesbeorh*), and was of sufficient merit to warrant claim by the abbeys of Glastonbury and Athelney, and by Tovi, the Sheriff of Somerset.

Why was St Michael's Hill significant, and why did the Saxon's choose to protect it by building a defensive structure of some kind upon its summit? The answer may lie in a manuscript entitled *De Inventione Sanctae Crucis Nostrae* that was written by a Canon of Waltham Abbey in the twelfth century. The manuscript recounts that in year 1035, during the reign of Cnut, a local blacksmith found a 'miraculous holy cross' buried on top of St Michael's Hill after it was revealed to him in a vision (Pooley, 1877). The cross was presented to Tovi, Lord of Montacute and Sheriff of Somerset, who carried the sacred relic by oxen cart to Waltham in Essex where he also owned land, and built a church to house it (Warbis, 1900, 9). When Tovi died the church and the cross passed to Harold Godwinson, the future king of England. Harold set great store by the cross, and believed himself to have been miraculously cured of sickness through its powers. He set about enlarging Tovi's church which, in time, grew to become Waltham Abbey. Later, Henry II further enlarged it, as part of his penance for the murder of Thomas à Becket, making it one of England's most powerful abbeys (Adkins, 1992).

The Holy Cross, or Holy Rood, became an object of popular veneration and pilgrimage, and Harold apparently believed that its powers would help him in his struggle against the Vikings and the Normans. The manuscript records that Harold prayed before the cross on the eve of the Battle of Hastings, and on the day itself, and that while he lay prostrate on the floor praying for victory, the Abbot noticed the head of the Christ bent down instead of up, and because of this ill omen two priests accompanied Harold onto the battlefield (Dean, 1973, 5). 'Holy Cross' was the battle cry of Harold's armies both at Hastings and Stamford Bridge, and when Harold was killed at Hastings his body was taken to Waltham Abbey where he was buried; a plain stone slab is believed to mark his grave. 'As for the holy cross, it remains shrouded in mystery. Despite its apparent failure at Hastings, it continued to work miracles and made Waltham Abbey a place of pilgrimage right up to the dissolution of the abbey in 1540' (Adkins, 1992, 25); after such times its fate is unknown.

It is feasible then that the hill known as *Logworesbeorh* was a place of immense religious significance to the Saxons, and this may have led to the construction of some kind of defensive or protective structure upon the summit. Later, the significance of the hill did not escape the attention of the Normans, and by 1068, Robert of Mortain had constructed a substantial motte and bailey upon the site. The erection of a castle upon the very spot where the legendary fragment of the 'True Cross' had been found must have inflicted a serious blow to the morale of the defeated Saxons; which was almost certainly the reason for the castle's construction.

Phenomenologists have recently argued that some castles functioned iconographically as symbols of Norman power and influence; a role which sometimes transcended their military importance (Johnson, 1996, 122-2; Lewis *et al.*, 1997, 231; Creighton, 2002, 65). The castle at Montacute falls into this category, as its military importance was evidently surpassed by its symbolic function, as a symbol of Norman dominion. 'A symbol of the Saxon's bondage and the living instrument of their oppression' (Trask, 1898, 30). It has also been suggested that the landscape surrounding castles often contained deliberately created components which embodied biblical iconography that would have been understood regardless of linguistic and cultural differences (Marten-Holden, 2001, 51-2). In the book of Genesis, God granted Adam dominion over the fish of the sea, the fowl of the air and the beasts that walk upon the earth. In the shadow of Montacute Castle there is an eleventh-century deer park, and a *c.*1102 Cluniac Priory, with associated fishponds and dovecote. Marten-Holden argues that this combination of features provided-symbolic representations of the facets of dominion granted to Adam, and subsequently claimed by the Norman lord of the manor (ibid.).

If, as seems likely, the castle at Montacute was intentionally erected over a Saxon holy site, and the surrounding landscape manipulated to graphically portray the Norman lord's god given right over the biblical facets of dominion, it can be concluded that the Normans were attempting to utilise symbolism to psychologically suppress the local Saxon population. 'The use of propaganda or other psychological means to influence or confuse the thinking, undermine the morale, etc. of an enemy or opponent', is the dictionary definition of psychological warfare (*Webster's New World Dictionary*, 1998). The Normans may have been utilising castles in symbolic or iconographic ways, as powerful psychological weapons.

There are two other castles in Somerset that may also embody symbolic elements: Cary (*21*, 11) and Neroche (*21*, 1). Leach and Ellis, discussing Cary, state that 'Norman castle builders whilst making use of existing features were also frequently aware of the symbolic importance of the sites chosen. This combination of motives can perhaps be seen in the use, common within the region, of prehistoric earthworks, as at Castle Neroche, Old Sarum or Malmesbury … It can [therefore] be argued that the Cary ringwork was also located at a site of significance to the Saxons associated with the source of the River Cary and perhaps with a continuing religious tradition from at least the Roman period' (2004, 122). Excavations in 1903 (Gray, 1903) and 1961-4 (Davidson, 1972) failed to uncover any evidence for prehistoric activity at Neroche however, and it is possible that the large Phase I earthwork (*19*) is in fact Saxon. Neroche, like Montacute, may also, therefore, have been constructed upon a site of Saxon, rather than Iron Age significance. In addition, the topography and landscape setting of Neroche is strikingly similar to that of Mortain itself. The fact that Robert of Mortain held the manor of Staple Fitzpaine (Williams & Martin, 2002, 250) which included Neroche, possibly suggests that the 'symbolic' aspect may have served a dual purpose here, Neroche symbolically reminding Robert of home.

The building of Robert's castle upon *Logworesbeorh* at Montacute must have been a massive affront to Saxon pride in the area. Unsurprisingly, in 1069, the men of Somerset and Dorset rose-up and attacked it, making Montacute one of the few castles in England to ever see military action at the hands of the Saxons. As Trask so poetically stated, 'It was around the walls of this castle on the peaked hill that Englishmen dealt the last blow for the freedom of the western shires … [and] it was there that the last patriotic rising was crushed by the heavy hand of Bishop Geoffrey of Coutances, with the help … of the English forces of the shires and cities which were already conquered' (1898, 30).

HOW THE WEST WAS WON: A CONCLUSION

> We cannot know what debates there may have been before the decision was taken to build a castle … but … the establishment of a castle must have been a matter for serious deliberation.
>
> Pounds, 1990, 54

For the Normans, Somerset was hostile territory indeed. Politically, before the conquest, Somerset had been one of King Harold's staunchest supporters, whilst topographically, the rich, waterlogged, reed-filled interior, made the county virtually impenetrable. This quality was successfully exploited in AD 878 by King Alfred, who used the fastness of the Levels to avoid the Danes, and rally an army to fight them off. For these reasons, until at least 1107, unlike many of England's other counties, not one Norman castle was constructed inside a Somerset town, and Somerset never received a royal castle at its heart. The Normans were forced to implement a full castle building programme in the county, and the vast majority of the castles they erected appear to have been positioned with strategic and or tactical considerations in mind. Each site was methodically selected so that the castle would have maximum influence over its primary objective, and, in addition, over its immediate environs and wider landscape setting, and, consequently, over the local Saxon populace. In several places, a proliferation of castles exists, such as those clustered around Bath or along the coast, suggesting that military tension in those areas ran high, the castles acting in concert rather than as individual units. In addition to which, William thought the county a serious enough threat to warrant despatching his own half-brother, Robert of Mortain, to deal with its suppression.

During the *Initial Invasion Period* (*15*), William of Mohun took, and then defended, the western coastal region (*17*), the passes over Exmoor and the Quantocks (*20*), and the royal estates along the coast at Carhampton and Williton (*27*). Walter of Douai took, and then defended, the northern coastal region (*17*), the routes north, and the approaches into Selwood Forest (*20*); whilst the south and east were taken, and then held, by Robert of Mortain (*17*), who guarded the county's borders (*20*) and the cross-country routes from Wiltshire into Devon (*23*), and was ready to defend against insurrection by the local Saxon militia.

It was stated, in chapter two, based upon rates of movement in the field for a mounted rider trotting, that the appropriate distance separating castles lay somewhere between 16 and 30 miles. Somerset's earliest castles (*17*) were mainly located upon the rough semi-circle of hills that form a natural perimeter enclosing the county, and the castles, on average, were spaced approximately 15 miles apart (24.13km). As these castles are below the appropriate distance apart, they again suggest that the area was hostile, the castles clustering close together for mutual support, shortening the length of time it took to ride between them: a mounted rider, trotting, could safely cover the distance in just under two hours. The castles are also roughly evenly distributed, meaning that in just four hours, riders setting out from each castle could have successfully scoured the vast majority of the county, a horse, trotting, taking eight minutes to traverse 1 mile (1.60km). The castle's spheres of influence, in combination, were wide-reaching enough to give complete territorial control to the Normans; their use of cavalry transforming the castle from a means of passive defence into an instrument for controlling the surrounding countryside. Lastly, the castles literally ring the county, effectively fencing in the native Saxon population.

These early castles, in their carefully chosen strategic positions, quickly gave the Normans command of Somerset's most important rivers, major ports, and road networks, and with them control over the county's systems of communication and supply, as well control of the border, and with it the passage of goods and people in and out of the county. This would have effectively tied the local Saxon population up in knots, as they would not have been able to move in, around, or out of the county without the Normans being aware of their journey. Indeed, any large Saxon force attempting to cross into, or out of, Somerset would have been easily detected. This early scheme, with its economic, yet highly effective use of a few well-positioned castles, was incredibly successful, as the capture of Exeter, the fall of Devon and Cornwall, the defeat of Harold's sons, the suppression of the rebellion at Montacute and the relatively trouble-free pacification of Somerset show.

It has been stated that 'the crucial factor' in the Norman selection of sites for castles 'does not appear to have been any abstract military thinking: the main reason for choosing a site was apparently convenience' (McNeill, 1992, 33). This statement is directly challenged by the above findings. The Normans did not cover Somerset in random 'castles of convenience', rather they positioned castles at carefully selected 'optimum sites' in the landscape, each chosen for its strategic and or tactical potential; the castles, in the vast majority of cases, fulfilled more than one military function, and operated simultaneously on several critical levels. These results are further strengthened by the fact that a similar pattern appears to have occurred in neighbouring Wiltshire. 'The early castles of Wiltshire … were suspended within the web of medieval landscape at a variety of levels. As military sites with strategic or tactical roles, mottes and ringworks were often sited to dominate key resources and routes of communication' (Creighton, 2000, 105).

With Somerset held tentatively in their grasp, the Normans began moving cautiously in towards the centre of the county (15), pressing home their advantage: the *Subjugation Period* witnessing the introduction of a 'Feudal System' so that 'a strategy of settlement might develop' (Platt, 1995, 1). By 1086, Walter of Douai held West Harptree manor and his son Robert of Bampton, from the newly built Richmont Castle [16], held, of the Count of Mortain, East Harptree manor, and together they controlled the routes across the Mendips. Alfred d'Epaignes constructed a motte at Over Stowey [14] and William of Falaise built a motte and bailey at Locking [13] further strengthening the Norman coastal defences. At the same time, William of Say constructed a motte and bailey at Bury [15] to protect Somerset's south-western border with Devon, to command the southern passes across Exmoor, and to control the River Exe, which flows south into Devon. The distribution and position of these new castles suggest that defence was still an important issue prior to *c*.1100, and that the Norman advance into the centre of the county was a slow one. The fact that the new castles cluster close to the earlier ones points to the continuing need for support, castle to castle, in the event of trouble.

After *c.*1100, the need for strategically placed military strongholds within the county gradually declined, as 'the period when castles were needed to protect the Normans against the English was ... quite short' (Costen, 1992, 161). From this point on, the Saxons appeared to pose less of a threat to the Normans, and consequently the locations chosen for the erection of new castles in the Somerset landscape slowly began to change. Castles were no longer built at locations with a purely military significance, emphasis instead shifting towards sites with influence over pre-Norman political and administrative units, existing towns and villages, and trade and commerce (4). For example, a castle and borough founded at this time at Stogursey [26], by William of Curci, quickly supplanted the importance and role of the former royal estate at Cannington (Aston, 1986, 64). Between 1107 and 1129, William Gifford erected a castle in Taunton [22] to replace the royal, and later episcopal centre at the heart of the vast Taunton estate. Between 1134 and 1154, Fitzharding erected a motte at Portbury [25] in order to exploit the possibility of trade with Bristol, its port, and the River Avon. Meanwhile, Neroche [1], Dunster [4], Culverhay [6] and Cary [11] were given additional, visually impressive, defences to increase their status. 'Thereafter, the spread of castle building went hand-in-hand with the emergence of feudal politics, and the struggle for control of land and vassals, signalled by rebellion and private war ... Castles formed the caputs of honours of the new landholders, at once the chief seat of the family and the centre of their administration' (Costen, 1992, 161).

The last castles that the Normans erected in Somerset have been appropriately termed 'Feudal Strongholds' (Dunning, 1995, 11). These castles could be defended, but their military significance, and consequently their tactical and strategic positioning, appears to take second place to their value as administrative or political centres. The castles of the *Colonisation Period* (15), unlike their predecessors, were not constructed in lofty, isolated, defensible locations, but in low-lying areas, very close to the people that the Norman lords elected to govern. Isabel de Chandos, the daughter of Alfred d'Epaignes, built a motte with two or, more probably, three baileys at Nether Stowey [19], to replace her father's ageing motte at Over Stowey [14]. The new castle, complete with stunning views of the Bristol Channel and the Quantock Hills, had a keep on the motte, built from the outset in stone. In 1202, a stone keep and bailey castle was built under royal licence at Bridgwater [27]. The castle was constructed on a low-lying site adjacent to the River Parrett, and was integrated into the 'New Town'. These new castles were no emergency structures; they were well planned and beautifully executed in stone, setting a precedent for the next phase of castle building in England: the awe-inspiring stone-built castles of the High Middle Ages. Other castles in Somerset, such as Dunster [4], Culverhay [6], Cary [11],

Taunton [22] and Stogursey [26] developed into feudal strongholds, the wooden tower on the motte at Stogursey, for instance, being replaced by a shell-keep.

All those who have previously adopted a *Strategic Approach* to castles have generally addressed the issue of Norman forward planning from one of two sides. Harvey (1925) and Beeler (1956 & 1966) argued that castles were part of an integrated scheme, planned and controlled from somewhere close to the king (Pounds, 1990, 54): Harvey stated that 'Castles were not isolated fortresses, but were arranged on a definite scientific plan' (1925, 3). Whilst, on the other side, Brown claimed that 'the basic geographical knowledge was not available for such strategic planning from the centre even had the basic political and economic structure of the kingdom made it conceivable' (1926, 189), Barlow added that 'castle building was deliberate policy … but it should not be thought that it was controlled by a strategic master-plan' (1961, 89). The evidence presented in this chapter appears to support the latter view, in the words of Painter, 'the Conqueror and his sons could not have had sufficient geographical knowledge to formulate a national scheme of castle building, and there was no need for such a plan' (1935, 321-2), to which can be added, 'because the use of castles in combination with military strategies, tactics and stratagems was plan enough to ensure a Norman victory over the Saxons'.

The Normans appear to have utilised a castle building scheme in Somerset that quickly afforded them control over the territory and its resources, leading swiftly to the subjugation of the local Saxon populace. This populace, once controlled, were unable to offer any kind of resistance to the introduction of a new form of political governance. In Somerset, a minority conquered the majority through stealth, strategy and military prowess: a scenario almost certainly played out in many of England's other counties. The impact upon the Saxons, as the Norman castle network spread out across the landscape, must have been dramatic, and one cannot help feeling a touch of pity for the Saxons, who were evidently out-smarted and overawed by the use of a new military technology.

4

Early castles in Monmouthshire

Almost nine hundred years ago, when the tide of Norman conquest rolled into the border shires and reached the frontier of the old Anglo-Saxon state ... It soon became clear to the conquerors that the existence of an independent Wales posed a serious problem. Sudden descents by the turbulent Welsh tribesman had terrorised the border for years, and Norman control over the region would never be secure as long as this threat remained unchecked.

Nelson, 1966, 4-5

THE TROUBLE WITH THE WELSH

In the seventh century, fierce Welsh resistance halted Mercian expansion into Wales. The Mercians were forced to stop short of the Cambrian Mountains, and gained only the foothills in the shadow of those heights. The barren uplands of Wales were apparently not worth the price the Mercians would have to pay for them. Due to the persistent Welsh threat, the Anglo-Saxon offensive turned rapidly into an exercise in the defensive, and King Offa (AD 757-96) was compelled to construct a dyke that spanned the entire neck of the Welsh peninsula in an effort to define and stabilise Mercia's western border. The stabilisation of this border proved difficult however, and was only retained over time through a continued Saxon military presence.

The security of the western border was at greatest risk during the 1040s and 1050s, due to an internal Welsh power struggle between Gruffydd ap Llewelyn of Gwynedd and Gruffydd ap Rhydderch of Deheubarth, both rulers being responsible for savage raids launched into English territory. In 1039, Gruffydd ap

Llewelyn seized the throne of Gwynedd and united it with that of Powys (*28*). He then led the combined Welsh forces against an unsuspecting Mercian army encamped upon the banks of the River Severn and crushed them completely. Following this impressive victory Gruffydd ap Llewelyn turned his attentions to the conquest of Deheubarth, but was unable to force a decisive encounter with its king, Hywel ap Edwin, until 1041. When the encounter finally occurred Hywel was defeated, and in a second encounter between the two – in 1044 – killed. This left Gruffydd ap Llewelyn in a position to unite the crown of Deheubarth with that of Gwynedd and Powys. In spite of this victory however, Deheubarth remained strongly provincial, especially Dyfed and Ystrad Tywy, and Gruffydd ap Rhydderch emerged as a leader to use this provincialism in an attempt to displace Gruffydd ap Llewelyn. Gruffydd ap Llewelyn was so threatened by Gruffydd ap Rhydderch's rise to power that he made a pact with an English border Earl, Swegen Godwinson, whose lands included both Herefordshire and Gloucestershire. Thus, in 1049, an allied Welsh and English force invaded Deheubarth and devastated the surrounding countryside. Gruffydd ap Rhydderch managed to survive the attack however, and continued to solidify local opinion against Gruffydd ap Llewelyn.

In 1047, as a result of Gruffydd ap Rhydderch's continuing propaganda, Gruffydd ap Llewelyn and his men were ambushed and defeated by the men of Ystrad Tywy. Gruffydd ap Llewelyn survived the encounter, but was temporarily forced into retirement in the north. Gruffydd ap Rhydderch then seized power for himself, and began a series of raids into English territory. In 1049, he struck up an alliance with a host of Irish Scandinavians, and with them raided into Herefordshire (*Anglo-Saxon Chronicle*; Whitelock, *et al.* 1961, 114), plundering the manor of Tidenham, and slaughtering a Saxon force sent against them by the Bishop of Worcester (*Florence of Worcester*; Thorpe, 1848-9, 203). It is possible that these raids, and the exposed position of Herefordshire, led to the establishment of Norman colonies in the region. 'Norman influences had been prominent in Edward's court for some time, and a number of Norman immigrants had risen to high position with the benefit of royal influence. A group of these immigrants … established themselves in Herefordshire … erecting the new type of fortress which had been perfected in Normandy' (Nelson, 1966, 16). Osbern Penticost established the lordship of Ewyas Harold in the Black Mountains, where he built one of the first castles in the country. Another Norman lord appears to have built Richard's Castle, a little to the south of Ludlow, and King Edward's nephew, Ralph, built himself a castle at Hereford (Rowley, 2001, 89).

In 1052, when King Edward banished the entire Godwin household from England in an attempt to break their growing power, Gruffydd ap Llewelyn was inadvertently released from his pact with Swegan. Having suitably recovered

28 The Kingdoms of early medieval Wales

from his defeat in 1048, he resumed his raids upon the Herefordshire border; attacking Earl Ralph's Normano-English army, he dealt them a bitter defeat, and returned to Wales loaded with booty and a greatly heightened status.

In 1056, Gruffydd ap Rhydderch was killed, and Gruffydd ap Llewelyn finally won the Welsh power struggle (*Brut y Tywysogyon*; Jones, 1952, 14 & 1955, 25). Gruffydd ap Llewelyn quickly reunited Deheubarth to his realms, thrusting the English border region into even greater danger. Shortly after regaining Deheubarth, Gruffydd ap Llewelyn was approached by Aelfgar, an exiled English nobleman. Aelfgar was intent upon regaining his lost lands, and to that end had raised an army from Ireland's Norse coastal towns. The two swiftly joined forces and marched upon Herefordshire. The combined Normano-English army, with Earl Ralph at its head, took flight before the allied Welsh, Danish and Irish force, leaving Aelfgar and Gruffydd free to plunder and burn Hereford itself.

The situation upon the border, and the threat posed to England's stability, had become extremely serious. This fast escalating crisis needed to be dealt with promptly and efficiently, and Harold Godwinson rose to the challenge. Harold invaded Wales, but was unable to make much progress at this time due to the unfamiliar and difficult terrain, which forced him to come to terms with his enemies (Lloyd, 1954, 365). Aelfgar was reinstated as earl of East Anglia, and Gruffydd appears to have been allowed to keep his border conquests.

In 1062, Aelfgar died, depriving Gruffydd of his powerful ally. Harold quickly acted upon this turn of events, and in 1063 led a contingent of land and sea levies into Wales. Gruffydd ap Llewelyn's seat at Rhuddlan was burnt, and Gruffydd was slain by his own men, who sent his head to Harold as a pledge of their submission. The *Anglo-Saxon Chronicle* records Harold placing another king on the throne (Whitelock *et al.*, 1961, 134), whilst *Florence of Worcester* states that Gruffydd was replaced by two kings, named Bleddyn and Rhiwallon (Thorpe, 1848-9, vol.1, 222).

By 1064, Harold had successfully managed to reduce the Welsh threat from one of national importance to one of mere border difficulties; but the problem persisted. In 1065, Harold led a Saxon force into troublesome Netherwent and, having subdued it, ordered the building of a hunting-lodge at Portskewett. 'So confident was he of the successful accomplishment of this work that he arranged that Edward should pay him a visit that summer to his new hunting-lodge, and saw to it that the place was fully provisioned' (Lloyd, 1954, 372-3). As the lodge was nearing completion however it was attacked and destroyed by Gruffydd ap Rhydderch's son, Caradog, who carried off the provisions intended for the royal household (*Anglo-Saxon Chronicle*; Whitelock *et al.*, 1961, 114). This is the only solid piece of evidence for Saxon occupation in Gwent, and demonstrates that 'the spirit of the Welsh remained unbroken and their independence was scarcely less ample than before' (ibid.).

Wales then, had always been a country divided, its princes were not subject to supreme authority, and its alliances and frontiers shifted with kaleidoscopic rapidity (Golding, 1994, 49). The Welsh had no effective central government, and short of making a treaty with every free Welshman, the English could not establish stable relations with them, making it virtually impossible to eliminate the threat of Welsh raids into England. 'Neither diplomacy nor terrorism could pacify the decentralised and intensely localistic Welsh for any length of time. Peace along the border could not be secured unless a Welsh leader emerged who was strong enough to enforce it among the turbulent tribesmen' (Nelson, 1966, 19). Unfortunately for the English, every time such a leader emerged, peace seems to have been the last item on the agenda, as the Welsh, once united, immediately became formidable opponents, threatening the security of the West of England time and again.

THE ARRIVAL OF THE NORMANS

Nor were hands wanting for the task of subduing the Welsh. For some invaders, at least, Wales represented not so much a threat as an opportunity. Beyond the border lay lands to be had for the taking; lands that were, to all intents and purposes, free and empty. Impelled by twin considerations of political expediency and personal gain, the Norman conquest of Wales began.

Nelson, 1966, 5-6

William the Conqueror must have been aware of the danger that Wales posed to the security and stability of England; the Normans no doubt placing the Welsh threat high on their list of possible barriers to the successful completion of their conquest of England. The Welsh problem, as past events had so readily shown, was threefold: if the Welsh tribesmen were united under a single ruler they immediately became formidable enemies; if they were kept in a continual state of disunity they would persist in raiding across the English border; whilst an alliance between an over-mighty frontier lord and a Welsh king could seriously threaten the overall security of the whole of England, as the alliance between Aelfgar and Gruffydd had done. These problems needed a solution and William appears to have found one.

William's solution was also threefold. First, he strove to keep the Welsh fragmented so that their overall threat was greatly lessened. Second, he was careful not to place too much power into the hands of any single Norman frontier lord. He created three compact, evenly sized earldoms and granted them to men he could trust. It is usual to refer to these three earldoms as 'palatinates'. A palatinate is a territory within which royal power had been delegated to a local prince, but in this case authority was less than palatine. Third, he established strong local forces that were given capable direction and considerable freedom of action thereby creating an effective defence against the Welsh raids.

The three palatinates centred on Chester, Shrewsbury and Hereford and each was defended by a network of castles both internally, and where possible, westwards into Wales. In the north, Hugh d'Avranches (d.1101) was installed as earl of Chester. He was given jurisdiction over an area of land roughly coinciding with the dimensions of the modern county of Cheshire, but with no boundary in the west, leaving him free to pass into and out of Wales as he wished. A forward defence was established at the borough of Rhuddlan, under his cousin Robert (d.1093). In the centre, Roger of Montgomery (d.1094) was installed as earl of Shropshire. He made the castle at Shrewsbury his seat and erected an outpost on the Welsh side of Offa's Dyke in the region of Montgomery, thereby securing his western flank (Rowley, 2001, 92). In the south, William fitz Osbern (d.1071) was installed as earl of Hereford. He made the castle at Hereford his seat, and was set the task of defending the Wye basin from his newly established castles at Wigmore, Clifford and Ewyas Harold. Each Earl was 'charged with the task of attempting the conquest and settlement of adjacent Welsh territory ... either by themselves or by encouraging lesser men to do so on their behalf' (Turvey, 2002, 41).

THE LIE OF THE LAND

> Physical geography ... has imposed its own complex pattern of fragmentation on Wales. It was a pattern which made for diversity, not for unity.
>
> Davies, 2000, 8

The Normans, in addition to dealing with fierce native resistance, had to contend with the difficulties presented by the Welsh landscape. Split by mountain ranges, cut by deep river valleys, and blanketed by thick woodlands, that sporadically gave way to marshlands, the country favoured the defender. The invader was invariably hampered by the difficult and unfamiliar terrain, and was largely denied the element of surprise. Methods of warfare used successfully elsewhere, became untenable in the rugged, fragmented and overgrown landscape. Instead, stealth, ambush and other guerrilla tactics, favoured by the Welsh, were preferable, as this style of combat was ideally suited to the environment. The Welsh understood the landscape that they occupied, and the landscape was instrumental in shaping their culture. To appreciate the difficulties that the Normans faced, and to understand the character of the native Welsh, a basic grasp of the country's topography and geography is essential.

Wales is dominated by mountains, which form its core. The central mountainous massif that is cut diagonally by numerous river valleys firmly divides north from south, and routes between the two regions are difficult and indirect. As a result, historically, little communication occurred between the two regions, and there is a marked difference in the Welsh spoken. Between east and west, there is an even greater topographical divide, and the inhospitable mountain core has restricted settlement to the coastal lowlands and river valleys. Wales is a country without a centre; its mountains force the population to live along its peripheries, isolated from each other in pockets, large and small.

Geographers tend to view Wales as a mountainous heartland, surrounded by the coastal regions of the north-west and Anglesey, the west, the south-west, the vale of Glamorgan and Gower, and the borderlands: northern, middle and south-eastern. These divisions align closely with Fox's 'Culture Provinces' of the eleventh and twelfth centuries (1932), where Wales was loosely divided into five major regions (28). In the north-west, in an area naturally protected from English incursions by mountains and estuaries, lay fiercely independent Gwynedd with Anglesey at its centre. In the south-west, beyond the Cambrian Mountains, lay Dyfed, its outlook for centuries remaining westwards toward Ireland. In the north-east lay Clywd, gradually establishing cultural, commercial and social links with lowland England, its orientation was slowly becoming eastward facing. In the central borderlands, in an area of river valleys that provided ready access from England into Wales, lay predominantly eastward-facing Powys; however, its rugged mountains, enclosed rounded-foothills and bleak moorlands offered shelter and protection to many hostile native Welsh. In the south and south-east lay the rich agricultural lowlands of Glamorgan, Gwent and Gwynllŵg, all exploited from an early date by English settlers (Davies, 2000).

The south-east was in many ways the most distinctive region of Wales. Sheltered by ridges of hills, which overhang its valleys, its agricultural land was rich, it was well populated, its economic and social structures were more differentiated and complex, its settlement patterns were more securely established, and its links with England were close. It was in this fertile, desirable and accessible region that the Normans made their first inroads into Wales.

HISTORIC MONMOUTHSHIRE

The historic county of Monmouthshire was not created until an 'Act of Union' in 1536, when the Tudor dynasty extended its rule over Wales and abolished the old political land divisions (29), establishing in their place 13 new shires based upon the English Model. The new county took its name from Monmouth, which was established as the county town at this time. The boundaries of the new county roughly corresponded to a group of Norman marcher lordships,

N

Cemais

Aberffraw

Rhosyl

Arllechwedd

Rhos

Tegeingl

Ystrad Alun

Hopedale

Arfon

Rhufoniog

Dyffryn Clwyd

Maelor Gymraeg

Maelor Saesneg

Lal

Eifionydd

Dinmael

Edeirnion

Swydd Y Waun

Llyn

Ardudwy

Penllyn

Oswestry

Deuddwr

Mochnant

Ystrad Marchell

Mechain

Gorddwr

Meirionydd

Caereinion

Llannerch Hudol

Cyfeiliog

Cedewain

Montgomery

Cwmwd Deuddwr

Penweddig

Arwystli

Ceri

Gwrtheyrnion

Anhuniog

Mefenydd

Maelienydd

Mebwynion

Caerwedros

Llythyfnwg

Gwynionydd

Pennardd

Buellt

Elfael

Is Coed

Glasbury

Hay

Emlyn

Cantref Mawr

Cantref Selyf

Cemais

Cantref Bychan

Talgarth

Ewias

Ergyng

Pebidiog

Daugl-eddau

Gwarthaf

Cantref Mawr

Gwent Uwch Coed

Rhos

Cedwell

Penfro

Gwyr

Gwent Is Coed

Gwrinydd

Penychen

Gwynllwg

Senghennydd

0   20 Miles

0   40 Km

29 The cantrefs and commotes of medieval Wales. These political land divisions were abolished by the 'Act of Union' in 1536. *After: Richards, 1969, nos. 1&3*

whose boundaries, in turn, had roughly corresponded to the Welsh system of commotes and cantrefs previously in existence in the region. Before the area was named 'Monmouthshire' it had unofficially been known as 'Gwent', the name deriving from the Celtic *Caer-Went*, for the Roman *Venta Silurum*.

As Monmouthshire's borders have been redrawn on several occasions in recent years it is important to define the geographical area that will form the basis for this chapter. Monmouthshire's oldest county boundary will be used, comprising Gwynllŵg, Gwent Uwch Coed, Ewias, the majority of Gwent Is Coed and the parish of Rhymney (part of Mid-Glamorgan since 1974) (*30*). Gwent Is Coed originally included Ystrad Hafren, or Tidenham, lying to the east of the River Wye (now part of Gloucestershire), but this area has been excluded as it did not develop into a full marcher lordship territory: the Normans passed swiftly through it and on into Gwent.

Situated on the northern shore of the Bristol Channel, the historic county of Monmouthshire, some 29 miles (46km) east–west and 42 miles (67km) north–south, encompasses a zone of transition from highland to lowland (*31*). The centre of the county has been likened to an amphitheatre, the Vale of Usk, surfaced with low twisting ridges and valleys, forming the arena. In the north-west, rising to 500m A.O.D., are the high coal measure uplands. In the north, rising to 300m A.O.D., are the Black Mountains, which are deeply trenched by the fertile parallel valleys of the Olchon, Escley Brook, Upper Monnow, Dulas and Dore. South-east of the Black Mountains, a gently rolling plateau is shot through by the Monnow river valley. The Monnow joins the Wye at Monmouth, and between them the two rivers form the county's north-eastern and south-eastern boundary. West of the Wye, is a region of rolling hills, and rising out of them, to over 300m A.O.D., are the Trellech Plateau and Wentwood Ridge. south of the Wentwood Ridge, are the coastal levels that stretch along the Bristol Channel: to the east of the Usk called the Caldicot Levels, and to the west the Wentloog levels. To the north of the Wentloog Levels, there is another region of rolling hills, and to the west, the River Rhymney forms the county's western boundary.

Monmouthshire's scenery today comprises rolling hills, quiet valleys, fields and hedgerows, but in the early eleventh century the landscape was much less ordered. The lowlands were largely untilled, undrained, bogs and marshes, containing dense thickets of reeds with no dry ground, and the valleys were covered with thorns and thistles (Davis, 1982, 12-13). Dense forests, dominated by great oaks, blanketed the plains, and the undergrowth, for the most part, consisted of gorse and bramble, presenting an almost impenetrable obstacle to travel and communication (Nelson, 1966; Davies, 2000, 139-71). The lowlands were, in addition, home to bears, wolves, wildcats and boars, which further added to the difficulties facing potential settlers (Nelson, 1966, 6).

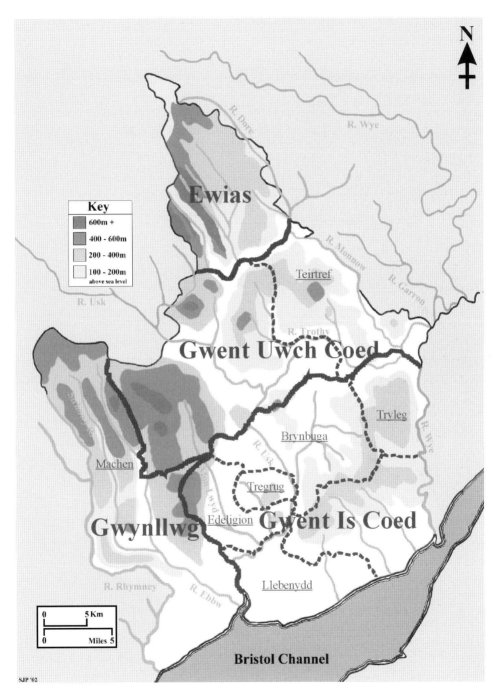

30 The cantrefs and commotes of Monmouthshire. The Welsh law books of the twelfth and thirteenth centuries show that Welsh administration before the Norman conquest was based upon kingdoms divided into cantrefs, which were in turn comprised of commotes

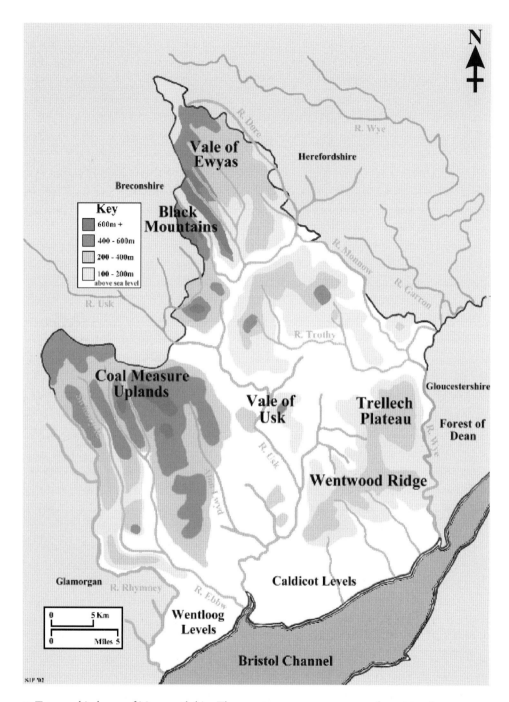

31 Topographical map of Monmouthshire. The county encompasses a zone of transition from highland to lowland, and its centre has been likened to an amphitheatre

Unsurprisingly, the majority of Welsh settlement tended to occur along the upper slopes of the interior, on the edge of the open moorland, where forest growth thinned out (Edwards, 1997, 1-11). In contrast to the lowlands, these areas were comparatively habitable, but they were not ideal. Often damp and boggy, they were exposed to the full force of the moisture-laden westerly winds, and the soil was characteristically thin and poor. To survive, the Welsh integrated the resources of upland and lowland to best effect. Practising transhumance from an early date, the communities availed themselves of the pastoral wealth of the uplands in summer and made maximum use of their limited arable and meadowland resources (Davies, 2000, 140). Monmouthshire was, and to a certain extent still is, composed of two quite distinct environments, each one harbouring a host of potential problems for the incoming Norman settlers.

MONMOUTHSHIRE'S NORMAN CASTLES

Between 1066 and 1262, the Normans built 58 castles in Monmouthshire. Figure *32* shows the locations of those castles and the period in which each was founded. The numbers allocated to the castles on figure *32* appear again in the first column of figures *33*, *34* and *35*, which list the castle's name, the type of castle first constructed at the site, the likely owner or builder of the castle, the probable date for the first phase of castle construction and any later or associated features. The identities of the castle builders and the dates of initial castle foundation derive from entries in Domesday Book, Pipe, Patent and Court Rolls, various medieval Calendars of Documents, contemporary sources like *Brut y Tywysogion*, *Gesta Regis Henrici Secundi*, and *Liber Landaviensis*, and the works of contemporary writers such as Orderic Vitalis and Giraldus Cambrensis. Numerous archaeological excavation reports were also consulted.

The eminent historian Sir John Edward Lloyd employed a series of useful chronological divisions in his book *A History of Wales from the Earliest Times to the Edwardian Conquest* (1954). 'The Norman Conquest – First Stage' (1066-1093) began with the Norman advance into Wales, led by William Fitz Osbern, Hugh d'Avranches and Roger of Montgomery, and ended with the advances made by Bernard de Neufmarché and Arnulf of Montgomery upon the death of Rhys ap Tewdwr in 1093. 'The Norman Conquest – Second Stage' (1094-1134) began with a Welsh uprising in 1095/6, following the escape from Chester prison of a hereditary chief of Gwynedd, Gruffydd ap Cynan. This uprising was gradually, but not entirely, suppressed by King Rufus, via a vastly expanded programme of castle building. The second stage ended with the death of Rufus in 1100, and the slow and steady consolidation of Norman power in Wales under Henry I. 'The

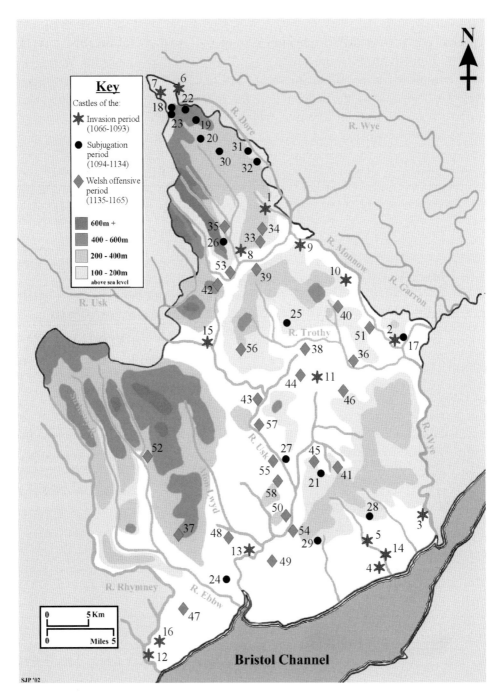

32 Monmouthshire's Norman castles. The castles have been divided into three phases – *Initial Invasion* (1066-1093), *Attempted Subjugation* (1094-1134) and *Welsh Offensive* (1135-1165) – based on the chronological divisions developed by Lloyd (1954)

National Revival' (1135-1165) began with the death of Henry I (d.1135), and covered the massive Welsh rebellion during the 'Anarchy' of Stephen (d.1154) and Matilda (d.1167). It ended in 1165, when Henry II invaded Wales, but was defeated by heavy Welsh resistance and the weather. Lloyd's chronological divisions will be used throughout this chapter, but the various periods have been renamed: *Initial Invasion*, *Attempted Subjugation*, and *Welsh Offensive*.

No.	Name	Earliest Phase	Probable Builder	Probable Date	Later or Associated Features
1	Ewyas Harold Castle	Motte and bailey	Osbern Penticost and later	1048, then	
			William fitz Osbern	1067-71	Shell-wall on the motte
2	Monmouth Castle (Mingui)	Motte or ringwork	William fitz Osbern	1066-69	Hall, curtain wall, gatehouse etc.
3	Chepstow Castle	Narrow keep and twin baileys	William fitz Osbern	1066-69	Numerous additions
4	Caldicot Castle	Motte and twin baileys	William fitz Osbern	c.1067	Round-keep, curtain-wall, etc.
5	Caerwent Motte	Motte	William fitz Osbern	1067-70	Defensive ditch system
6	The Bage (Bach Motte)	Motte	William fitz Osbern	1067-71	Possible bailey
7	Mouse Castle (Cusop)	Motte and bailey	William fitz Osbern or	1067-71 or	
			Roger de Lacy	1085-96	Outer ramparts
8	Walterstone	Motte with ?three baileys	Walter de Lacy	1067-71	Possible tower or shell-keep
9	Grosmont Castle	Ditched earthwork platform	William fitz Osbern	c.1070	Hall block, curtain-wall, etc.
10	Skenfrith Castle	Earth and timber castle	William fitz Osbern or	c.1070 or	
		and wet-defences	possibly King Stephen	1135-54	Thirteenth-century stone castle
11	Raglan Castle	Motte and bailey	Walter Bloet	c.1070	Fifteenth-century stone castle
12	Rumney Castle	Ringwork	?Robert fitz Hamon	1081 or 1093	Timber buildings, palisade, tower
13	Caerleon Motte	Motte	Turstin fitz Rolf	pre-1086	Twin barbican and towers
14	The Berries, Ballan Moor	Motte and bailey	The Ballon family	1086-1106	Wet-ditch

15	Abergavenny Castle	Motte & Bailey	Hamelin de Ballon	c.1090	Stone Keep, Curtain Wall, etc.
16	Caer Castle – St Mellons	Motte or Ringwork	?Robert fitz Hamon	c.1093	Outer Ditch

33 Table of details for Norman castles built in Monmouthshire during the *Initial Invasion Period* (1066-1093)

Having established dates for the first phase of castle construction at each site throughout the county, it is possible to create phased distribution maps. Figure *36* shows the castles constructed by William fitz Osbern between 1066 and 1071. The importance of William fitz Osbern and his role in the Norman invasion of Wales will be discussed at length below, here concern lies with the usefulness of the map itself. This map clearly highlights the areas in the county first infiltrated by the Normans, as well as giving an insight into the various locations selected for initial castle construction.

No.	Name	Earliest Phase	Probable Builder	Probable Date	Later or Associated Features
17	Dixton Mound	Motte with wet-defences	Uncertain	Eleventh century	None
18	Mynydd-brith	Motte and bailey	Uncertain	Eleventh century	Possible stone tower
19	Snodhill Castle	Motte and bailey	The Chandos family	Eleventh century	Shell-keep, round-towers etc.
20	Urishay Castle	Motte and bailey	Uncertain	Eleventh century	Stone causeway, bridge etc.
21	Beiliau Llangwm	Small motte or ringwork	Uncertain	Eleventh century-twelfth century	None
22	Dorstone Castle	Motte and bailey	The de Sollers	Eleventh century-twelfth century	?Large shell-keep and gate-tower
23	Nant-y-Bar (Dorstone)	Motte and bailey	Uncertain	Eleventh century-twelfth century	?Shell-keep and outer enclosure
24	Stow Hill Castle	Motte	Robert of Hay	c.1100	None
25	The White Castle	Earthwork platform	Hugh de Lacy, or possibly	c.1100 or	
		Bailey wet-moat	Payn fitz John	1120-35	Square keep, moats, curtain wall
26	Pont-Hendre	Motte and bailey	Payn fitz John	1118 to 1137	None

27	Usk Castle	Earthwork platform and bailey	?The de Clare's	pre-1120	Square keep, curtain wall, etc.
28	Dinham Castle	?Earth and timber castle	Walter fitz Richard de Clare,		
		or Geoffrey de Ivry	c.1128	Tower and stone buildings	
29	Penhow Castle	Ringwork	Uncertain	pre-c.1129	Pele-tower / enclosure castle
30	Cothill Tump	Motte and bailey	Uncertain	?pre-1134	Possible tower
31	Chanstone Tumps	Motte and bailey	Uncertain	?pre-1134	Shell-keep and wet-defences
32	Bacton (Newcourt Farm)	Motte and bailey	Uncertain	?pre-1134	Stone-tower and forebuilding

34 Table of details for Norman castles built in Monmouthshire during the *Attempted Subjugation Period* (1094-1134)

No.	Name	Earliest Phase	Probable Builder	Probable Date	Later or Associated Features
33	Llancillo Motte	Motte	The Scotney (Escotot) family	1138-54	Octagonal keep
34	Rowlestone Motte	Motte and possible bailey	The ?Turbeville family	1138-54	None
35	Longtown Castle	Motte and rectangular enclosure	Hugh de Lacy	c.1175	Curtain-wall
36	Mill Wood Castle Mound	Motte and bailey	Uncertain	pre-1182	None
37	Twyn-Bar-Lwm Castle	Motte and bailey	Uncertain	Twelfth century	None
38	Coed-y-Mount, Penrhos	Motte with double bank and ditch	Uncertain	Twelfth century	Traces of an outer bailey
39	Goytre Wood Castle Mound	Motte	Uncertain	Twelfth century	None
40	Newcastle	Motte and bailey	Uncertain	Twelfth century	None
41	Cwrt-y-Gaer Ringwork	Ringwork	Uncertain	Twelfth century	None
42	Pen-y-Clawdd Motte	Motte with wet-defences	Uncertain	Twelfth century	Glacis-bank and ditches
43	St Mary's Yard Mound	Motte and bailey	Uncertain	Twelfth century	None

44	Wern-y-Cwrt Castle Mound	Motte	Uncertain	Twelth century	None
45	New House Ringwork	Ringwork	Uncertain	Twelth century	None
46	Trecastle (Llangovan)	Motte and bailey and wet-moat	Uncertain	Twelth century	None
47	Wentloog Castle	Motte	Uncertain	Twelth century	None
48	Graig Wood Motte	Motte	Uncertain	Twelth century	None
49	Langstone Court Mound	Motte and bailey	Uncertain	Twelth century	Square-tower, ditch and bank
50	Kemeys Inferior Motte	Ringwork	Uncertain	Twelth century	Motte and bailey
51	Rockfield Castle	Motte and bailey	Uncertain	Twelth century	None
52	St Illtyd's Motte	Small motte	Uncertain	Twelth century	None
53	The Moat – Treveddw	Motte and bailey	Uncertain	Twelth century	None
54	Caer Licyn	Motte and bailey	Uncertain	Twelth century	None
55	Graig Foel	D-shaped ringwork	Uncertain	Twelth century	None
56	Hendre Hafaidd	Ringwork	Uncertain	Twelth century	None
57	Trostrey	Ringwork	Uncertain	pre-1225	Enclosure castle
58	Llangibby Castle Mound	Ringwork	Gilbert de Clare	pre-1262	None

35 Table of details for Norman castles built in Monmouthshire during the *Welsh Offensive* (1135-1165)

NORMAN CASTLE BUILDING STRATEGIES IN MONMOUTHSHIRE

As previously mentioned, until relatively recently, the castle's military role went largely unchallenged, and as such, the strategies associated with castle usage remain, for the most part, unexplored. Nowhere is this factor more evident than in Wales. The Norman use of castles in Wales is well documented, but hardly anywhere is there discussion of the various strategic or tactical functions of these castles or, more importantly, discussion of the stratagems lying behind the choices of site selected for their construction.

Pettifer, in a recent book on Welsh castles, avoids the issues of strategy and tactics completely (2000), whilst King offers his opinion of what the distribution of castles in the landscape *do not represent* (1983, 1, xxxv). Renn, in passing, mentions William fitz Osbern's castles as protecting England's western frontier, with Chepstow, Hereford and Monmouth castles lying about 15.5 miles (25km) apart along a medieval road, further suggesting that the site for the castle at

Wigmore was probably selected to control the Roman road to Hereford (1987, 57). Nelson briefly covers the usefulness of castles: in forming defensive border lines, in providing a refuge for men and goods, and as a form of retro-defence employed to stop homeward bound, booty-laden, Welsh raiders from entering their valleys after pillaging in England. He also points to the combination of castle and borough forming an economic unit of unprecedented vitality (1966). Rowley is a little more forthcoming on the subject, discussing the symbolic function of castles; their usage as strategic centres 'from which Norman political control was exercised and military dominance clearly demonstrated'; and their role in 'providing bases for active operations'; stating that their 'distribution … was to some extent determined by the locations of … various uprisings against Norman control' (2001, 93-4); whilst Walters suggests that, 'if castles were frequently found along roads and rivers [in Wales] it is only because most of the medieval population was found near them' (1968, 83). Most surprising though is Pounds, who, despite an entire chapter on 'A Pattern of Castles' (1990, 54-71), offers little by way of explanation for the siting of castles in the Welsh landscape: stating simply that 'there was no overall plan of defence … [as] each castle could have been circumvented too easily for that'; he argues instead that 'they served only for local protection against an enemy who came by stealth and at night to forage and loot' (1990, 70). Thus a study of castles in a Welsh landscape, from a military perspective, is long overdue.

Pivotal points

The importance of 'tactically significant' and 'strategically significant' locations have already been discussed: tactically significant locations are highly defensible, topographically or geologically strong, points in the landscape, and strategically significant locations are points in the landscape which, due to their geographical positions, afford control of 'key strategic elements'. Both types of location, because of their inherent advantages, compel the military to acquire them, and then hold them via the construction of fortified places: 'as the possession of such points [is] indispensable for carrying on the war' (Wagner; in Shaw & Pilkington, 1872, 6). The modern British army tends to refer to such locations as 'nodal' or 'pivotal points'.

Utilising the criteria established in chapter two, it is possible to take a map of a given region and plot onto it the locations of the critical 'pivotal points'. A map of castles existing in the region can then be compared with it, meaning that it is possible to suggest whether or not the castles in the landscape are at locations that are considered to be of strategic or tactical significance. Figure *37* shows the pivotal points in Monmouthshire's landscape. There are 18 pivotal points plotted, and when this is compared with the map of castles existing in the region (*32*),

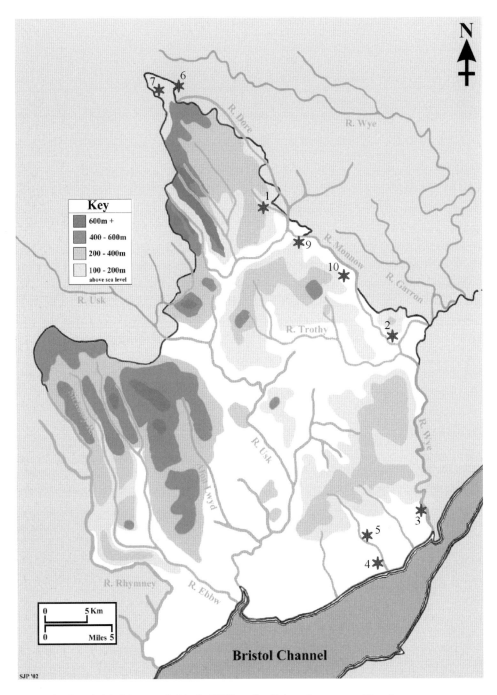

36 Castles founded in Monmouthshire by William fitz Osbern between 1066 and 1071

1 The castle at Nether Stowey, Somerset, is situated on high ground, on the northern slopes of the Quantock Hills, and has stunning views of the surrounding landscape and Bristol Channel. *Photograph: M. Aston*

2 Dunster Castle, set high on a rocky cliff above an inlet of the sea, was constructed between 1067 and 1086 by William of Mohun to defend the Somerset coastline against invasion. *Photograph: M. Aston*

5 Recent excavations at Castle Cary, Somerset, have provided evidence for an early castle and have demonstrated the nature of that fortification. Walter of Douai appears to have founded a D-shaped ringwork on the site *c.*1067. *Photograph: M. Aston*

Opposite above: 3 Fenny Castle, near Wells, on the Somerset Levels, appears to have been constructed to control portage-routes leading from the Sheppy, Rivers Brue and Axe to Glastonbury and Wells

Opposite below: 4 Cockroad Wood Castle, near Wincanton, lay on an important portage-route between the Rivers Cale and Brue, close to the Dorset, Wiltshire and Somerset borders. *Photograph: M. Aston*

6 Culverhay Castle, near Bath, Somerset, was built close to a major road junction, between the Roman road from Poole Harbour and the Fosseway. This would have given the Normans a degree of control over traffic on these important route-ways. *Photograph: M. Aston*

7 In the past Wimble Toot, in Somerset, has been listed as a barrow or windmill mound, but is almost certainly an early Norman castle, built at the request of Robert, Count of Mortain, to watch over the Cary Valley and Fosseway

8 Burrow Mump, a natural hill adjacent to the Rivers Parrett and Tone, in Somerset, was scarped to form a flat-topped motte. The motivation for the construction of the castle was the Anglo-Saxon burh at nearby Athelney. *Photograph: M. Aston*

9 The tree-covered motte on St Michael's Hill, Montacute, Somerset, where, in 1035, according to a twelfth-century manuscript from Waltham Abbey, a local blacksmith unearthed a 'miraculous holy cross'

10 The value of the site by the Nedern Brook at Caldicot, Monmouthshire, was recognised by the Normans as early as 1067. They built a motte with two baileys and a deep surrounding ditch to control this portion of South Wales. Caldicot was held in 1067 by William fitz Osbern

11 In the south-east corner of the Roman town wall at Caerwent, Monmouthshire, 400m from the Nedern Brook, William fitz Osbern erected a motte that was defended via a system of both Roman and contemporary ditches. The castle was erected between 1067 and 1070

12 There was a motte and bailey castle at Raglan, in Monmouthshire, as early as *c.*1070. From its position, on an elevated point of land, the castle watched over the stretch of Roman road from Monmouth to Usk

13 Grosmont Castle, Monmouthshire, was founded *c.*1070 on a hill overlooking the point where the Roman road from Kenchester to Abergavenny fords the River Monnow

14 Abergavenny Castle, in Monmouthshire, was founded *c.*1090 on a defensible point of land overlooking the Usk and Gwenny rivers, close to the intersection of two Roman roads

15 Wern-y-Cwrt Castle Mound, Monmouthshire, overlooks an east–west route that is probably of great antiquity, which ran from Abergavenny at least as far as Raglan, and may have continued all the way to Monmouth and beyond

16 Skenfrith Castle, in Monmouthshire, probably began *c.*1070 as an earth and timber castle. The masonry is early thirteenth century, the work of Hubert de Burgh. Skenfrith was one of the castles that formed the 'Three Castles Lordship', an important strategic triangle that remained in one ownership until the last century

17 Chanstone Tumps motte and bailey, Monmouthshire, was founded pre-1134 on rich land in Ewias. The castle is situated close to the Roman road from Kenchester to Abergavenny. The motte is crowned with the buried remains of a shell-keep

18 The Moat, Treveddw, Monmouthshire, comprises a tall motte with bailey. The castle, which overlooks the Monnow and a Roman road that follows the river's southern bank, was built during the turbulent years of the *Welsh Offensive*, 1135-65

19 Longtown Castle, Monmouthshire, built *c.*1175, was the new castle of the second Hugh de Lacy (d.1186). The castle, which replaced the nearby, ageing, Pont Hendre Castle, commanded the north–south route-way between Hay-on-Wye and Abergavenny

20 Mill Wood Castle Mound, Monmouthshire, is situated in highly defensible location at the terminus of a steep point of land between the River Trothy and a subsidiary valley with a stream. The castle, which sits beside a modern bridge, would have guarded an important river crossing

21 Coed-y-Mount motte and bailey, Monmouthshire, is situated in a commanding and highly defensible position, atop a ridge. The castle overlooks the valley of the River Trothy to the north and is defended by streams on both its northern and southern sides

22 Drumcondra motte and bailey, Co. Meath, sits in the trees atop a defensible steep-sided hill surrounded on three sides by water. The castle guarded the ends of two passes through the hills, which entered Meath from the north-west and north-east and controlled a section of the River Dee's environs

23 Nobber motte and bailey, Co. Meath, sits on a pronounced ridge surrounded on all sides by water. The castle guarded the Dee river-valley and a gap in the hills to the north-west, down which ran an ancient route-way that forded the Dee to the north-west of the castle

24 Drogheda motte and bailey, Co. Meath, is situated at the eastern end of the River Boyne, only 4 miles (7km) inland from the Irish Sea, overlooking a port. The castle's presence ensured Anglo-Norman control of the Boyne estuary, allowing provisions and supplies to be shipped directly from England

25 Trim Castle, Co. Meath, was strategically positioned at the western end of the navigable section of the River Boyne, at a fording point, adjacent to an Early Christian monastery. Together the castles of Drogheda and Trim gave the Anglo-Normans control over the majority of Meath's waterways

26 Clonard Motte, Co. Meath, viewed from the modern bridge over the River Kilwarden. The motte was strategically positioned to overlook the river, a ford and the *An tSlighe Mhór*. Anglo-Norman control of the routeway was further reinforced by Mulphedder Ringwork [39] on the opposite (southern) side of the road

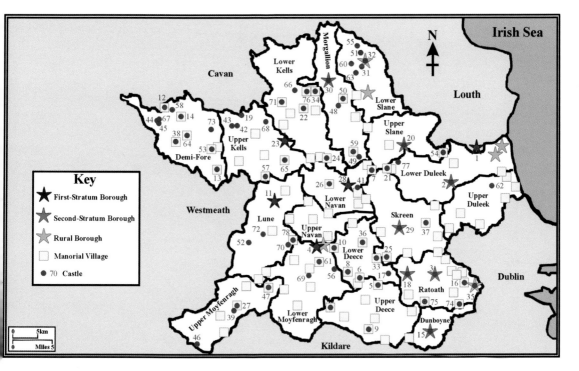

27 Meath's baronies, castles and boroughs. Thirty-six of Meath's manorial villages and 14 of its boroughs have associated castles, which demonstrates the castle's usefulness as a centre for administration, justice and social organisation, whilst additionally underlining the castle's continuing role as a mechanism for control.
After: Graham, 1975, 50

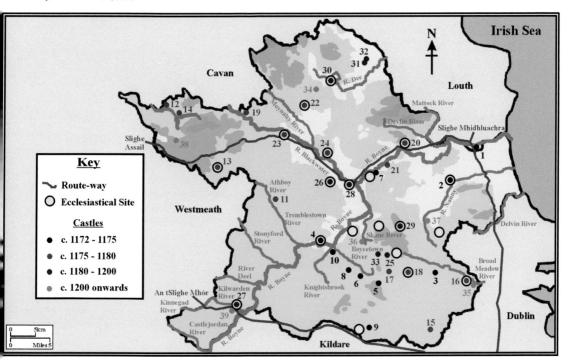

28 Phased map of Meath's datable Anglo-Norman castles. Of Meath's 78 castles, 39 can be ascribed accurate dates, and these divide logically into four chronological periods, which were determined by the historical events

29 View from Ardmulchan Motte, Co. Meath, looking west down the River Boyne. The river formed the initial Anglo-Norman frontier in the region, and the castle, from its elevated position, was able to perform several strategic functions simultaneously

30 The donjon at Colchester, Essex, was the first to be built in England (*c.*1075-80), is by far the largest, and was undoubtedly intended to act as a symbol of Norman dominion and Anglo-Saxon oppression. Its construction also suggests that the Normans were identifying with the Roman past

it can be seen that at 14 of the pivotal points there are indeed castles; at three there are castles within a couple of miles radius (all in Ewias); and at only one of the pivotal points there exists no castle whatsoever (at the juncture of the River Ebbw's upper tributaries). There is a strong probability then, that many of the castles in Monmouthshire's landscape were sited with military considerations in mind.

Topography, geology and castle locations

It has been suggested that in certain circumstances underlying geology may have had a direct effect upon the locations selected for castle erection and upon the types of castle constructed (Halsall, 2000; Spurgeon, 1987; Neaverson, 1947). In neighbouring Glamorgan, for instance, a geological determinant seemingly dictated the type of castle that could be constructed in certain areas, due to the presence or absence of glacial drift. All of Glamorgan's mottes are located to the north of the 'Port Way' – the medieval name for the main east–west Roman road across South Wales that roughly follows the southern edge of a large glacial drift deposit – whilst most of the county's ringworks lay to the south (RCAHMW, 1991, 7 & 34-6). The theory is that mottes could not be raised upon the shallow soils over rock to the south of the Port Way, as their construction required the presence of a suitable substratum that could be rapidly fashioned into conical mounds. Ringworks were thus erected in their stead.

Monmouthshire's underlying geology is very diverse, but, overall, a variety of castle types occur randomly across this geological spectrum, suggesting that geology was not a particularly significant factor in the siting of the county's castles. This is to be expected though, as few areas display the abrupt and distinctly separate zones of drift and shallow soils over rock found in Glamorgan. There is one interesting exception, however. In the Vale of Usk, there is a concentrated group of seven ringworks [21, 29, 41, 45, 50, 55, 58]. A quick glance at their details (34 and 35) rules out the erection of these ringworks as part of a single campaign, as they range in date from the eleventh to the thirteenth century. Spurgeon states that 'this singular group of ringworks has yet to be tested for any possible geological anomaly' (1987, 35).

Two of the ringworks, Penhow [29] and Graig Foel [55], are situated over limestone. Limestone largely consists of calcium carbonate, which is easily dissolved by rainwater, leaving little parent material to form soils. Soil deposits over limestone tend, therefore, to be relatively shallow in nature (less than 28-30cm thick). This factor could easily account for the erection of the two ringworks as the substrata in the area was unsuitable for the construction of mottes. The other five ringworks [21, 41, 45, 50, 58] are situated over Old Red

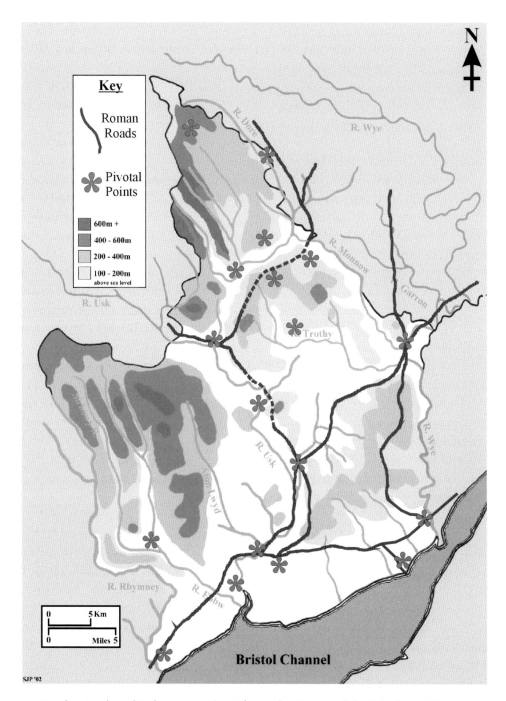

37 Map showing the militarily important 'pivotal points' in Monmouthshire's landscape. These points were determined using the criteria established in chapter two. If the Norman campaign was to succeed, the possession of these points was critical

Sandstone, which gives rise to a sandy-textured, deep (70-200cm), fertile, Acidic Brown Earth; ideal conditions, in fact, for the construction of mottes. Why then were five ringworks built in an area perfectly suited to the construction of mottes? The answer appears to lie with the choice of castle site. The ringworks were all constructed at the crests of steep slopes, where, due to the action of certain geological processes, the soils are likely to be restricted to very shallow depths – called lithomorphic or ranker soils (less than 30cm deep). Localised geological conditions therefore made the erection of mottes impossible. Why did the Normans choose to build these castles at the summits of steep slopes? There is really only one answer to this question, due to the continuing Welsh threat in the area, it was necessary to erect castles in elevated, tactically defensible, locations overlooking the Usk valley: the choice of location, and associated local geology, dictating the construction of ringworks.

Moving to topography, at first glance it appears that the majority of Monmouthshire's castles were erected in the lowland zone (*32*). As the county contains strong contrasts in both geography and geology, the use of the term 'lowland' must be applied with some caution however. In reality, only 27 per cent of Monmouthshire's castles were erected below 50m A.O.D., the majority of castles lying between 50m and 150m A.O.D., with a mere 7 per cent above 300m A.O.D.. In effect then, most of Monmouthshire's castles were founded in the zone of transition between upland and lowland, in a region which Davis terms 'the fertile plain' (1982, 12-13). Wales was not a land of easy opportunity or great reward, so the prospect of exploiting the rich fertile plain of Monmouthshire for its agricultural potential, once it had been deforested, must have been a great boost to Norman morale; and Norman interest in that direction is clearly evidenced by the distribution of many of the region's castles.

In Monmouthshire, the Normans constructed the largest proportion of their castles in the fertile river valleys, or upon the lands overlooking the profitable coastal regions. Where the Normans did manage to retain land, they introduced a manorial structure, founded nucleated villages with open field systems, brought in large numbers of English settlers or French colonists, reclaimed land from the sea, and founded new towns and boroughs. Monmouthshire's new agrarian communities prospered by exploiting the region's rich soils, woods and fisheries, and consequently the towns, whose weekly markets served to stimulate the local economy through trade, also thrived.

The Normans had little interest in settling the comparatively barren uplands, and these were left to the Welsh to inhabit. Thus, by the end of the twelfth century, Wales was a country of two peoples, Welsh and Anglo-Norman, and 'the territory was often divided into the 'Englishry' and the 'Welshry', the latter lying above the 120m mark. In these upland areas Welsh laws and customs and Welsh agricultural practices survived' (Thomas, 1977, 20). The Normans transformed Wales – in terms of political mastery, social configuration and cultural influence – more profoundly than any other group or movement up until the industrial revolution (Davies, 2000, 82). Before all this could begin though, the Normans first had to take and then hold the land, and it is essential to remember that there are also some highly significant tactical and strategic reasons for positioning castles in river valleys, or near the coastline: castles in such locations afforded their garrisons control over trade, and command of the region's routes of transport, communication and supply.

CASTLES, RIVERS AND THE BRISTOL CHANNEL

> Nowhere can a fortress serve so many purposes or play so many parts as when it is located on a great river.

> Clausewitz; in Howard & Paret, 1984, 399

It is clear from a quick glance at the map of Monmouthshire, that many of the county's castles lie adjacent to waterways (*32*). This fact is not particularly surprising however, as it is difficult to walk more than 4 miles (6.43km) in Monmouthshire without having to cross a river; whilst a garrison's demands for access to a ready supply of potable water tended to force castle construction close to rivers. Figure *32* also shows that there was a chain of castles stretched out along the coastline. Along the coast of the Bristol Channel there is, in fact, a more or less continuous line of castles as far as Pembrokeshire. In order to determine which of Monmouthshire's castles were primarily associated with waterways then, more information is required.

The Pigot & Co Directory for South Wales 1844, states that 'the Wye, which rises in Radnorshire, and the Usk, [which rises] in Brecknockshire, are amongst Wales' navigable waterways'. Whilst *Kelly's Directory for Monmouthshire 1901*, notes that 'the Usk is navigable as far as the ancient city of Caerleon'. The Usk is actually navigable as far as Newbridge, which is approximately 3 miles up-river from Caerleon. *The Pigot & Co Directory for Monmouthshire 1850*, further states that 'the county of Monmouth is abundantly watered with fine rivers, the principal of which are the Severn, the Wye, the Monnow (or Munnow), the Rumney, the Usk, and the Ebwy'; adding that 'the ... Severn [is a] powerful auxiliary of commerce', and that 'the River Wye ... is navigable for barges to Monmouth, and ships of considerable berth come up to Chepstow'. A recent DEFRA paper (*Wye Navigation Order 2002*), suggests though that 'by normal

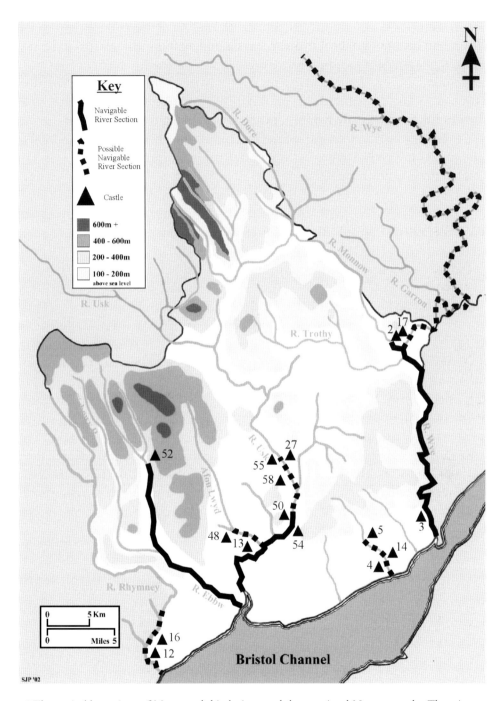

38 The navigable sections of Monmouthshire's rivers and the associated Norman castles. There is a significant correlation between many of the county's most prominent and influential castles and the navigable stretches of its waterways

standards the Wye is not a navigable river for large craft due to its long stretches of shallow streamy water … the upper river contain[ing] many rocky stretches'. Since the seventeenth century however, there has been some form of legislation permitting and protecting navigation on the Wye and an undisputed right of navigation exists by statute as far upriver as Hay on Wye (ibid.). Furthermore, *A Map of Navigable Waterways*, dated 1818, by Longman *et al.*, appears to show that the Ebbw was navigable as far upriver as Llanhilleth. Lastly, Courtney states that 'in 1324, Usk was referred to … as a port' (1983, 134).

Using the information above, it is possible to ascertain the navigable sections of Monmouthshire's rivers, and the castles associated with those sections (*38*). It is clear that there is a significant correlation between many of Monmouthshire's most prominent and influential castles and the documented navigable stretches of its waterways. For example, Monmouth Castle [2] lies adjacent to a navigable stretch of the Monnow; Chepstow Castle [3] lies adjacent to a navigable stretch of the Wye; Rumney Castle [12] lies adjacent to a navigable stretch of the Rhymney, and Caerleon Motte [13] lies adjacent to a navigable stretch of the Usk. It must also be remembered that many of these rivers would have been navigable by smaller vessels much further upstream, a fact that would increase this correlation.

As previously stated, the optimum location for a castle designed to exert influence over a river is on an area of higher ground close to, and overlooking, the watercourse. In Monmouthshire, almost every castle associated with a navigable waterway was positioned at a tactically defensible location, on an area of higher ground, overlooking the navigable section of the river (*39*). The Normans were clearly employing their *stratagem of optimum site selection*, and their objective is readily apparent. They strove to gain control of the region's navigable waterways, as this would have given them access to a means of transportation, communication and supply, whilst conversely enabling them to observe and control enemy movement along the river valleys.

No.	Name	Nearest River	Proximity	Location
2	Monmouth Castle	River Monnow	Adjacent to it	On bluff overlooking Wye and Monnow rivers
3	Chepstow Castle	River Wye	Adjacent to it	Mid ridge, overlooking River Wye
4	Caldicot Castle	Nedern Brook	50m	On low-lying site beside the Nedern Brook
5	Caerwent Motte	Nedern Brook	400m	SE corner of Roman town wall, beside the Nedern Brook

12	Rumney Castle	River Rhymney	100m	Atop a steep scarp, overlooking River Rhymney and floodplain
13	Caerleon Motte	River Usk	200m	Beside River Usk, adjacent to remains of Roman Isca
14	The Berries, Ballan Moor	Nedern Brook	100m	On a dry spur, in a marshy area, beside the Nedern Brook
16	Caer Castle, St Mellons	River Rhymney	1300m	Edge of south-eastern facing scarp, overlooking Levels and Bristol Channel
17	Dixton Mound	River Wye	300m	On Roman site beside Wye floodplain
27	Usk Castle	River Usk	250m	On promontory between two rivers, on Roman fort site
48	Graig Wood Motte	Afon Llwyd River	250m	Above floodplain, on south bank of Afon Llwyd River
50	Kemeys Inferior Motte	River Usk	100m	On western side of steep scarp slope rising from River Usk floodplain
52	St. Illtyd's Motte	River Ebbw	700m	On high promontory above confluence of Ebbw Fach and Ebbw rivers
54	Caer Licyn	River Usk	700m	On commanding ridge, overlooking River Usk
55	Graig Foel	River Usk	500m	On steep spur, high above River Usk flood-plain
58	Llangibby Castle Mound	River Usk	1700m	Above River Usk flood-plain, protected north and south by streams and valleys

39 Table showing the castles in Monmouthshire associated with navigable stretches of river. In most cases these castles were positioned at tactically defensible locations, on areas of higher ground, overlooking navigable river sections

The Monnow and Wye rivers were the first to be secured, and may have been taken as early as 1066-7. Monmouth Castle [2] was constructed on the navigable lower reaches of the Monnow, and Chepstow Castle [3] was constructed on the lower reaches of the navigable River Wye. This gave the Normans a supply route that stretched from the Bristol Channel in the south around the whole of the eastern edge of the county. It has been suggested that the ideal site for a medieval castle was an isolated rocky hillock, 100-300m in diameter, sited alongside a navigable river or marine harbour (Halsall 2000, 5). Chepstow Castle undeniably fits this description (*9*). The castle at Chepstow was supplied with provisions from the port at Bristol, and those provisions entered the castle by way of a stout pulley arm projecting out of the doorway of the cellar over the river: the supplies were winched up from boats beached within a cave below. William fitz

Osbern, the founder of Chepstow Castle, no doubt reached and secured the area initially by way of the sixty ships he contributed – and filled with his own men – for the Norman Conquest of England. Shortly after the appropriation of the River Wye, the castles of Caldicot [4] and Caerwent [5] were constructed (*colour plates 10* and *11*), apparently in the shadow of safety cast by Chepstow Castle. Both these castles lie close to the Nedern Brook, and the sites were probably first reached via this watercourse – perhaps in small boats. The Normans then moved westwards along the coast, and by way of the River Usk, reached Caerleon, establishing a motte [13] there by 1086. Usk Castle [27] was later established at the river's northernmost navigable point – before 1120.

The Norman invasion of southern Wales is generally perceived as an east to west, land-based affair, the Normans presumably moving across the country by way of the old Roman roads, such as the east–west Port Way. It is equally likely however, that the invasion was a waterborne one, as the castles strung out along the coastline suggest (*32*). The traditional version of events is that 'fitz Osbern moved down into Gwent, established the lordship of Strigoil and fortified Chepstow and Monmouth. By the time of his death in 1071 he had reached the Usk' (Thomas, 1977, 20). Considering that the Normans had a seaworthy armada at their disposal, and that the easiest access route into south-east Wales was across the Severn estuary, the traditional version of events seemingly makes little sense. Nelson adopts a similar stance, arguing that there is strong evidence that Robert fitz Hamon launched his attack on Wales from his lands across the Bristol Channel [in Gloucestershire] (1966, 105). It is more likely that the invasion came from both land and sea, with the earliest Norman invaders seeking out the best sites for their castles along existing lines of communication. Robert fitz Hamon appears to have sailed up the River Rhymney in 1093, and on Monmouthshire's western border, he established both Rumney Castle [12] and Caer Castle [16]. These castles, lying close to the tidal inlet, could be supplied or relieved in an emergency by sea.

It has been stated that 'there was an advantage in siting a castle close to a navigable waterway, though the Normans were somewhat slow in learning it' (Pounds, 1990, 162): this does not seem to apply in Monmouthshire. The principal castles of the lordships of Newport, Chepstow, Abergavenny, Monmouth, Caerleon and Usk were all situated at important river crossings, the last four at confluences – which would have added natural strength to their defences – with only Abergavenny and Usk castles lying upon un-navigable sections. The Normans, in this way, were able to ensure permanently safe river crossings for themselves, whilst preventing their enemies from crossing within a radius of several miles of their castles. This strategy bolstered castle defence, turned rivers into impassable barriers, and in South Wales halted almost all west–east movement. The Normans also gained the capacity to safely shelter their own ships, won control over all river traffic, and could intercept and restrict movement on the roads that followed the riverbanks or crossed the rivers themselves. 'In being thus master of the rivers, one thereby obtains command of the whole country: one may divert their course, if occasion shall require it; may be readily furnished with supplies of provisions; may have magazines formed, and ammunition, or other sorts of military stores transported to you with ease' (Saxe, 1787, 84).

CASTLES, ROMAN ROADS AND ANCIENT TRACKWAYS

Communications are an obvious factor involved in the conquest, settlement and subsequent domination of any region.

RCAHMW, 1991, 5

Monmouthshire was dissected by five Roman roads: the road from Kenchester (Herefordshire) to Abergavenny, the road from Brecon – via Abergavenny, Usk and Llantrisant – to Caerleon, the road from Weston under Penyard (Herefordshire) – via Monmouth and Usk – to Caerleon, the road from Hereford – via Monmouth – to Chepstow, and the road from London to Carmarthen – which is often referred to in Wales as the Port Way. The Port Way branched beyond Silchester to reach Caerwent either via Cirencester and Gloucester, or via Bath and a Severn crossing from Sea Mills in the estuary of the Bristol Avon (*40*). The Roman roads in Monmouthshire are different in nature from those found in England, as they do not form the straight lines one would usually expect to see plotted onto maps associated with Roman engineering. It is clear, however, that many of the county's castles were situated along their routes.

In Wales, Roman roads did not run in straight lines for considerable distances, as the hilly nature of the country prevented actual straightness for any but short distances, although the general direction towards their objective was always maintained as far as conditions would allow. In addition, the roads were often not as well constructed as their English counterparts, as Roman roads in Wales often comprised only a single layer of metalling, made up of coarse quarried gravel, whilst those in England generally consisted of about five layers of differing materials (O'Dwyer, 1934, 5). The roads may have been different in nature from their English counterparts, but they played a significant role in the Norman campaign in Wales.

In Monmouthshire, there is a highly significant correlation between the network of Roman roads in the region and the sites selected for castle erection

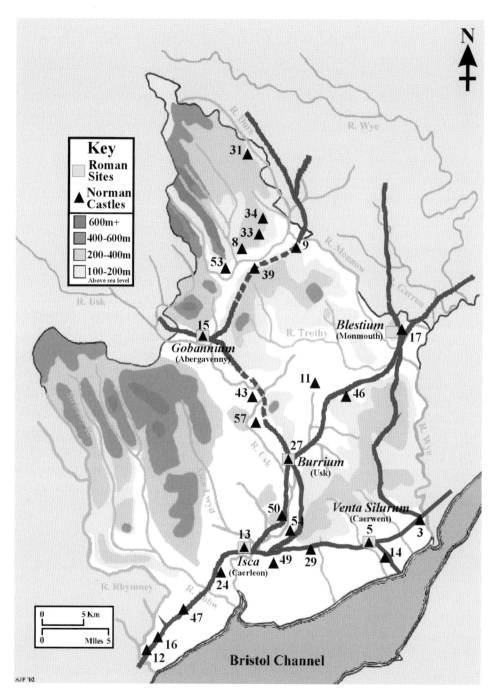

40 Monmouthshire's Roman roads and sites and associated Norman castles. The Roman roads, which do not follow usual straight lines, may be different from those seen in England, but their continuing importance is suggested by the number of castles positioned along the routes

(*41*). Twenty-six of Monmouthshire's castles, or 45 per cent, were strategically located on or near Roman roads, and the vast majority of these castles were positioned at tactically defensible locations overlooking the roads themselves, with 15 castles on or near *pivotal points*. This suggests that, in Monmouthshire at least, the Roman road network was still very much in use and of great importance, especially militarily. It has been stated that 'the Normans made good use of the decayed Roman road network in the south-east' (Davies, 2000, 92). The evidence in Monmouthshire visibly substantiates this claim.

No.	Name	Probable Date	Location
3	Chepstow Castle	1066-69	Mid ridge, at 'pivotal point', overlooking River Wye and Roman road
5	Caerwent Motte	1067-70	Extreme south-eastern corner of Roman town wall
8	Walterstone	1067-71	North bank of River Monnow, overlooking Roman road to south
9	Grosmont Castle	*c*.1070	On a hill, at 'pivotal point', where Roman road from Kenchester to Abergavenny fords River Monnow
11	Raglan Castle	*c*.1070	On a crest, near junction of Roman road from Abergavenny to Monmouth and Monmouth to Usk
12	Rumney Castle	1081 or 1093	Atop steep scarp, at 'pivotal point', where Roman road to Cardiff fords River Rhymney
13	Caerleon Motte	pre-1086	At 'pivotal point', beside River Usk, adjacent to remains of Roman Isca
14	Berries, Ballan Moor	1086-1106	On spur beside Nedern Brook, near 'pivotal point' and Roman road from ferry crossing (Sudbrook to Sea Mills)
15	Abergavenny Castle	*c*.1090	At 'pivotal point', on promontory, overlooking River Usk and River Gwenny, near intersection of Roman roads
16	Caer Castle, St Mellons	*c*.1093	Edge of south-east-facing scarp, overlooking Levels and Bristol Channel, near Roman road from Caerleon to Cardiff
17	Dixton Mound	Eleventh century	On Roman site, at 'pivotal point' beside Wye floodplain, overlooking main Roman road to England
24	Stow Hill Castle	*c*.1100	At 'pivotal point', between River Ebbw and River Usk, near major east-west Roman road, overlooking the port
27	Usk Castle	pre-1120	On Roman fort site, at 'pivotal point', between two rivers, at crossing of Roman roads
29	Penhow Castle	pre-*c*.1129	Overlooking small valley, which provides a route for Roman road from Caerwent
31	Chanstone Tumps	pre-1134	Near 'pivotal point' and close to Roman road from Kenchester to Abergavenny

33	Llancillo Motte	1138–54	North bank of R. Monnow, near 'pivotal point', overlooking Roman road to south
34	Rowlestone Motte	1138–54	North bank of R. Monnow, overlooking floodplain & Roman road to south
39	Goytre Wood	Twelth century	On spur high above R. Monnow, at 'pivotal point', overlooking Roman road
43	St Mary's Yard Mound	Twelth century	W. bank of R. Usk, at 'pivotal point', beside Roman road from Caerleon to Abergavenny
46	Trecastle	Twelth century	At head of a valley, close to Roman road
47	Wentloog Castle	Twelth century	Overlooking east–west Roman road across Monmouthshire
49	Langstone Court Mound	Twelth century	On high ground, at 'pivotal point', overlooking major east–west Roman road
50	Kemeys Inferior Motte	Twelth century	W. side of steep scarp, above Usk floodplain, overlooking Roman road from Usk to Caerleon.
53	The Moat, Treveddw	Twelth century	North bank of R. Monnow, at 'pivotal point, overlooking floodplain & Roman road to south
54	Caer Licyn	Twelth century	On high ridge, overlooking R. Usk & Roman road, at point where valley narrows
57	Trostrey	pre 1225	On spur-end, overlooking R. Usk & Roman road

41 Table of details for the locations of castles associated with Monmouthshire's Roman roads

The geographical locations and dates of foundation of the castles associated with Monmouthshire's Roman roads are useful when considering the question of a Norman land-based or seaborne invasion of Wales. As the positions and dates of the castles are known, it is possible to work out the routes initially taken by the Normans, and their advance along those routes.

It is widely accepted that the medieval Port Way followed the line of a major Roman road across South Wales, and that many important early castles lay along this route; often within or adjacent to Roman forts. This is certainly true in Monmouthshire, as the two earliest castles in the county, Chepstow [3] (1066-69) and Caerwent [5] (1066-67), lay upon this route, along with seven others, two of which are inside Roman fortifications (Caerwent [5] and Caerleon [13]). The Port Way was arguably the first road in the territory utilised and secured by the Normans, as it formed the most natural invasion route for them to have followed. Nelson, writing upon the invasion of Glamorgan, is in accord, stating that the Normans entered the region by way of 'the Roman road leading from Caerleon to Cardiff and then through the Vale of Glamorgan along the line now followed by the A48 highway' (1966, 106). Viewed in isolation this could be used to imply that the Port Way formed the main route for the Norman invasion of South Wales. If this were true, however, one would expect the conqueror of

Glamorgan to be also Lord of Gwent, which was not the case. The conqueror of Glamorgan was Robert fitz Hamon, who was lord of the lands lying directly across the Bristol Channel from the region invaded. Thus, the argument for a largely sea-borne invasion is further strengthened.

Following the advance along the Port Way, it appears that the next inroad for the Normans into Monmouthshire was either the route from Weston under Penyard or the one from Hereford, with Raglan Castle [11] in existence and watching over the stretch of road from Monmouth to Usk by *c.*1070 (*colour plate 12*). This was closely followed by the appropriation of the road from Kenchester (Herefordshire) to Abergavenny, with Grosmont [9], Walterstone [8] and Abergavenny [15] castles all in existence by *c.*1090 (*colour plates 13* and *14*), after which, with these strategically positioned strongholds in place, the Normans were free to usurp the rest of the road network at their leisure.

It is also interesting to note that Caerleon [13], Abergavenny [15], Monmouth [2], Usk [27] and Caerwent [5] castles were all located at the sites of important Roman centres (*40*). Courtney argues that 'it is possible that this reflects continuity of these settlements as administrative centres from Roman times (1983, 69). It is more likely however, that these sites were occupied because the Roman roads continued to play an important role in the region's communication system, and that the Romans had sited their bases at vital strategic points, and these points retained their value into Norman times.

The Roman road network was not the only land-based system for transport, communication and supply in use when the Normans entered Monmouthshire. The lines of Norman advance and Welsh counter-attack were more often the drier and more practicable mountain trackways. Unfortunately, there is no record of the locations of these early trackways, and many are probably now beneath modern roads, but the positions of several Norman castles may indicate the whereabouts of some of these route-ways.

Wern-y-Cwrt Castle Mound [44] overlooks an east–west route that is almost certainly of great antiquity (*colour plate 15*). The track probably ran from Abergavenny at least as far as Raglan, and may have continued all the way to Monmouth and beyond. Its route from Abergavenny is now followed by the modern B4598 as far as Llanvihangle Gobion, and then by minor roads to Raglan, and it seems likely that both the northern ends of the Roman roads from Caerleon to Abergavenny, and Caerleon to Monmouth, overlie it.

The motte at Newcastle [40] is situated in an elevated position atop a north–south ridge now used by the B4347 road. This road continues north up the Golden Valley, to become the B4348, and, along with the B4293 to the south, may represent the remains of an ancient trackway stretching all the way from Chepstow to Hay-on-Wye. The track runs directly past seven early

Norman castles and passes within 2 miles (3.21km) of 12 others. One of the castles on route is Rockfield Castle [51]. Rockfield is situated in an isolated location overlooking the Monnow river valley, but its position suggests that it was better suited to guarding the col now used by the B4233 road. The B4233 runs due east from Abergavenny to Rockfield, deviating only slightly at Llantilio Crossenny. Llantilio (medieval *Llanteylo* or *Llandeilo Gresynni*) means 'the church of St Teilo', the Welsh saint whose principal monastery was at Llandeilo Fawr in Carmarthenshire, and it is likely that the church here may have formed the centre of a large ecclesiastical estate belonging to the Bishop of Llandaff. Llantilio however, may have had prior religious significance, as the church stands atop an entrenched mound, possibly indicating Christian reuse of an earlier, perhaps pagan, site (Thomas, 1977, 132). Either way, it is clear that the road respects the antiquity of the settlement at Llantilio, swinging around it in a large arc to the north and it is feasible that this route represents another ancient trackway.

Finally, O'Dwyer mentions an ancient track that passes close to the old church at St Illtyd (1937, 21) and it is perhaps possible that a trackway ran north–south, first down the Ebbw Fach and then down the Ebbw river valley, from Brecon all the way to the estuary of the River Usk. The route was probably monitored and controlled by a garrison stationed at St Illtyd's Motte [52], which was set high on a promontory overlooking the junction of the two rivers.

It is clear that the vast majority of castles in Monmouthshire were erected in locations that can be associated with the winning, and subsequent monitoring and control, of road and river systems. It is therefore highly likely that these systems formed the focus for the Norman campaign in the region.

THE NORMAN 'INVASION' OF MONMOUTHSHIRE

It has been stated that 'the detailed transactions by which the Normans effected their penetrations … of the Welsh March are hidden from view' (Edwards, 1956, 157), and that 'the conquest of Gwent by the Normans is poorly documented' (Courtney, 1983, 48). Having now established the principal focus of the Norman castle building programme in Monmouthshire, as well as a chronological sequence for the various phases of castle construction at each site throughout the county, it is possible, in combination with what little historical documentation there is left in existence, to construct a convincing narrative for the Norman invasion of the region.

Initial Invasion Period (1066-1093)
The Norman invasion of Wales began when William I created three palatinates centred on Chester, Shrewsbury and Hereford. By the 1070s, Hugh d'Avranches

had extended Norman control along the north coast as far as the Conway estuary, and Roger of Montgomery had begun a slow advance up the Severn valley, but it is generally agreed that the most impressive gains were made by William fitz Osbern. The majority of accounts of the Norman advance into Wales state that 'the most immediate gains were made by William fitz Osbern. He crossed the River Wye and overran much of Gwent before his death in 1071' (Pettifer, 2000, xii). The facts do not appear to fully support this statement however.

Judging by the locations of the castles that William fitz Osbern constructed between 1066 and 1071, it appears that his gains were not perhaps as immediate as was previously supposed (36). The castles that can definitely be attributed to him, The Bage [6], Ewyas Harold [1], Grosmont [9], Monmouth [2], Chepstow [3], Caldicot [4], and Caerwent [5], along with those that he may have constructed, Mouse Castle [7] and Skenfrith [10], suggest only minor excursions into Monmouthshire at this time, as the majority of the castles lay upon the very edge of the county. Indeed, it is far from certain how far William fitz Osbern penetrated into Gwent. The *Brut y Tywysogyon* records that in 1072, Meredud ap Owain of Deuheubarth was defeated on the banks of the River Rhymney by Caradog ap Gruffydd and a Norman knight named Roger de Breuteuil (Jones, 1952, 16 & 1955, 27-8). Caradog was the son of Gruffydd ap Llywelyn Gruffydd ap Rhydderch, the former ruler of Deheubarth. Caradog is documented as ruling Gwent Uwch Coed, Ystradyw and Gwynllŵg during the reign of William I (*Liber Landaviensis*; Rees, 1840, 279), and is further recorded as ruler of Morgannwg in a *Llandaff Charter* of *c*.1075. It is therefore likely that the Normans did not pursue any major invasions into south-east Wales until Caradog's death in 1081. Caradog probably negotiated some kind of temporary alliance for mutual gain with his Norman neighbours.

The same situation seems to have existed in Gwent Is Coed and Ewias. The *Liber Landaviensis* (Rees, 1840, 279) states that during the reign of William I both of these areas were ruled by the cousin and rival of Caradog ap Gruffydd, Rhydderch ap Caradog, and it is possible that both Walterstone Castle [8], built *c*.1067-71 by Walter de Lacy, and Raglan Castle [11], built *c*.1070 by Walter Bloet, were constructed in agreement with the local Welsh ruler, rather than, as previously supposed, to conquer and suppress him. Caradog and Rhydderch continued to rule their respective areas, but accepted the Normans as overlords. In 1071, William fitz Osbern was slain at the battle of Cassel in Flanders and his lands passed to his youngest son Roger, an entry in *Liber Landaviensis* for 1072 referring to Roger fitz Osbern as 'Lord of Gwent' (Rees, 1840, 272-4).

Rhydderch was killed in 1076 by a member of his own family, who may have sided with his rival and cousin Caradog, and Caradog was himself killed in an inter-Welsh battle in 1081. It is only after these two events that the Norman advance into Monmouthshire can be seen to gather momentum (*32* and *42*). In *c*.1086, the Ballon family (?Winebald de Ballon) constructed 'The Berries' [14] motte and bailey on Ballan Moor and Turstin fitz Rolf constructed Caerleon motte [13]; both castles lying in Gwent Is Coed, on land formerly belonging to Rhydderch. By *c*.1090, Winebald's brother, Hamelin de Ballon, had established a motte and bailey at Abergavenny [15], close to the border with Talgarth, presumably in support of the conquest of Brycheinog by Bernard Neufmarché. The castle lay on a highly defensible spur of land overlooking the Rivers Usk and Gwenny, in the cantref of Gwent Uwch Coed, on land that had previously belonged to Caradog. Hamelin probably entered the region by way of the old Roman road from Herefordshire, and must have been a very brave individual indeed, for his newly established castle lay deep within enemy territory. A charter of 1100-6 records Hamelin giving his lands and castle for a *bourg* to the Abbey of St Vincent and St Lawrence (near Le Mans): 'He gave the tithes of all *Wennescoit* [?Gwent Uwch Coed] both of his own demesne and those lands which he had given or would give in fee' (*Cal. Docts.*, Round, 1899, 395-416).

Finally in this period, during widespread Norman advances into Wales following the death of Rhys ap Tewdwr in 1093, Robert fitz Hamon (d.1117) annexed the lowland regions of Gwynllŵg, after conquering the majority of the neighbouring kingdom of Morgannwg (Glamorgan). Robert established both Rumney Castle [12] and Caer Castle [16] on Monmouthshire's western border, close to the River Rhymney, on land that had previously belonged to Caradog. Robert carried out his conquests with the aid of troops stationed in his lands directly across the Bristol Channel. The *Brut y Tywysogyon* records that the Welsh of Brycheiniog, Gwynllŵg and Gwent Uwch Coed were in revolt in 1096, apparently indicating that by this time Robert had conquered Gwynllŵg, and Hamelin de Ballon had conquered Gwent Uwch Coed (Jones, 1952, 20 & 1955, 35). Gwynllŵg – the Newport lordship – and Glamorgan remained in the hands of the fitz Hamon family until 1183, when a daughter, Isabel, the wife of King John, inherited. After the death of Isabel in 1217, the lordship passed into the hands of Richard de Clare.

Attempted Subjugation Period (1094-1134)

It is often assumed that by 1100 the Normans had conquered the majority of Monmouthshire. As Kightly states, 'Following in the footsteps of the Conqueror's Earls, the Normans succeeded in overrunning almost the whole of south and west Wales during the latter part of the eleventh century' (1975, 95). Again however, this generalisation is not supported by the evidence. William is not documented as 'Lord of Monmouth' until 1101-2 (*Cal. Docts.*, Round, 1899, 406) and even then he was still very far from being master of it all. The locations of

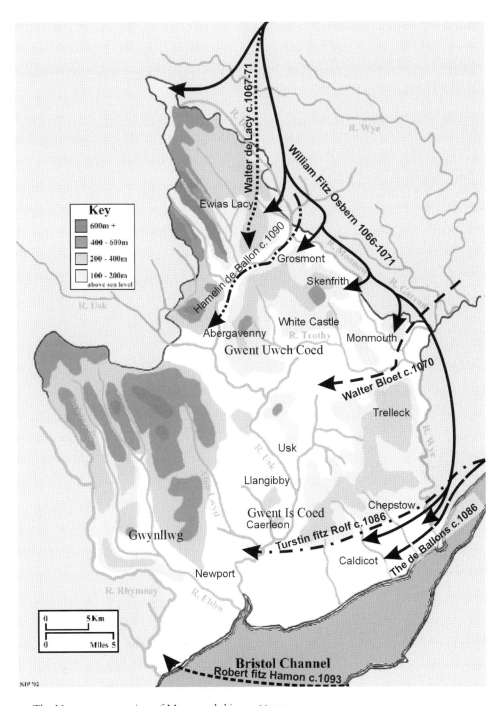

42 The Norman penetration of Monmouthshire, 1066–1093

their castles show that by 1093 the Normans were not in complete control of Monmouthshire, as large areas of land remained wholly unoccupied (*32* and *42*). The Vale of Usk, the western half of Ewias, the northern half of Gwent Uwch Coed, the Caldicott Levels and the valleys of the River Ebbw (i.e. the commote of Machen), contained no castles, and were nodoubt still under Welsh rule. Added to which, as mentioned above, in 1096, the Welsh of Brycheiniog, Gwynllŵg and Gwent Uwch Coed revolted, successfully defeating the Norman army that was sent into Gwent to crush the rebellion, suggesting that the Normans actually lost some ground at this point.

During this period, the Normans were forced to rely heavily upon their castles. Areas already conquered were governed from the sanctuary of existing castles, whilst in previously unoccupied territory new castles were founded to shelter the men engaged in the winning of land (*32*). Usk Castle [27] was most likely built by the de Clares sometime before 1120, and appears to represent the first Norman advance into the amphitheatre-like arena of the Vale of Usk. Militarily, Usk Castle was ideally sited, as it was strategically located at the crossing of two Roman roads and tactically positioned on area of land between two rivers. In Domesday Book, Turstin fitz Rolf is recorded as holding six carucates of land beyond the Usk in 1086; this is unlikely however, as the territory beyond the Usk was not under direct Norman control at this time. Turstin's lands more likely lay near Caerleon, which he is known to have taken during the *Initial Invasion Period*. Winebald de Ballon is recorded as granting lands in Caerleon to Montacute Priory in Somerset in 1129 (*Liber Landaviensis*; Rees, 1840, 30 & 54), suggesting that by this time he had become Lord of Caerleon. In *c.*1128, in an area that would eventually belong to the lordship of Caldicot, Walter fitz Richard de Clare or Geoffrey de Ivry founded Dinham Castle [28]; whilst, in what would later become the lordship of Usk, the castle of Beiliau Llangwm [21] was constructed. These two castles, along with Penhow [29], which was built pre-1129 in the lordship of Chepstow, appear to indicate further Norman annexations of the area around the Wentwood Ridge.

In the developing lordship of Monmouth, Dixton Mound [17] was erected, presumably in an effort to control movement along the Roman road that crosses the River Wye into England via a ford between Walford and Goodrich. The castle was, in all probability, founded to protect England's borders in direct response to the Welsh uprisings of 1096. Another motte constructed for similar reasons was Stow Hill Castle [24]. Stow Hill was Newport's earliest castle. It was founded as a safety precaution following the Welsh uprisings and became the administrative centre of the caput of Newport. Stow Hill Castle was built was built by Robert of Hay in *c.*1100 on land given to him by Robert fitz Hamon. Militarily, Stow Hill Castle sat perfectly in the landscape, it was tactically positioned between the

Rivers Ebbw and Usk, it lay strategically close to the major east–west Roman road across Monmouthshire; it overlooked the port, and it had fine views to the south and south-west.

Another interesting castle of this period is the White Castle [25], built by either Hugh de Lacy (c.1100) or Payn fitz John (1120-35). The White Castle was constructed on a hilltop in open countryside, and at first glance appears to be oddly placed. The other castles often associated with it, Skenfrith [10] (*colour plate 16*) and Grosmont [9], are both located in the Monnow valley adjacent to the river, but the White Castle is 0.621 miles (1km) away from an un-navigable section of the River Trothy, and there is no obvious associated Roman road or ancient trackway. Furthermore, the White Castle, unlike the castles of Skenfrith and Grosmont, is not situated next to a village or parish church: the nearest village being Llantilio Crossenny, 1.5 miles (2.40km) to the south-east.

The church at Llantilio appears to have formed the centre of a large pre-Norman ecclesiastical estate, which belonged to the Bishop of Llandaff, and its existence could account for the White Castle's unusual location. The White Castle was probably constructed upon the nearest unoccupied land beyond the bounds of the ecclesiastical estate. Why build a castle in this area in the first place? The morphology and architecture of the castle suggests an answer to this question. The White Castle has little grace or comfort about it, and it is plainly a functional military structure, which served as a base, store and arsenal. Looking at the castle's imposing bailey it is not difficult to imagine a garrison encamped within the walls, ready to sally forth at a moment's notice, in the event of trouble, either south into the Vale of Usk or north into the Monnow valley.

Between 1219 and 1232, Hubert de Burgh rebuilt the castles of Skenfrith and Grosmont to make them more comfortable and habitable, whereas at the White Castle he simply improved its defences, adding further weight to the argument that it served as a functional military edifice. In the thirteenth century, a garrison stationed at the White Castle closed the routes into Herefordshire and north Monmouthshire. This was done to stop the Welsh, who were operating out of the remaining native lordships of Gwent Is Coed, striking through the Gap of Abergavenny. It is likely that the White Castle's earlier role was very similar.

Finally, during this period, a host of castles emerge in the landscape of Ewias. Ewias would later become the lordship of Ewias Lacy, which was founded no earlier than 1175. Walter de Lacy built Walterstone Castle [8] in Ewias between 1067 and 1071, when he was granted the bulk of the commote by William fitz Osbern, as a reward for being his main follower. Walter died in 1085 and was succeeded by his son Roger. In 1096, King Rufus exiled Roger for his part in the Mowbray Rebellion and his lands were conferred upon his younger brother Hugh de Lacy. Little is known of the acts of Hugh, except for his re-founding of Llanthony Priory in 1108, and it seems likely that he died shortly after this, as a writ sent by Henry I to Bishop Reinhelm of Hereford [1102-1115] sometime between 1108 and 1115, orders the monastery of St Peter to hold all the grants of Walter, Roger and Hugh Lacy in peace (Remfry, 1997, 5).

The castles founded in Ewias between c.1094 and c.1134 were Pont-Hendre [26], built by Payn fitz John, Snodhill [19], built by the de Chandos family, Dorstone [22], built by the de Sollers, and Mynydd-brith [18], Urishay [20], Nant-y-Bar [23], Cothill Tump [30], Chanstone Tumps [31] (*colour plate 17*) and Bacton [32]. It could be argued that the construction of nine castles within a relatively small area, at roughly the same time, is unlikely. It must be remembered, however, that the Olchon, Escley Brook, Upper Monnow, Dulas and Dore rivulets flow through incredibly fertile, narrow, parallel valleys that would have been attractive to Norman settlers from the first, as they were ripe for exploitation and comprised ideal locations for planned towns. Also, in hostile regions, it is not uncommon to find large numbers of castles clustering close together for mutual support, such castles acted in concert against the common enemy. It has been suggested that Ewias, during this period, 'was populated, like Archenfield, by friendly Welsh ... who ... were acting as clients of the Normans and interpreters between the races' (Remfry, 1997, 4). Considering the fact that the construction of castles was an expensive and significant undertaking, this suggestion seems unlikely, but there are two other possible explanations for the large number of castles erected in the region at this time. First, with the death of Hugh (d.1108-15), it is known that the de Lacy estates disintegrated, leading to a period of in-fighting between the relatives and descendants of the first Walter de Lacy; Payn fitz John remained the main contender up until his death in 1137. Second, the Welsh rebellion was slowly gathering pace, even in the previously peaceful commote of Ewias.

The Welsh Offensive (1135-1165)

By the beginning of the twelfth century, it seemed as if, despite occasional reverses, the Norman invaders were on the verge of conquering the whole of Wales. However, with the death of Henry I in 1135, the Welsh rose-up against the Normans on the southern March. In 1136, the Welsh, led by Owain Gwynedd in the north and Gruffydd ap Rhys in the south, fell upon the Norman intruders and overran their castles, until at one stage only Pembrokeshire remained in Norman hands. The Welsh of western Brycheiniog revolted and raided into Gower, inflicting a massive defeat upon the Norman forces set to defend the region, and Iorwerth ab Owain ap Caradog ap Gruffydd ambushed and killed Richard fitz Gilbert de Clare, Lord of Ceredigion. The countryside was again at the mercy of the Welsh. King Stephen mounted two expeditions into Wales to try to quell the rebellion, but both failed dismally. After this, the Marcher Lords were left to deal with the crisis themselves, Stephen essentially abdicating royal leadership in Wales. In 1154, Stephen died and the mighty Henry II ascended the throne. Henry managed to contain the Welsh princes' advances, but was unable to rectify the situation completely. By the end of the century, Henry had forged an uneasy peace with the Welsh. The Anglo-Normans were left holding the low-lying south and east of the country, whilst the Welsh held most of the mountainous north and west.

During these troubled times, the Normans intensified their castle building programme (32). Twenty-six castles were erected, in comparison to 16 in the *Initial Invasion Period* (1066-1093) and 16 in the *Attempted Subjugation Period* (1094-1134). Beginning in the north of the county, four castles were constructed in Ewias: The Moat [53] 1135-54 (*colour plate 18*), Llancillo Motte [33] 1138-54 by the Escotot family, Rowleston Motte [34] 1138-54 by the Turbeville family, and Longtown Castle [35] (*colour plate 19*) *c.*1175 by the second Hugh de Lacy. In 1119, the nobles of the commote of Ewias – as recorded by the Bishop of Llandaff – were Robert de Chandos (Golden Valley), and Geoffrey Broi and Payn fitz John (Ewias Lacy) (*Liber Landaviensis*; Clark, 1910, 93-4). Following the death of the childless first Hugh de Lacy (d.1108-15), Payn fitz John had married Sibyl, Hugh's niece, and through her gained the rights to the de Lacy lands. Payn remained lord of the majority of Ewias until his death in 1137, after which, the de Lacy lands, with the blessing of the recently enthroned Stephen (1135), passed to Cecily, Payn's daughter, and Roger, her new husband (the son of Miles of Gloucester). Gilbert de Lacy, the son of the banished Roger de Lacy, took affront at this decision however, seeing it almost as a declaration of war by Stephen, as he had been in the Royal Court at the time pressing for the reinstatement of his family's lands.

In 1138, Gilbert de Lacy seized Ludlow Castle and presumably declared in favour of the Empress Matilda. In the following year, Stephen besieged Ludlow and eventually managed to oust the rebels, but Gilbert escaped. Around this time, The Moat [53], Rowleston Motte [34], and Llancillo Motte [33] were erected; the latter by the Scotney (*Escotot*) family who became prominent barons of the de Lacys in the late twelfth and early thirteenth centuries. The majority of the magnates of the March sided with Matilda, so that a solid wall of their personal armies completely blocked the way into Wales against any campaign that King Stephen might care to mount against them. Interestingly enough, The Moat, Llancillo and Rowleston castles were all constructed on the northern bank of the River Monnow overlooking the floodplain, ostensibly to impede the progress of any troops along the low-lying river valley that provided ready access into the region via a Roman road situated on the river's southern bank. Rowleston

Motte additionally monitored the Cwm Brook, whose valley afforded passage onto the higher grounds in the south of the commote. In 1149, Gilbert was finally granted that which he sought, his hereditary dues in Herefordshire along with the castles in Ewias, as part of a general anti-King Stephen settlement, and with most of the Marcher lords siding with Matilda, there was precious little Stephen could do to rectify the situation. With the death of Stephen in 1154, Henry II assumed the crown without opposition, and in c.1155, upon the death of Roger, the son of Miles of Gloucester, officially granted the majority of the lordship of Ewias to Gilbert.

In 1160-2, Gilbert (d.1163+) granted his estates to his son, the second Hugh de Lacy, and it was during the next 10 years that Hugh obtained a charter confirming Ewias Lacy and other lands to him. Hugh was an outstanding soldier and seasoned campaigner and during his lifetime became one of Henry II's favourites. In October 1171, as part of a royal expedition, Hugh set sail for Ireland, and remained there after Henry II returned to England in April 1172. Hugh was made Lord of Meath, Constable of Dublin and Justiciar of Ireland, to counterbalance Richard fitz Gilbert de Clare's growing power, eventually rising in 1177, to the rank of Procurator-general of Ireland. In c.1175, Hugh erected Longtown Castle [35], probably to replace the ageing motte and bailey at Pont-Hendre [26] that had been built by Payn fitz John between 1118 and 1137, and established a borough befitting his status. Giraldus states that Hugh 'was the first to succeed in deriving any profit from that which had brought others nothing but trouble' (Scott & Martin, 1978, 191). Hugh held his lands in Ewias until his death in 1186, after which they were briefly seized by the crown, later to be returned to Hugh's son and heir Walter, in 1189.

Moving south from Ewias, we enter the lordship of the Three Castles, which was founded during this period. Following the death of Henry I in 1135, and the subsequent Welsh revolt, it is often stated that:

> two or three years later Stephen reunited the territory of the Three Castles in his own hands *by exchange*, to make a single unit for purposes of defence. In this way, the Three Castles came to be a single lordship, a block of territory which was to remain in one ownership until the last century. (Knight, 1987, 47)

This view is supported by documentary evidence, which shows that throughout the eleventh and twelfth centuries Crown officials administered the lordship. However, in a charter of 1137-8, Grosmont and Llantilio (White Castle) are confirmed as belonging to Roger, son of Miles of Gloucester, and his wife Cecily: 'lands which belonged to her late father, Payn fitz John, by acquisition or inheritance' (Round, 1888, 35-8). It is feasible then that a mutually beneficial *exchange* took place between Stephen, on the one hand, and Roger and Cecily, on the other. The marriage between Cecily and Roger had been arranged by their fathers, Payn fitz John and Miles of Gloucester, in an effort to protect Payn's de Lacy holdings – Cecily was to take the fiefs as dower. Unfortunately for Cecily, Payn was killed whilst chasing a Welsh raiding party and the marriage was halted. After a brief inquiry, Stephen decided, in December 1137, to let the marriage between Roger and Cecily go ahead, with all that it entailed for the Lacy estates. Stephen's blessing did not come without a price, however, and in this case, the price was almost certainly Cecily's holdings of Grosmont and Llantilio (White Castle). Stephen combined these holdings with the one at Skenfrith and thereby gained a block of strategically placed Marcher lordship territory, and into the bargain made a powerful enemy – Gilbert de Lacy.

It is possible that the previously mentioned castles, The Moat [53], Rowleston Motte [34] and Llancillo Motte [33], were raised in southern Ewais in direct response to Stephen's founding of the lordship of the Three Castles. The castles, instead of defending the Normans against the Welsh, were defending Gilbert de Lacy's pro-Matilda barons in Ewias, from Stephen's troops stationed in the lordship of the Three Castles. These events could also account for the construction of the Goytre Wood Castle Mound [39], which was erected in the north-western corner of the lordship of Grosmont at this time. Goytre Wood Castle was tactically positioned on an isolated spur high above the River Monnow. It was erected at a strategic point overlooking a Roman road and lay directly across the valley from de Lacy's Walterstone Castle [8]. It was sited midway between The Moat [53] and Llancillo Motte [33]. Any movement along the Monnow valley would have been easily detected by the garrison, due to the castle's ideal location. Stephen may have instigated the construction of this castle in order to protect the northern border of his Three Castles lordship.

Moving further south, Rockfield Castle [51], Newcastle [40], and Mill Wood Castle Mound [36] *(colour plate 20)* were founded in the lordship of Monmouth, and their highly defensible locations are indicative of the troubled times in which they were constructed. Newcastle and Rockfield castle appear to have been built to monitor and control movement along two ancient trackways, one stretching from Chepstow to Hay-on-Wye and the other running from Abergavenny to Rockfield itself. Mill Wood Castle Mound, on the other hand, lies beside a modern bridge across the River Trothy and may once have guarded a river crossing into the south-west corner of the Monmouth lordship. As the Monmouth lordship borders England, it is often assumed that it fell swiftly into Norman hands. However, the church of Llangattock and its chapel of St Maughans and Llanllwyd are not documented in Norman hands until a papal Bull of 1146, which suggests that the Normans did not gain complete control of the lordship until the early twelfth century. The strategic and tactical locations chosen for the castles erected during this period support this suggestion.

A similar pattern of castle building can be observed in the remainder of the old cantref of Gwent Uwch Coed, in the fast-developing lordship of Abergavenny. Castles in this area were likewise erected at important strategic locations. Pen-y-Clawdd Motte [42] was constructed in a tactical location, at the foot of the steep eastern slopes of the mountain of Bryn Arrw, next to one of the sources of the River Gwenny, 0.621 miles (1km) away from and overlooking the River Monnow. The castle's location indicates a purely military function, observing movement along the Monnow and Gavenny Valleys leading from Abergavenny towards Herefordshire. It is also interesting to note that Pen-y-Clawdd Motte lies directly across the river from The Moat [53], suggesting that its builder may have sympathised with either Gilbert de Lacy or Stephen.

St Mary's Yard Mound [43] was erected on the west bank of the River Usk, adjacent to a Roman road from Caerleon to Abergavenny, on a 'pivotal point', monitoring the area's communications routes. Similar functions were performed in the east of the lordship by Coed-y-Mount [38] (*colour plate 21*), which was constructed atop a ridge in a highly defensible position commanding the valley of the River Trothy, and Wern-y-Cwrt Castle Mound [44], which was erected in a valley overlooking an east–west route-way of great antiquity. Both castles were designed to counter easy passage into the region along the river valleys. The Hendre Hafaidd [56] ringwork was tactically positioned between two brooks on an elevated spur of land at the very heart of the Abergavenny lordship. Its isolated location suggests that it served in a similar capacity to that of the White Castle, as a military base, store and arsenal. St Illtyd's Motte [52], which was built upon the western extremity of the lordship, probably lay within the bounds of the Newport lordship (Gwynllŵg) and as such will be discussed below. Lastly, if doubts prevail over the military significance of the region's castles, it is worth remembering that in 1184 Abergavenny Castle was attacked and taken during a Welsh revolt. The Welsh used scaling ladders to enter the bailey and captured the castle's constable, his wife and most of the garrison (Giraldus; Thorpe, 1978, 111-13).

South of the nascent lordship of Abergavenny, in the lordship of Usk, the Normans founded five new castles, four of which have discernible military functions. New House Ringwork [45] was constructed atop a hillock, in an isolated location, with commanding views northwards up the valleys of the Olway and Nant-y-Wilcae to Raglan. The D-shaped ringwork of Graig Foel [55] was erected on a steep-sided spur projecting from high ground above the flood-plain of the River Usk. Both of these castles were positioned in tactically defensible locations, at key strategic sites connected with the control of the region's rivers. Whilst Trecastle [46], situated at the head of a valley, and Trostrey [57], erected on the tip of a prominent spur overlooking the Usk valley, were both built to monitor and control movement along the Roman roads that pass close to them.

It has been argued that the castles founded near Usk at this time reflect the continuing 'process of Normanisation' (Courtney, 1983, 141). This implies that the lordship was stable enough to support the introduction of Norman principles and doctrines, ideologies and strictures, but the locations of the newly built castles suggest an unstable area, which was still very much at risk. In truth, signs of integration and permanent settlement within the region do not occur until the thirteenth century. An inquisition of 1296, reveals, for the first time, the existence of both English and Welsh fees in the lordship (*Cal. Inq. p. m.*, 3, Edw. I, 371). The construction of the fifth castle, Cwrt-y-Gaer Ringwork [41], in the late twelfth century, at a site with no obvious military significance, can perhaps be seen as heralding the dawn of peaceful coexistence and settlement within the region. Cwrt-y-Gaer is situated between Pill Brook and another minor tributary of the River Usk, on the eastern end of a ridge, overlooking the church and hamlet of Wolvesnewton. The area comprises some of the lordship's richest soils, and is ideal for arable cultivation, as the nearby 'Model Farm' demonstrates (ST 444 987). Furthermore, Wolvesnewton 'the new *tun* of the Wolf family', is the lordship's only major English place name.

Moving west, we enter the small lordship of Llangibby, which may have been based upon a Welsh cantref named Tregrug (Rees, 1930, 194). The lordship was clearly independent, as documentation from the late thirteenth century shows that Llangibby was eventually administered as part of the Usk lordship (*Min. Acc.*, 1262-3; SC6/1202/1), but was held separately from the King (*Inq. p. m.*, Edw. I, 1307; C133/130/62). In the centre of the lordship, during the *Welsh Offensive*, Llangibby Castle Mound [58] was constructed. The ringwork was built high above the floodplain of the River Usk, and was protected on both its northern and southern sides by valleys and streams. The castle's tactical location reflects the continuing strategic importance of the Usk Valley. To the south of Llangibby, on the western edge of the lordship of Chepstow, Caer Licyn [54] was erected, and again there is no disputing the castle's military potential. It was built on a commanding ridge overlooking the River Usk and a Roman road that runs south from Usk itself, at the point where the valley narrows considerably. The location is faultless tactically and strategically the castle is ideally situated to monitor and control the nearby systems of transport, communication and supply.

The reason for the construction of these two castles is apparent. Llangibby Castle Mound secured Llangibby itself, and in addition protected the western border of the lordship of Usk, whilst Caer Licyn protected the western border of the lordship of Chepstow. The borders of both lordships were at risk of attack from the east at the time, as in 1154 the Normans had lost Caerleon to the Welsh. The Sheriff of Gloucester was allowed 40s for crown lands granted to Morgan ap Owain in Caerleon (*Great Pipe Roll*, Henry II, 1155-8, 49), and this probably represents acceptance by the newly enthroned Henry II of the military seizure of Caerleon by the Welsh. Caerleon remained in Welsh hands until William Marshall seized it in 1217, after which the de Clare family purchased it.

The fact that Caerleon was attacked and taken by the Welsh accounts for the construction of three castles within the lordship itself at this time. Graig Wood [48] was constructed high above the floodplain of the Afon Llwyd in order to monitor and control the river valley, Langstone Court Mound [49] was erected at a 'pivotal point', on high ground immediately to the south of and overlooking a major east–west Roman road across Monmouthshire, and Kemeys Inferior Motte [50] was built in a naturally defensible location, on the western edge of a steep scarp slope, overlooking the Usk valley. Each of these castles bears the hallmarks of military endeavour and their dates of foundation place them in the period immediately preceding the *Welsh Offensive* – pre 1154.

Finally, moving west, we enter the lordship of Newport, which is perhaps the most interesting of all the lordships during this period. In *c.*1114, Robert of Hay appears to have relinquished the lordship of Newport (the southern half of the old cantref of Gwynllŵg) to Robert, earl of Gloucester, who ruled it, along with Morgannwg, until his death in 1147. In 1135, Robert granted 300 acres of the coastal levels in his demesne at Rumney to the sons of the Welsh prince of the commote of Machen (the northern upland half of the old cantref of Gwynllŵg). This was, in all probability, a diplomatic effort to restore peace to the area following the widespread violence that had erupted with the death of Henry I. It has recently been suggested that Machen came under the control of Robert fitz Hamon as early as *c.*1093 (www.castlewales.com/glam_rum.html). Other evidence indicates however, that Machen, which formed the northern upland area of the Newport lordship, remained under Welsh rule until the late thirteenth century.

In the Newport lordship, there was a clearly defined frontier. The Normans occupied the low-lying coastal regions to the south and the Welsh occupied the high uplands to the north (*43*). The stone castles of Twyn Tudor, Castle Meredydd and Castell Taliorum, which were built by the Welsh in the Machen uplands, signify continuing Welsh rule in the area. The Welsh also constructed earth and timber castles in the commote, as they quickly learnt to imitate the Normans in their construction of castles. From the late eleventh century onwards, both Normans and Welsh were engaged in building and capturing castles. Between 1135 and 1165, in an effort to protect the lowland lordship of Newport from Welsh incursions, the Normans appear to have raised Twyn-Bar-Lwm Castle

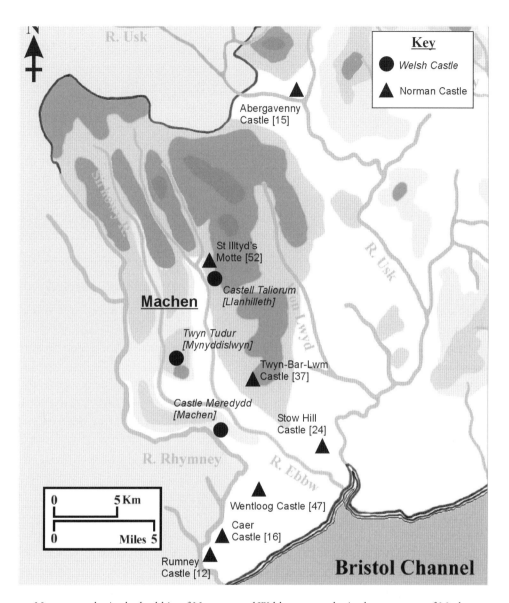

43 Norman castles in the lordship of Newport and Welsh stone castles in the commote of Machen. From the late eleventh century onwards, both the Normans and the Welsh were engaged in building and capturing castles

[37], within a large Iron Age enclosure atop a coal-measure mountain, St Illtyd's Motte [52]. It was raised upon a high promontory to the east of and overlooking the divide of the Ebbw Fach and Ebbw rivers, and Wentloog Castle [47], situated in a relatively low-lying position overlooking the main east–west Roman road that crosses Monmouthshire.

Twyn-Bar-Lwm, at 404m A.O.D., and St Illtyd's, at 350m A.O.D., are Monmouthshire's most elevated Norman castles, and their positions are highly instructive. To the west of the castles lies the Ebbw river valley, which forms a natural north–south pass, through which, passing close to the old church at St Illtyd, runs an ancient trackway, possibly stretching all the way from Brecon in the north, via the Ebbw Fach, to the estuary of the River Usk in the south. This track formed a perfect route for invasion of the lowland lordship of Newport by the Welsh of the uplands. The Normans, in order to protect themselves, sealed this passage with the construction of two strategically positioned castles. To the north, at the point where the trackway emerged from the Ebbw Fach river valley, St Illtyd's Motte was erected, and to the south, at the point where the trackway emerged from the Ebbw river valley, Twyn-Bar-Lwm Castle was erected.

As these castles were situated close to hostile territory, in remote and exposed locations, they relied upon the region's mountainous terrain for their defence. Norman engineers carefully singled out two elevated, naturally defensible, positions for the construction of the castles. The elevation afforded the garrisons an impressive view of the surrounding landscape, and an approaching enemy would have been easily spotted. With the castles in place, the Normans gained control of the route-way, blocked passage to the Welsh, and thereby protected the Newport lordship from harm. Furthermore, if an approaching Welsh force were too large for the garrison to sensibly deal with, signal fires could be lit to attract aid and serve warning. On a clear day, a beacon fire lit on Twyn-Bar-Lwm would be visible not only in the lowland Newport lordship, but could be seen from the English side of the Bristol Channel.

As explained in chapter two, fortifications were often built on or near an enemy's side of the mountains as a means of keeping a military presence in a remote or distant area. A fortification on the 'away side' was frequently supported by another fortification built on the 'home side' of the watershed, which served as a rearward barrier and a base of operations. It seems reasonable to suggest that St Illtyd's in the north and Twyn-Bar-Lwm in the south were functioning in this way: acting in concert for mutual support.

A similar system of control has been noted in the neighbouring lordship of Glamorgan (Morgannwg), which was also ruled by Robert, earl of Gloucester. Glamorgan, like Newport, comprises a fertile lowland zone and an inhospitable upland interior, and 'the castles on the southern fringes of the uplands primarily served to stiffen the outer perimeter of the lowlands' (RCAHMW, 1991, 5). In the later period, after the annexations, very few castles were founded or improved in the uplands, those that were being works of an essentially military nature acting as advanced garrison-castles (ibid.).

Finally, at this time, Wentloog Castle [47] was constructed to protect the Port Way: the main east–west Roman road across South Wales. It was vitally important to guard the Port Way as, descending from the uplands, the Welsh could easily, by way of this route and a river crossing near Rumney Castle [12], have attacked Cardiff. Again, it is clear that this system of control extended into neighbouring Glamorgan (Morgannwg), as many of the lordship's earliest castles are positioned along the route of the Port Way.

The Norman strategies of castle building in the Newport lordship appear to have been fairly successful, as Robert continued to rule it until his death in 1147, after which it passed into the hands of his son and heir, William, who ruled until his own death in 1183. The lands then passed, for a time, into royal custody. The Welsh of the commote of Machen continued to present problems to the Normans however. In 1236, Gilbert Marshall seized the castle at Machen from Morgan ap Hywel, although he quickly restored it through fear of Llywelyn, despite the fact that he had made a great dyke or fortification around it (*Cal. of Pat. Rolls*, 1, Henry III, 160). By 1251, the commote was still in Welsh hands, the possession of Maredudd ap Gruffydd (Lloyd, 1954, 713, n.113).

COMMOTES, CANTREFS AND CASTLES: A CONCLUSION

The land through which the Normans moved was made up of cantrefs, which they occupied one by one, replacing the chieftain's llys with the lord's castle, taking over the obligations of the native Welsh, and transforming them into feudal dues.

Pounds, 1990, 156

The Welsh law books of the twelfth and thirteenth centuries show, if somewhat theoretically, that Welsh administration before the Norman Conquest was based upon kingdoms divided into cantrefs, which were in turn comprised of commotes. The law books specify two commotes per cantref, but this probably represents an idealised picture. The commote was approximately equivalent to the English hundred and was in turn composed of townships or trefydd (sing. tref). At the head of each commote was the tywysog or prince, and his home, the llys, was generally a purpose-built timber hall where he held court and ruled over his small patrimony. Monmouthshire itself was divided between four such cantrefs, Ewias, Gwent Uwch Coed, Gwent Is Coed and Gwynllŵg, and these were further subdivided into commotes (*30*).

It has long been argued that commotes formed 'units of penetration' for the Normans, who, instead of obtaining Welsh lands in a somewhat piecemeal fashion, intentionally sought to acquire commotes, or groups of commotes. Pounds states that 'when the Normans began to conquer Wales they occupied commotes, one at a time, so that these units remained the building blocks of which feudal Wales was made' (1990, 154). Edwards believed that the commote was bound up with the Welsh institution of the tywysog (prince), and that the Normans, 'by adopting the procedure of seizing commotes … were acquiring more than land: they were acquiring 'lordship'' (1956, 169-70). A view also upheld by Nelson, who stated, 'the marcher lords derived their powers directly from the Welsh chieftains whom they replaced' (1966, 158-9).

No.	Name	Parish	Cantref	Commote	Lordship
7	Mouse Castle (Cusop)	Clifford	?Gwent Uwch Coed	Ewias	Ewias Lacy
23	Nant-y-Bar (Dorstone)	Dorstone	?Gwent Uwch Coed	Ewias	Ewias Lacy
18	Mynydd-brith	Dorstone	?Gwent Uwch Coed	Ewias	Ewias Lacy
19	Snodhill Castle	Peterchurch	?Gwent Uwch Coed	Ewias	Ewias Lacy
20	Urishay Castle	Peterchurch	?Gwent Uwch Coed	Ewias	Ewias Lacy
26	Pont-Hendre	Longtown	?Gwent Uwch Coed	Ewias	Ewias Lacy
8	Walterstone	Walterstone	?Gwent Uwch Coed	Ewias	Ewias Lacy
30	Cothill Tump	Turnastone	?Gwent Uwch Coed	Ewias	Ewias Lacy
31	Chanstone Tumps	Vowchurch	?Gwent Uwch Coed	Ewias	Ewias Lacy
1	Ewyas Harold Castle	Ewyas Harold	?Gwent Uwch Coed	Ewias	Ewias Lacy
6	The Bage (Bach Motte)	Clifford	?Gwent Uwch Coed	Ewias	Ewias Lacy
22	Dorstone Castle	Dorstone	?Gwent Uwch Coed	Ewias	Ewias Lacy
32	Bacton (Newcourt Farm)	Bacton	?Gwent Uwch Coed	Ewias	Ewias Lacy
15	Abergavenny Castle	Abergavenny	Gwent Uwch Coed	Uwch Coed	Abergavenny
25	The White Castle	Llantilio Crossenny	Gwent Uwch Coed	Teirtref	White Castle
9	Grosmont Castle	Grosmont	Gwent Uwch Coed	Teirtref	Grosmont
10	Skenfrith Castle	Skenfrith	Gwent Uwch Coed	Teirtref	Skenfrith
2	Monmouth Castle	Monmouth	Gwent Uwch Coed	Teirtref	Monmouth
17	Dixton Mound	Monmouth	Gwent Uwch Coed	Teirtref	Monmouth
27	Usk Castle	Usk	Gwent Is Coed	Brynbuga	Usk
11	Raglan Castle	Raglan	Gwent Is Coed	Brynbuga	Usk
21	Beiliau Llangwm	Llangwm	Gwent Is Coed	Brynbuga	Usk
13	Caerleon Motte	Caerleon	Gwent Is Coed	Edeligion	Caerleon

5	Caerwent Motte	Caerwent	Gwent Is Coed	Is Coed	Chepstow
14	The Berries, Ballan Moor	Caerwent	Gwent Is Coed	Is Coed	Chepstow
3	Chepstow Castle	Chepstow	Gwent Is Coed	Is Coed	Chepstow
29	Penhow Castle	Penhow	Gwent Is Coed	Is Coed	Chepstow
28	Dinham Castle	Dinham	Gwent Is Coed	Is Coed	Caldicot
4	Caldicot Castle	Caldicot	Gwent Is Coed	Is Coed	Caldicot
12	Rumney Castle	Rumney	Gwynllŵg (Morgannwg)	Newport	
16	Caer Castle – St Mellons	Rumney	Gwynllŵg (Morgannwg)	Newport	
24	Stow Hill Castle	Newport		Gwynllŵg (Morgannwg)	Newport

44 Table showing the cantref, commote and lordship for castles constructed in Monmouthshire between 1066 and 1134

Edwards' theories derived from a study of the lordship of Cardigan, where he observed that 11 castles and the associated castelries, which were founded between 1100 and 1136, correlated closely with the 10 commotes of Ceredigion (1956, 165-9). The situation in Monmouthshire is entirely different. Between 1066 and 1134, the Normans founded 13 castles in the commote of Ewias, one in Uwch Coed, five in Teirtref, three in Brynbuga, six in Is Coed, and three in the cantref of Gwynllŵg, whilst in the commotes of Tryleg, Tregrug and Llebenydd no Norman castles were constructed (*44* and *45*).

This inconsistent distribution indicates that the Normans were adhering to a different strategy within the region. Judging by the results of this chapter, the primary objective of the Norman campaign in Monmouthshire was the appropriation of the county's systems of communication, transportation and supply, which suggests an active military take-over. The evidence from Ceredigion, on the other hand, suggests a more politically orientated campaign, which focused upon the appropriation of individual commotes.

Lordship	Cantref from which the Lordship was carved	Associated Commotes	Date of initial occupation	First occupied by
Abergavenny	Gwent Uwch Coed	Uwch Coed	*c.*1090	Hamelin de Ballon
Caerleon	Gwent Is Coed	Edeligion, Llebenydd	*c.*1086	Turstin fitz Rolf
Caldicot	Gwent Is Coed	Is Coed	*c.*1067	William fitz Osbern
Chepstow	Gwent Is Coed	Is Coed	*c.*1066-9	William fitz Osbern

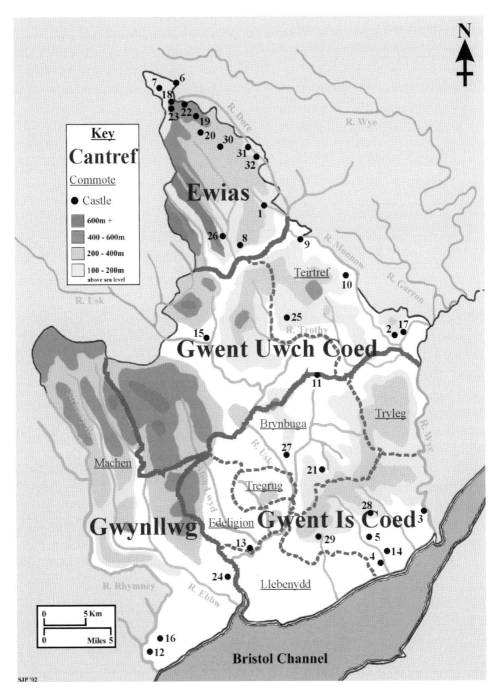

45 Monmouthshire's cantrefs, commotes and castles constructed between 1066 and 1134. No Norman castles were constructed in the commotes of Tryleg, Tregrug and Llebenydd at this time

Ewias Lacy	?Gwent Uwch Coed	Ewias	c.1067	Walter de Lacy
Grosmont	Gwent Uwch Coed	Teirtref	c.1070	William fitz Osbern
Llangibby	Gwent Is Coed	Tregrug	pre-1262	Gilbert de Clare
Monmouth	Gwent Uwch Coed	Teirtref	c.1066-9	William fitz Osbern
Newport	Gwynllŵg (Morgannwg)	Machen	c.1093	Robert fitz Hamon
Skenfrith	Gwent Uwch Coed	Teirtref	c.1070	William fitz Osbern
Usk	Gwent Is Coed	Brynbuga	c.1120	Walter fitz Richard de Clare
White Castle	Gwent Uwch Coed	Teirtref	c.1100 or 1120-35	Hugh de Lacy or Payn fitz John
Trelleck	Gwent Is Coed	Tryleg	?1230	?the de Clare's

46 Table showing the relationship between Norman lordships and pre-Norman land divisions in Monmouthshire

This chapter has shown that the Normans were active at a wide variety of locations across Monmouthshire from an early date (46). This further discredits the notion that the Normans occupied the region's cantrefs or commotes one at a time. Edwards argues that William fitz Osbern and his son Roger de Breuteuil held the two cantrefs of Gwent Uwch Coed and Gwent Is Coed between 1066 and 1075 (1956, 162-3), but Domesday Book does no more than record that they had been active in the region, between the Rivers Monnow and Usk (Williams & Martin, 2002, 446), presumably because neither one held any area of land substantial enough for the Domesday Commissioners to describe. The boundaries of the cantrefs and commotes did eventually provide a basic framework for the new system of lordships established in Monmouthshire (30, 47, and 48), and in due course the Norman castelries, knight's fees, mesne lordships and manors gradually distorted or obliterated the old Welsh divisions.

Throughout their campaigns in Monmouthshire, the Normans rigorously adhered to tried and tested military techniques. Relying upon their detailed knowledge of strategy and tactics, the Normans built castles in naturally defensible locations overlooking the region's major rivers, roads and trackways, whilst others were founded close to important passes, fords and key sections of coastline. 'The castles, almost without exception, displayed the Norman talent for choosing strategic sites to maximum military and territorial advantage (Davies, 2000, 90). Then, with the lines of transport, communication and supply assured, the Normans reorganised the landscape to form lordships or castleries, each one centred upon a major castle. From this position, the Normans were safe to reap the benefits of their conquests.

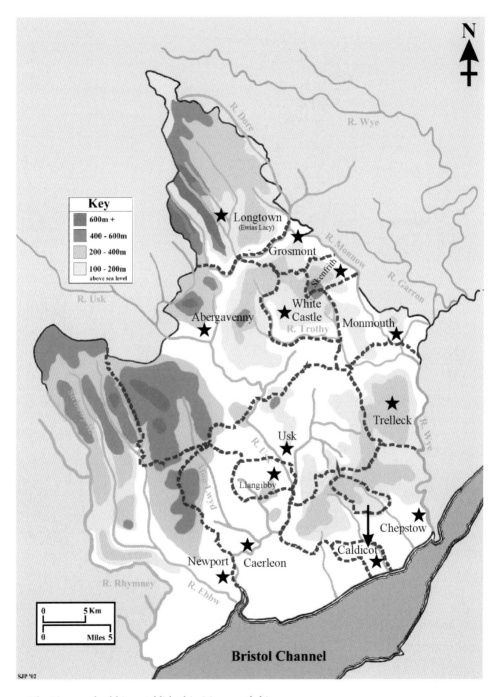

47 The Norman lordships established in Monmouthshire

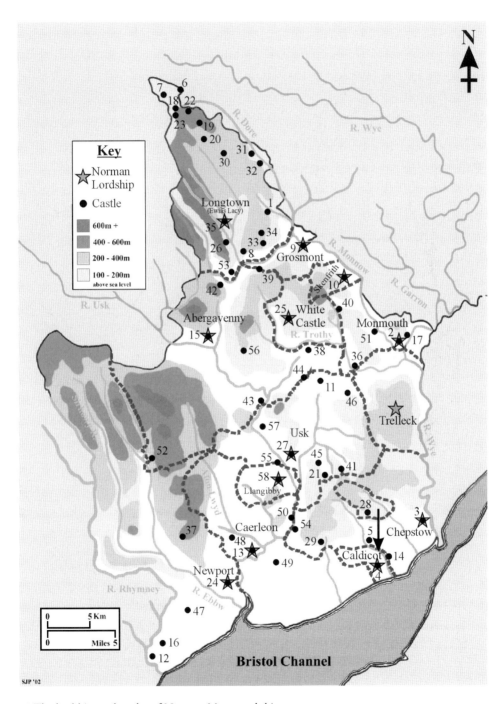

48 The lordships and castles of Norman Monmouthshire

The Norman conquest of Monmouthshire was not a single event planned and co-ordinated by a king, or powerful lord, but consisted instead of many campaigns, carried out by numerous individuals, at a variety of locations, across a broad time span. This, in effect, demonstrates just how well established the principles behind the Norman castle building programme were and explains why the campaign was not a complete success. The Norman Conquest was the idea of one man, which was accomplished in less than 20 years, and embraced the whole of England. The Norman conquest of Wales was achieved piecemeal, over the course of some 120 years, and only ever extended permanently to half of Wales; broadly speaking, the southern half. The Norman campaign in Wales was thwarted partly by the country's hostile terrain, thick forests, dense undergrowth and unforgiving weather, partly by the strength of the Welsh resistance, and partly by the fact that the Welsh were afforded time to adapt. Giraldus records that it was from the Normans that the Welsh learnt how to use arms, construct castles and fight on horseback (Giraldus; Thorpe, 1978).

5

Early castles in Meath

The Celts came from a land beyond the sea,
And settled at last on Erin's shore,
And sang their songs of simple glee
And loved and fought in the days of yore.
But the Normans came with their feudal lore
To banish forever the life they knew,
Earl and Marshall – and something more –
Sheriff and Bailiff and hangman too.

from *The Ballade of Law and Order* by Colm O'Lochlainn
(in Brady, 1961, 38)

WAR, KINGSHIP AND TREACHERY

The Early Middle Ages (*c.*400-1200) have long been considered a 'Golden Age' in Ireland's history. In a country newly converted to Christianity, literature, learning and the arts flourished. The rural landscape was neatly divided into units, interspersed with wealthy proto-urban monastic centres, and society was neatly divided into a hierarchy. The lower classes lived in scattered farmsteads, sometimes inside defended enclosures, in comfortable dwellings, and reared cattle and pigs, and grew cereal crops. At the upper levels of society, Irish kings employed chancellors and issued charters, acquired houses in Norse sea-ports or monastic centres, constructed naval fleets, fielded large well-organised armies, which they could provision and keep in the field for months at a time, presided over reforming synods of the church – gatherings which might also issue regulations on secular matters – and claimed territorial ownership over the kingdoms which they ruled. A far cry from the 'primitive', 'barbarous', 'uncultivated', 'axe wielding', 'treacherous', 'wild and inhospitable people', portrayed by Giraldus, who further claimed that the Irish 'lived like beasts' and went 'naked and unarmed into battle' (O'Meara, 1985). Although an obvious form of early propaganda, the writing of Giraldus does contain an element of truth, the Irish *were* a warlike nation.

The backdrop that formed the setting for the arrival of the Anglo-Normans in Ireland was in many respects similar to the situation that had existed in Wales prior to their invasion: a patchwork of rivalry, infighting and continual aggression. The history of Ireland in the eleventh and twelfth centuries was the history of a nation evolving its monarchy. The armies of provincial kings marched and counter-marched across a 'trembling sod' in an attempt to secure for their leader a most elusive goal, the High-Kingship of all Ireland (Byrne, 1993). Warfare then, or at the very least an absence of peace, was central to the Irish historical experience (Bartlett & Jeffery, 1996), and the relentless struggle for power resulted in alliances and boundaries that shifted continually.

In 1072, Conor O'Melaghlin, king of Meath, killed the over ambitious king of Leinster, Dermot MacMaelnamo, only to be slain himself the following year. The deaths of these two influential men had a dual outcome. First, the way was cleared for the king of Munster, Toirrdelbach O'Brien, to rise to power, and second, the previously potent kingdom of Meath went into a decline.

From 1086 to 1114, the most dominant provincial king in Ireland was Muirchertach O'Brien of Munster (*49* and *50*). Muirchertach and his father Toirrdelbach had, between them, come close to achieving true High-Kingship in Ireland from their capital at Limerick. Commanding most of the country, they instigated friendly relations with the Norwegian king of the House of Ivar at Waterford, established trading links with Rouen, the capital of the Duchy of Normandy, and encouraged ecclesiastical reform. Their pretensions to the monarchy of Ireland were held in check by Domnaill MacLochlainn of Ailech (in The North) however, who, being militarily more powerful, remained a rival claimant to the High-Kingship from 1083-1121. This stalemate continued until 1114, when Muirchertach fell ill and was deposed by his brother Diarmait. Diarmait made a secret peace with Turlough O'Connor, king of Connacht – a former ally of MacLochlainn's – and upon the death of Muirchertach in 1119, Turlough partitioned Munster between the sons of Diarmait and Tadg MacCarthaig, thereby destroying the power of the O'Briens. With Munster greatly weakened, Turlough then threw his energies into making himself High-King of Ireland.

Putting aside for a moment Meath's strategic, economic and ecclesiastical importance, the county held a huge symbolic significance for any would-be

49 The political divisions of Ireland, c.1169. *After: Byrne, 1993 & Walsh, 2003*

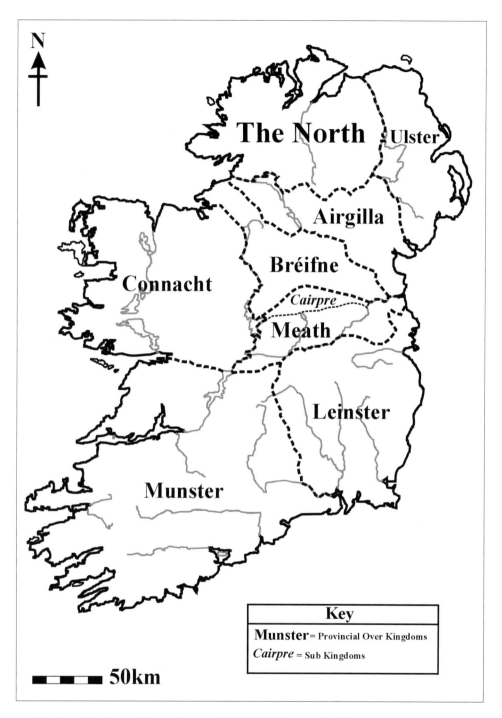

50 Ireland's political geography on the eve of the Anglo-Norman invasion

High-King. Tradition suggests that from the second century AD, Meath was known as the Royal County, territory of the High-Kings of Ireland whose traditional residence was the Hill of Tara. Meath figures predominately in any narrative on Ireland's history. In the years 1115, 1125, 1127 and 1138 the ever ambitious Turlough made attempts to oust Murrough O'Melaghlin (*Murchad*) (*51*), king of Meath, to secure the kingdom for himself. On each occasion however, Murrough managed to hold off Turlough's advances, and continued to rule until his capture by Turlough's ally, Tiernan O'Rourke, king of Bréifne, in 1143. Meath was then divided into three. Tiernan managed to push the borders of his kingdom of Bréifne as far south as Kells and Slane, 'and was styled not altogether incorrectly as "King of the Meath Men" by Giraldus' (Scott & Martin, 1978, 25). Tiernan's enemy, and uterine brother, Donncadh O'Carroll, king of Airgialla – and nephew of Murrough – occupied the ancient Brega kingdom of Fir Arda Ciannachta (Co. Louth). Whilst to the south, Dermot MacMurrough, king of Leinster – and Tiernan's greatest adversary – extended the borders of his kingdom into southern Brega. In 1150, Donncadh managed to retake Dermot's gains from him, restoring Murrough O'Melaghlin to the western half of Meath in 1152. Melaghlin (*Maelechlainn*), Murrough's son, was then given the eastern half of Meath, and together father and son ruled jointly as kings. Murrough's rule of West Meath was short-lived, as he died in 1153, after which Melaghlin claimed to be sole king of Meath.

Melaghlin ruled Meath until he was poisoned in 1155, at which point Donnell O'Melaghlin (*Donnchad*) seized the crown. Donnell's right to kingship was contested by his brother Dermot (*Diarmaid*), and as a result Donnell was deposed by the men of Meath and Dermot set up in his place. Over the next four years, Meath became a war-zone, as the two brothers – each a puppet of a powerful ally – fought over the crown. In 1159, Donnell finally gained 'all of Meath from the Shannon to the sea', but was slain the very next year by the king of Delbna Mór (in Westmeath), the kingship reverting for a time to Dermot.

In 1156, Turlough O'Connor, king of Connacht, died, and upon his death supreme power in Ireland passed to Muirchertach MacLochlainn, the king of Tír Eógain (in The North). Muirchertach was quick to ally himself with Dermot MacMurrough, king of Leinster, against his main opponent, Turlough's son and heir, Rory O'Connor of Connacht, whilst unsurprisingly, Dermot's mortal enemy, Tiernan O'Rourke, king of Bréifne, allied himself with Rory. The north–south alliance between Muirchertach and Dermot proved successful, and Muirchertach held the upper hand in Ireland for the next 10 years. During this period Dermot, with the support of his ally, again expanded the northern borders of his kingdom into southern Brega (Meath), but this programme of aggressive expansion brought him once more into conflict with Tiernan of

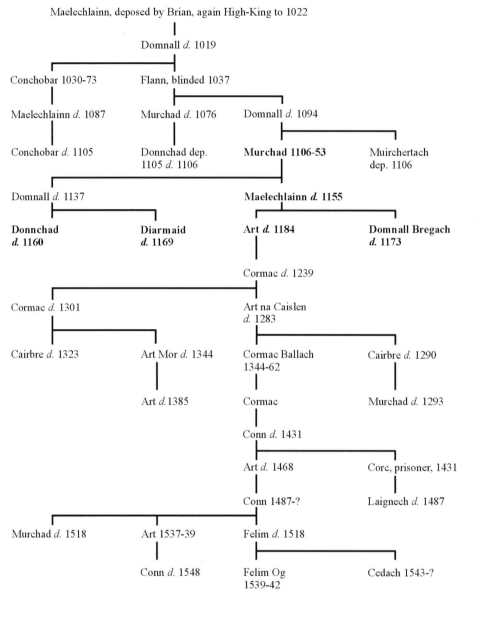

Maelechlainn, deposed by Brian, again High-King to 1022

Domnall *d.* 1019

Conchobar 1030-73   Flann, blinded 1037

Maelechlainn *d.* 1087   Murchad *d.* 1076   Domnall *d.* 1094

Conchobar *d.* 1105   Donnchad dep.   **Murchad 1106-53**   Muirchertach
1105 *d.* 1106   dep. 1106

Domnall *d.* 1137   **Maelechlainn *d.* 1155**

Donnchad   **Diarmaid**   **Art *d.* 1184**   **Domnall Bregach**
***d.* 1160**   ***d.* 1169**   ***d.* 1173**

Cormac *d.* 1239

Cormac *d.* 1301   Art na Caislen
d. 1283

Cairbre *d.* 1323   Art Mor *d.* 1344   Cormac Ballach   Cairbre *d.* 1290
1344-62

Art *d.* 1385   Cormac   Murchad *d.* 1293

Conn *d.* 1431

Art *d.* 1468   Corc, prisoner, 1431

Conn 1487-?   Laignech *d.* 1487

Murchad *d.* 1518   Art 1537-39   Felim *d.* 1518

Conn *d.* 1548   Felim Og   Cedach 1543-?
1539-42

Of unknown descent: Magnus, who became King of East Meath in 1173 with the death of Domnall Bregach.
Magnus was hanged in 1175 at Trim by the Anglo-Normans for his part in the 1174 uprising.

Maelechlainn Beg, styled King of Temair in 1189, when he made submission to the King of
Connacht. Banished in 1213.

51 Genealogical table of the Ua Maelechlainn Kings of Meath. The kings that feature in this chapter
are shown in bold. *After: Walsh, 2003, 106*

Bréifne, and a bitter hatred grew between the two men – hatred strengthened by the fact that in 1152, during the course of yet another dispute over territory in Meath, Dermot had abducted Tiernan's wife, Dervorgilla.

In 1166, Muirchertach MacLochlainn was slain in battle and Dermot MacMurrough lost his ally and protector. With Muirchertach dead, Rory O'Connor saw his chance at High-Kingship, and Tiernan O'Rourke saw an opportunity to avenge himself upon his old enemy. Rory and Tiernan marched through Meath – receiving hostages from Dermot O'Melaghlin – to Dublin. The Ostmen (Norsemen) of Dublin submitted to Rory, and he was quickly inaugurated as High-King of Ireland. From Dublin, now accompanied by Ostmen, Rory and Tiernan moved to Mellifont, and there received hostages from Donncadh O'Carroll, king of Airgialla. Then only one man stood in Rory's way, Dermot MacMurrough king of Leinster. Rory and his allied forces marched on Leinster, and with their coming the princes in the north of the kingdom, the Ostmen of Wexford, and the majority of Dermot's chief vassals abandoned him. Dermot was forced to submit to the new High-King and lay aside his title of 'king of Leinster', Rory allowing him to retain Uí Ceinnsealaigh, his hereditary principality. For Tiernan O'Rourke this was not punishment enough however, and in late September 1166, aided by the Ostmen of Dublin and Dermot O'Melaghlin, king of Meath, he stormed into Uí Ceinnsealaigh. Deserted by almost everyone, and seeing no hope of a successful resistance, Dermot MacMurrough, the prince of Uí Ceinnsealaigh, set sail for England.

THE PRINCE, THE EARL, THE KING AND THE JUSTICIAR

The prince

> Diarmait was tall and well built, a brave and warlike man … whose voice was hoarse as a result of constantly having been in the din of battle. He preferred to be feared by all rather than loved. He treated his nobles harshly and brought to prominence men of humble rank. He was inimical towards his own people and hated by others. All men's hands were against him, and he was hostile to all men.
>
> Giraldus; in Scott & Martin, 1978, 41

Having been abandoned by his allies in Ireland, and losing first his kingdom and then his princedom, Dermot MacMurrough set sail for Bristol on the 1 August 1166 to seek assistance from the Normans in England. After a brief stopover in Bristol with Robert fitz Harding, Dermot travelled to the continent to meet with Henry II. In 1167, Dermot caught up with Henry in Aquitaine and swore fealty and allegiance to him and, in return, the king gave Dermot a letter of patent giving him permission to recruit volunteers from among the Norman colonists in Wales to assist him in regaining his kingdom in Leinster. Dermot returned to Bristol, and then travelled into Wales, attempting to gain support for his proposed venture. Initially, he was unsuccessful, and it was not until he approached one of the greatest lords of the Welsh marches, Richard earl of Clare, nicknamed 'Strongbow', that he found the support he needed.

The earl

> The Earl … had reddish hair and freckles, grey eyes, a feminine face, a weak voice and a short neck, though in almost all other respects he was of a tall build. He was a generous and easy-going man. What he could not accomplish by deeds he settled by the persuasiveness of his words … In peace time he had more the air of a rank-and-file soldier than of a leader, but in war more that of a leader than a true soldier. When acting on the advice of his followers he was brave enough for anything … When he took up a position in the midst of battle, he stood firm as an immovable standard round which his men could re-group and take refuge. In war, he remained steadfast and reliable in good fortune and bad alike. In adversity, no feelings of despair caused him to waver, while lack of self restraint did not make him run amok when successful.

> Giraldus; in Scott & Martin, 1978, 87-9

Strongbow, or Richard fitz Gilbert de Clare, lord of Strigoil, was the head of an influential Norman family, and a seasoned campaigner. His father, Gilbert de Clare, had been earl of Pembroke, and his grandfather, Richard de Clare, had fought at Hastings in 1066, and was descended from Godfrey, a natural son of Richard I of Normandy. In 1167, Strongbow was a troubled man however, as Henry II had confiscated much of his family's land and had denied him his title as earl of Pembroke in retribution for his support of King Stephen. In Dermot, Strongbow saw a chance to recoup his fortunes. Strongbow's support was not easily won however, as to gain his assistance Dermot had to offer his own daughter, Aoife, in marriage, and the prospect of the kingdom of Leinster in succession to himself.

After winning Strongbow over to his cause, Dermot visited Rhys ap Gruffydd, prince of South Wales, to gain the freedom of Robert fitz Stephen, a 'knight of great renown', who was being held captive. At the request of Robert's half-brothers, David (bishop of St David's) and Maurice fitz Gerald, Robert was released on the condition that he went to Ireland to assist Dermot. With Strongbow and Robert fitz Stephen now on his side, other Cambro-Normans quickly began to flock to Dermot's cause, and by the summer of 1167 he had achieved the promise of substantial aid.

Having achieved his goal, Dermot returned to Ireland in August 1167, accompanied by a small force of Welsh and Flemish troops, under the command of Richard fitz Godebert, and there quickly re-established himself in his princedom of Uí Ceinnsealaigh. On 1 May 1169, Robert fitz Stephen landed near Wexford with 30 knights, 60 armoured sergeants and 300 archers, and on the following day Maurice de Prendergast landed with a force of around 200 to reinforce fitz Stephen's group. Over the next 12 months, fitz Stephen was followed by his cousins Maurice fitz Gerald and Raymond le Gros, who between them brought 20 more knights and 200 archers. Finally, Strongbow himself landed near Waterford on 23 August 1170, with 200 knights and 1000 other troops.

Between 1168 and 1171, Dermot, with the backing of his Anglo-Norman allies, managed to re-conquer his kingdom of Leinster, capture the Norse-Irish towns of Wexford, Waterford and Dublin, invade the neighbouring province of Meath, and harry Tiernan O'Rourke's kingdom of Bréifne. Dermot's victories were short-lived however, as he died suddenly in May 1171, leaving Strongbow and the other Anglo-Normans in a very difficult predicament.

The king

> Henry II … had hair that was almost red in colour, grey eyes, and a large round head. His eyes were bright, and in anger fierce and flecked with red. He had a fiery complexion, his voice was husky, his neck bent forward a little from the shoulders, and he had a broad chest and powerful arms … He was moderate and temperate … a most eloquent prince … and he was well read … in war a man of valour, and in time of peace a most prudent statesman … He treated the unruly with ferocity, but showed mercy towards those he conquered … for a long time he enjoyed success and everything turned out just as he wished.
>
> Giraldus; in Scott & Martin, 1978, 125-33

On 17 October 1171, Henry II landed in Ireland, near Waterford, accompanied by a large army, which comprised 400-500 knights and up to 4000 men-at-arms. There were several reasons for Henry's appearance in Ireland at this time. First, the original letter of patent which Henry had granted to Dermot covered only the recovering of his own territories, but before his death, Dermot had gone far beyond those terms, and may even have been contemplating the conquest of all Ireland. Second, the taking of Wexford and Waterford and the capture of Dublin – Ireland's political centre and richest town – by Strongbow, had made him a major power in the land. In addition to which, on 25 August 1170, Strongbow had married Aoife, and with the death of Dermot in May 1171, had become lord of Leinster. Third, the decision of the Anglo-Norman leaders not to return to Wales, nor to seek to enter the service of another Irish king upon the death of Dermot, but to set up their own lordship over Leinster and Dublin, suggests an attempt to create a political entity that would have spanned the Irish Sea. Henry II journeyed to Ireland to prevent Strongbow establishing a rival state that could have seen both Chepstow and Kilkenny under the same master.

Henry's ploy was successful, Strongbow immediately submitted, ceding Dublin, Waterford and Wexford to him, and in return gained royal recognition of his possession of a trimmed-down Leinster, which was to be held as a fief in return for homage, fealty, and the service of 100 knights. The Irish turned to Henry for protection against the turbulent Anglo-Norman barons. Henry remained in Ireland until 17 April 1172, and during that time received oaths of fealty from many of the Irish kings: including Dermot MacCarthy, king of Desmond, Donal Mor O'Brien, king of Thomond, Murchadh O'Carroll, king of Airgialla, Tiernan O'Rourke, king of Bréifne, and Donn Sleibhe MacDunleavy, king of Ulaid, as well as from the Ostmen of Wexford. In fact the only Irish kingdoms not to submit at this time were mid and west Ulster, and possibly Connacht, under Rory O'Connor. Finally, before departing Ireland for the Continent, Henry carried out an act that was specifically designed to safeguard his position. Henry knew that Strongbow was by far the most powerful baron in Ireland, and one with royal aspirations, and to counterbalance his power, Henry enlisted the help of a trusted ally, Hugh de Lacy.

The justiciar

> Hugh's complexion … was dark, with dark, sunken eyes and flattened nostrils. His face was grossly disfigured down the right side as far as his chin by a burn, the result of an accident. His neck was short, his body hairy and sinewy … he was a short man … misshapen … and … his character, resolute and reliable, restrained from excess by French sobriety. He paid much attention to his own private affairs, and was most careful in the administration of the office entrusted to him and in his conduct of public affairs. [He was] well versed in the business of war … and more ambitious for his own advancement and pre-eminence than was proper.
>
> Giraldus; in Scott & Martin, 1978, 193

In 1172, Henry II made Hugh de Lacy 'Constable of Dublin' and 'Justiciar of Ireland' and granted him 'the lands of Meath – from the Shannon to the sea – with all its appurtenances … to be held by him and his heirs for the service of 50 knights; to have and to hold … as fully as Murchad Ua Mael Sechlainn held it or any other before him' (*Gormanston Reg.*, f.5, 177). This appointment made Hugh, arguably, the most powerful man in Ireland, and in keeping with his nature, he immediately sallied forth to stamp his mark upon his newly won territories. Thus began the conquest for Meath, and the Anglo-Normans, having learnt valuable lessons in Wales and the Marches, came armed with an infallible plan of action.

THE LIE OF THE LAND

It has been stated that 'much of the history of Ireland is the story of how invaders coped with the physical problems posed by the island' (Edwards, 1973, 21). The Irish landscape, which is liberally supplied with rivers, lakes, bogs, mountains, drumlins and inhospitable coastline, contains numerous insuperable obstacles, any of which could prove fatal to the unwary intruder. To appreciate the difficulties that the Anglo-Normans faced, and to understand the character of the native Irish, a basic grasp of the country's topography, geography and geology is essential.

Giraldus Cambrensis (*c.*1146-1223), the celebrated chronicler and clergyman, provides a good starting point. Giraldus, as his name suggests, was born in Wales, of Norman and Welsh parents, into one of the leading Norman families involved in the invasion of Ireland. He first visited Ireland in 1183 and returned again, in the company of Prince John, two years later. In 1185, he wrote an account of Ireland and its early history that was published as *Topographia Hibernica*, which forms an important resource for the study of medieval Ireland. This was followed, in 1189, by an account of the Anglo-Norman Conquest of Ireland, the *Expugnatio Hibernica*. Giraldus, through blood or marriage relations, was able to learn a great deal about the pioneering years of the first Norman lords who came to Ireland, and this makes his work invaluable. In *Topographia Hibernica*, Giraldus describes Ireland thus:

> Ireland – The largest island beyond Britain, is situated in the western ocean about one short day's sailing from Wales … a country of uneven surface and rather mountainous. The soil is soft and watery, and there are many woods and marshes. Even at the tops of high and steep mountains you will find pools and swamps … here and there [are] some fine plains, but in comparison with the woods they are

indeed small … The land is fruitful and rich in its fertile soil and plentiful harvests. Crops abound in the fields, flocks on the mountains, and wild animals in the woods. The island is, however, richer in pastures than in crops, and in grass than in grain … for this country more than any other suffers from storms of wind and rain. (O'Meara, 1985, 33-4)

Ireland is remarkable for a topographical variety disproportionate to its size. This diversity of landscape is the product of a complex geographical history. Unlike many other European countries, Ireland has no central mountainous area; instead the uplands are mainly coastal and form a sharp contrast to the poorly drained central lowlands. Many rivers rise in the central lowlands, and they divide the island into sections with their long courses; whilst the mountains, although remarkably varied, rarely rise above 900m.

To the north of Meath's rich pastures, running from Dundalk Bay in the north-east to Donegal Bay in the north-west, is a broad curving band of glacial drumlins, low rounded hills, heavy in gley soils, shot through with a maze of small lakes and streams, forming the agriculturally limited borderlands of Ulster (52). To the south-west of this band lies the flat limestone escarpment of Ben Bulbin, and to the north-west the precipitous cliffs of Slieve League, and the harsh and rocky landscape of Donegal; whilst in the north-east, are the rich lowlands around Lough Neagh, hemmed in by the rounded ridges of the Mourne Mountains, the Sperrin Mountains, and the high cliffs formed by the Antrim Mountains.

To the west of Meath, beyond ancient routes that follow raised gravel eskers into the heartland of Ireland, is the River Shannon. Beyond this, to the north-west, are the distant mountains of West Connacht, skirting a landscape of barren blanket bog interrupted only by brown peaty lakes; to the west, the bare limestone karst of the Burren; and to the south-west, the sandstone and shale lowlands of West Clare.

To the south of Meath, on the borders of Leinster, are the older granite Wicklow Mountains, the treacherous Bog of Allen, and the flat sandy plains of the Curragh. Beyond these, are the fertile river valleys of the Barrow, Nore and Suir, whose rivers discharge into the sea at Waterford. To the south-west, in Munster, the landscape is a patchwork of hills and valleys, and beyond that, lakes and mountains stretch towards a ragged coastline projecting far out into the Atlantic Ocean (Edwards, 1999, 6-8; O'Meara, 1985, 33-7).

Strategic considerations

Ireland was extensively wooded in the medieval period, and these large forests formed virtually impenetrable barriers to effective progress across much of the

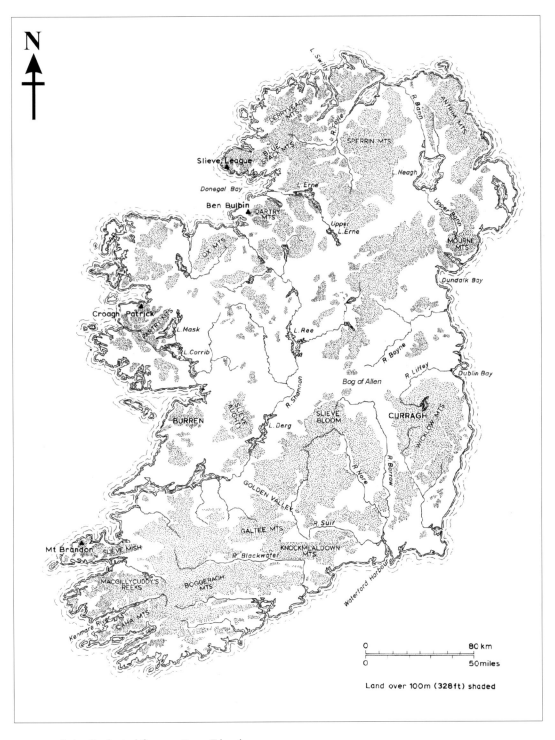

N

52 Ireland's physical features. *From: Edwards, 1999, 7*

country. North-east Ulster and south-west Munster were practically inaccessible due to vast tracts of woodland, and extensive detours were necessary to reach many parts of Connacht. In Leinster, the mountainous and wooded areas of Wicklow made military manoeuvres difficult, and to the west, the Shannon posed a formidable obstacle to any advancing army, although it could be forded at some points.

The most naturally defended province in Ireland however was Ulster, and the strength of its physical defences probably explains why Gaelic rule continued in much of the region until 1603. There were only three entry routes into Ulster, two lay close together in the south-west, where Ulster and Connacht were separated by the River Erne, and the third lay to the south-east, between Dundalk and Newry. The first entry point was via a crossing on the River Erne near Ballyshannon, the second via a route between the lakes at Enniskillen, and the third via a gorge in the hills, through which the Slighe Mhidhluachra ran. This pass is known collectively as 'The Gateway to Ulster', 'The Moyry Pass' and 'The Gap of the North' (Edwards, 1973, 33-4).

The multiplicity of the landscape and the diversity of the countryside had a profound effect upon the development of early Irish society, and it is worth mentioning here that the Irish knew their landscapes well and utilised the terrain to utmost effect in times of war. The Irish would not fight in the open unless absolutely pressed to do so. Instead, they favoured the fastness of woods, peaks, bogs and fens, and relied upon the use stealth, ambush and other guerrilla tactics, which were better suited to the difficult terrain. The Irish saw forests, mountains and marshes, not as deserted wastelands, but as zones of refuge and retreat.

CO. MEATH

> The territory of Meath I shall describe to you, and the territory of the powerful Breagha, from the Shannon with bright cormorants to the sea.

> From a c.1200 manuscript, in the Bodleian Library, Oxford
> (Rawlinson B 512 / folio 25)

The Midhe granted to Hugh de Lacy comprised the whole of East and West Meath, the northern half of Co. Dublin, the whole of Co. Longford, the baronies of Kilcoursey, Garrycastle, Eglish, Ballyboy, Ballycowan and Geashill, and the parish of Castlejordan in the barony of Warrenstown, in Offaly (formerly King's County) (53). By the fourteenth century, the Anglo-Normans had established the basic political divisions of Ireland, but during the Tudor and Elizabethan periods Ireland's political geography underwent several changes, eventually emerging in the reign of James I as the system of four provinces – subdivided into counties – recognisable today. In fact, the only difference between the contemporary divisions and those of the sixteenth century are that Connacht was much larger, comprising, in addition to its modern counties, of Cavan and Longford, while Ulster included Louth. In the reshuffles Midhe was gradually slimmed down, was finally delimited in 1542, and currently comprises the counties of East and West Meath, in the province of Leinster.

East Meath is today known simply as County Meath, or Meath, and this area forms the basis for this chapter. Mention will be made of West Meath, but it has been largely omitted from this present study, as County Meath alone contains 78 Anglo-Norman castles, which is a more than adequate sample for study.

Meath is approximately 36 miles (58km) north-south, 45 miles (73km) east–west, and is bounded in the north by Cavan, Monaghan and Louth, in the east by the Irish Channel and Dublin, in the south by Kildare, and in the west by West Meath (54). It has a rich drift-covered landscape of undulating lowland pasture, watered by many rivers and tributaries, and is noted for its fine horses and cattle; whilst on the Loughcrew Hills sheep are reared. Meath has always been a prosperous agricultural county, composed of some of the best land in Ireland; its soil, a rich fertile loam, commonly supports wheat, oats, barley, clover, flax and root-vegetables.

Geologically, Meath lies within an extension of the central limestone plain of Ireland, comprising limestones from the Upper Carboniferous period which underlie the fertile plains surrounding Navan and the River Boyne. In the northern part of the county, there is a zone of movement, with a series of faulting associated with the Longford-Down inlier. This zone contains older rocks of the Devonian Series, with some limestone, which has given rise to a landscape of low undulating hills.

There are several upland areas in the county, the largest of which, with an average height of more than 180m above sea level, occurs in the north-west along the border with Cavan. Other upland zones include Slieve Na Calliagh (Hill of the Witches) in the Loughcrew Hills to the south-east of Oldcastle, and an area on the border with Louth, to the north of Slane. Although there are not many hills in the county, there are three of major importance: the Hill of Tara was the site of residence of the High-Kings of Ireland, it was on the Hill of Slane that St Patrick reputedly lit the Paschal Fire and the Loughcrew Hills contain extensive megalithic tombs.

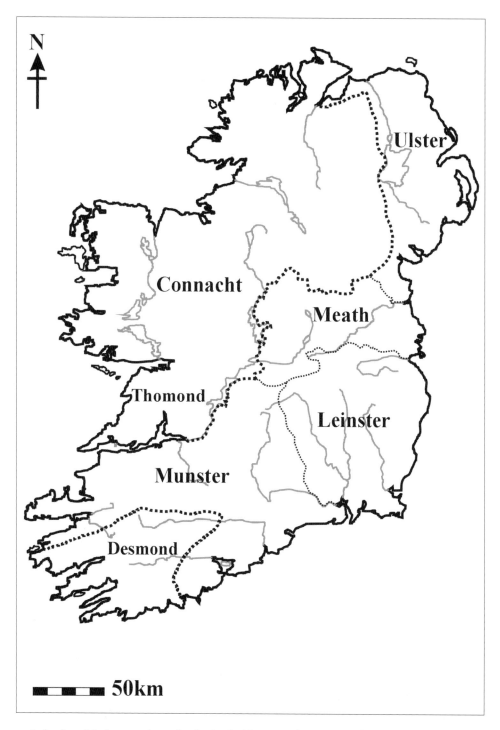

53 Ireland's political geography under the Anglo-Norman colony, c.1210. The colony comprised
Ulster, Meath, Leinster and Munster

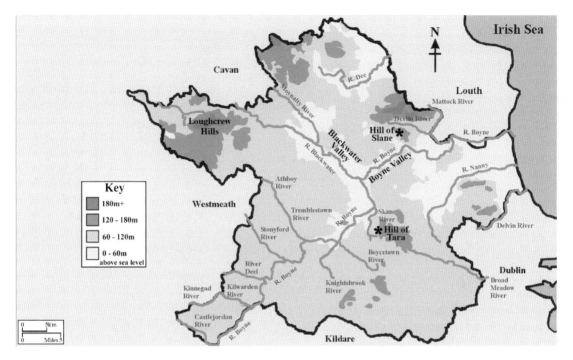

54 The topography and rivers of Meath. There are several upland areas in the north, but the majority of the county comprises undulating lowland pasture, watered by numerous rivers and tributaries.

MEATH'S ANGLO-NORMAN CASTLES

The Anglo-Normans built 78 castles in Meath. Figure 55 shows the locations of those castles. The numbers allocated to the castles on figure 55 appear again in the first column of either figure 56 or 57, which list the castle's name, the type of castle first constructed at the site, any associated features, and, if known, the probable date for the first phase of castle construction, along with the likely owner or builder.

In previous chapters, phased distribution maps have been used to show the period in which each castle was founded. Unfortunately, in Ireland, this is somewhat problematic, as there is a distinct lack of medieval documentation, largely due to the fact that many original archives were lost in 1922 with the destruction of the Public Record Office in the Four Courts, Dublin, during the Irish Civil War. The loss of these archives has created an information vacuum in Irish Medieval Studies, and to fill this void undue dependence is placed upon calendared summaries, which are often of dubious accuracy and limited detail. In addition, it is not possible to examine archaeological reports for dating evidence, as only sixteen mottes have been excavated in the whole of Ireland (McNeill, 2000, 63), and the morphology of the castles cannot be used as an aid to dating, as the earthworks are all of similar type.

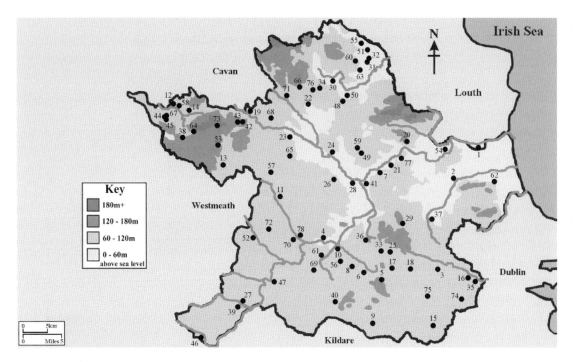

55 Meath's Anglo-Norman Castles

No.	Name	Earliest phase	Probable builder	Probable date	Associated features
1	Drogheda	Motte and bailey	Hugh de Lacy	c.1172-4	Borough
2	Duleek	Motte	Hugh de Lacy	c.1172-4	Irish monastery, borough
3	Ratoath	Motte and bailey	Hugh de Lacy	c.1172-4	Borough
4	Trim	Motte or ringwork	Hugh de Lacy	c.1172-4	Irish monastery, borough
5	Culmullin	Motte	Hugh de Lacy or Leonisius de Bromiard	c.1172-5	Church
6	Derry Patrick	Castle site	Hugh de Lacy or Leonisius de Bromiard	c.1172-5	Field system, church
7	Ardmulchan	Motte	Hugh Tyrrell	c.1174	Church
8	Galtrim	Motte and bailey	Hugh de Hussey	c.1174	Church
9	Rodanstown	Ringwork	Hugh de Hussey	c.1174	None

10	Scurlockstown	Motte	The Scurlocks of Pembrokeshire	c.1174	Church
11	Athboy	Motte	William de Muset	c.1174–82	Borough
12	Castlecor	Motte and bailey	Matthew or Richard de Tuit	c.1174–82	Church
13	Newtown	Motte and bailey	Richard de Tuit	c.1174–82	Castle, field system, church
14	Oldcastle	Motte and bailey	Richard de Tuit	c.1174–82	Church
15	Dunboyne	Motte	William Petit or Hugh de Lacy	c.1174 or c. 1182-7	Borough
16	Donaghmore	Motte	Leonisius de Bromiard	c.1175	None
17	Knockmark	Motte	Leonisius de Bromiard	c.1175	None
18	Dunshaughlin	Motte	Leonisius de Bromiard	c.1175 or c.1182	Borough, church
19	Derver	Motte and bailey	Hugh de Lacy	c.1175–80	None
20	Slane	Motte and possible bailey	Richard the Fleming	c.1175–80	Irish monastery, church, borough
21	Dollardstown	Motte or ringwork	Adam Dullard	c.1176	Church
22	Kilbeg Upper	Motte and bailey	Thomas de Craville	c.1176	Irish monastery, church
23	Kells	Motte	Hugh de Lacy	c.1176–8	Irish monastery, borough
24	Donaghpatrick	Motte and Bailey	Roger le Poer	c.1180	Irish monastery, church
25	Killeen	Motte	Hugh de Lacy	c.1181	Castle
26	Ardbraccan	Motte	Jocelin de Angulo	c.1182	Irish monastery, church
27	Clonard	Motte and possible bailey	Hugh de Lacy	c.1182	Irish monastery, church, field system
28	Moathill	Motte and bailey	Jocelin de Angulo or Hugh de Lacy	c.1182	Borough
29	Skreen	Motte and possible Bailey	Adam de Futepoi or Hugh de Lacy	c.1182	Irish monastery, borough
30	Nobber	Motte and Bailey	Gilbert de Angulo or Hugh de Lacy	c.1186–96	Borough
31	Drumconrah	Motte and Bailey	Walter de Lacy	c.1200	Borough

32	Dunsany	Motte and castle	Hugh de Lacy [the third]	c.1200	Castle, church
33	Cruicetown	Motte and bailey	Stephen de Cruys	Early 1200	Church
34	Greenoge	Motte	William de Lacy	Prior to 1204	Borough, church
35	Kilmessan	Motte	Uncertain	Early thirteenth century	Church
36	Rathfeigh	Motte and possible bailey	Uncertain	Prior to 1224	None
37	Milltown	Motte and possible bailey	Uncertain	Pre-1275	Castle, church
38	Mulphedder	Ringwork	Uncertain	Late thirteenth Century	None
39	Agher	Motte and bailey	Uncertain	Unknown	Deserted settlement, field system, church

56 Table of details for datable Anglo-Norman castles built in Meath

Due to a dearth of medieval documentation, many of Meath's castles are undatable. Of the 78 castles in the county, only 39 can be ascribed dates (*56*). Fortunately, the small number of medieval documents that have survived for Meath are both accurate and reliable. Sources include Irish Pipe Rolls, Calendars of Documents, Deeds, Abbey Registers and Charters, contemporary accounts such as *The Annals of Clonmacnoise, The Annals of Loch Ce, The Annals of the Four Masters, The Annals of Ulster* and *The Song of Dermot and the Earl*, and the works of contemporary writers like Giraldus Cambrensis (*Topographia Hibernica and Expugnatio Hibernica*).

No.	Name	Earliest phase	Probable builder	Probable date	Associated features
40	Athlumney	Motte and possible bailey	Uncertain	Unknown	Church
41	Balgree	Motte	Uncertain	Unknown	None
42	Ballyhist	Motte and bailey	Uncertain	Unknown	None
43	Ballymacad	Motte and possible bailey	Uncertain	Unknown	Castle site, church
44	Ballymacad	Motte and possible bailey	Uncertain	Unknown	None
45	Castlejordan	Motte and bailey	Uncertain	Unknown	Castle/tower house, church
46	Castlerickard	Motte	Uncertain	Unknown	Field System, church
47	Castletown	Motte and bailey	Uncertain	Unknown	None

48	Castletown Kilberry	Motte	Uncertain	Unknown	None
49	Castletown Kilpatrick	Motte	Uncertain	Unknown	Church
50	Clonbarton	Motte and possible bailey	Uncertain	Unknown	Irish monastery, church, field system
51	Coolronan	Motte and bailey	Uncertain	Unknown	None
52	Diamor	Motte and bailey	Uncertain	Unknown	Church
53	Dowth	Motte	Uncertain	Unknown	Church
54	Drumbride	Motte and possible bailey	Uncertain	Unknown	Church
55	Ginnets Great	Motte	Uncertain	Unknown	None
56	Girley	Motte	Uncertain	Unknown	Church
57	Glenboy	Motte and bailey	Uncertain	Unknown	None
58	Kilberry	Motte	Uncertain	Unknown	Church
59	Killadden	Motte and bailey	Uncertain	Unknown	None
60	Laracor	Motte	Uncertain	Unknown	Church
61	Lisdoran	Motte	Uncertain	Unknown	None
62	Loughbrackan	Motte	Uncertain	Unknown	None
63	Loughcrew	Motte and possible bailey	Uncertain	Unknown	Church
64	Milltown	Motte	Uncertain	Unknown	None
65	Moat (ME005 080)	Motte	Uncertain	Unknown	Foundations of a large building
66	Moat (ME008 032)	Motte and bailey	Uncertain	Unknown	None
67	Moat (ME010 039)	Motte and bailey	Uncertain	Unknown	None
68	Moat (ME042 005)	Motte and bailey	Uncertain	Unknown	None
69	Moat Town	Motte	Uncertain	Unknown	None
70	Moynalty	Motte and possible bailey	Uncertain	Unknown	None
71	Moyrath	Motte and bailey	Uncertain	Unknown	None
72	Patrickstown	Motte and possible bailey	Uncertain	Unknown	None
73	Priest town	Motte	Uncertain	Unknown	Church
74	Rathbeggan	Motte	Uncertain	Unknown	None
75	Robertstown	Motte	Uncertain	Unknown	Church
76	Thurstianstown	Motte	Uncertain	Unknown	None
77	Tremblestown	Motte	Uncertain	Unknown	Tower house, church

57 Table of details for undatable Anglo-Norman castles built in Meath

Because of the lack of dating evidence, the information presented in this chapter will be dealt with in a different way from that in the previous two. Discussions on stratagems, tactics and strategies will include all 78 Anglo-Norman castles, whilst discussion on Hugh de Lacy's campaigns in Meath will utilise only the castles directly attributable to that period.

ANGLO-NORMAN CASTLE BUILDING STRATEGIES IN MEATH

The less remote part of the country, as far as the river Shannon, which divides the three eastern parts of the island from the fourth in the west, should be secured and protected by the construction of many castles. But the more remote area should for the moment be coerced by levying an annual tribute.

Giraldus; in Scott & Martin, 1978, 249

The importance of 'tactically significant' and 'strategically significant' locations has been continually emphasised throughout this work, but it is worth repeating here the meaning behind each of the terms. Tactically significant locations are highly defensible, topographically or geologically strong points in the landscape, and strategically significant locations are points in the landscape which, due to their geographical positions, afford control of 'key strategic elements', such as rivers, roads and mountain passes. The armed forces, who call such places 'pivotal points', are often required to win possession of these locations, and then, because of the military advantages gained through their occupation, are compelled to hold them via the construction of fortifications.

Figure 58 shows the pivotal points in Meath's landscape. Because of the elaborate river systems in the county, it would be necessary to occupy numerous points in the landscape in order to gain effective military control. There are 30 pivotal points plotted, and when these are compared with the locations of Meath's Anglo-Norman castles (55), three notable details arise. Firstly, it can be seen that at 23 of the pivotal points there were indeed castles. The castles of Drogheda [1], Duleek [2], Trim [4], Culmullin [5], Ardmulchan [7], Rodanstown [9], Athboy [11], Oldcastle [14], Derver [19], Slane [20], Kilbeg Upper [22], Kells [23], Moathill [28], Nobber [30], Drumcondra [31], Rathfeigh [36], Milltown [37], Mulphedder [38], Athlumney [40], Castlerickard [46], Coolronan [51], Ginnets Great [55] and Lisdoran [61] were all located at pivotal points. Secondly, at two of the pivotal points there were castles within a couple of miles: Ratoath [3] was 1.12 miles (1.80km) away from one, and Donaghpatrick [24] was 1.57 miles (2.53km) away from another. Thirdly, at only five of the pivotal points plotted were no castles found to exist: namely, a point on the hills to the north-east of Grangegeeth overlooking the Devlin River; a point to the south-west of Ballivor overlooking the River Deel; a point on the hills to the north of Crossakeel overlooking the ancient Slighe Assail route-way; a point to the south-east of Tara, at the pre-Anglo-Norman ecclesiastical centre of Trevet, overlooking the source of the Broad Meadow River; and a point to the north of Innfield, on the hills to the north of, and overlooking, the ancient An tSlighe Mhór route-way. These results strongly suggest that many of the Anglo-Norman castles founded in Meath were sited in the landscape predominantly with military considerations in mind.

Geology, land-use and castle locations
The simplest way to establish which factors influenced Anglo-Norman decisions concerning the positioning of castles in Meath's landscape is to firstly dismiss those elements that played no discernible part. Meath's underlying geology is quite diverse, but a variety of castle types occur randomly across the county's geological spectrum, which indicates that no clear-cut divisions exist between the two.

It was mentioned in the previous chapter that limestone, consisting largely of calcium carbonate, is easily dissolved by rainwater, which leaves little parent material to form soils, and the resulting substratum, which was often unsuitable for motte construction, sometimes led to the erection of ringworks. Meath's underlying geology largely comprises carboniferous limestone, but it is drift covered in this instance and the soils are deep, so Meath's landscape is unsurprisingly rich in mottes. There are however, two definite ringworks in Meath, Mulphedder and Rodanstown, and two others that may have been fashioned initially in this form, Dollardstown and Trim, but these earthworks are situated where mottes could just as easily have been erected. Underlying geology then does not appear to have been a significant or determining factor in the siting, or morphology, of Meath's Anglo-Norman castles.

Directly related to the topic of geology are soils and land-usage. The development of farming and the associated growth of settlement in Ireland were affected by regional variations in climate, soils and the resulting vegetation. Meath was intensively settled from an early date, as farming communities based in the area would have had little difficulty producing their livelihood in its lush fertile pastures. Based on similar reasoning, it is often assumed that the Anglo-Normans also chose to settle in the most fertile areas, erecting castles to protect their newly won prime agricultural lands. This in turn lead to the growth of settlements around the fortifications, which in some cases developed into manorial villages, towns or even boroughs. There is little doubt that the Anglo-Normans wished

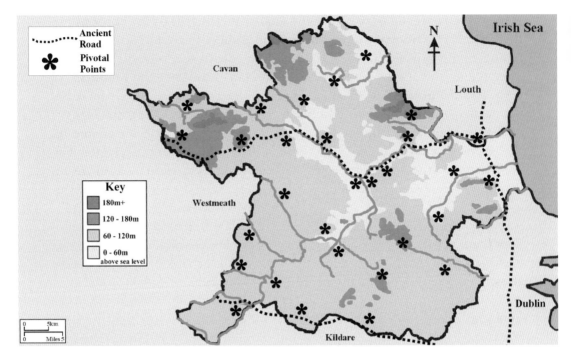

58 Map showing the militarily important 'pivotal points' in Meath. Because of the elaborate river systems in the county, it would be necessary to occupy numerous points in the landscape in order to gain effective military control. At 23 of the pivotal points shown there were Anglo-Norman castles

to 'use the land which was most suitable for agriculture because the somewhat inadequate documentary record indicates that from the earliest period of the colonisation and settlement of Meath, they were engaged in a mixed-farming economy which probably had a semi-commercial basis' (Graham, 1975, 234). The Anglo-Normans exported agricultural produce and manufactured products from Meath to Chester and Liverpool via the river port at Drogheda, which subsequently developed into one of Ireland's principal medieval ports. The question at hand however, is whether soil quality directly influenced the siting of castles in the landscape.

Barrett has demonstrated a close correlation between many Irish ring-forts, essentially, farmsteads and soil quality (1982, 250-1), and if the Anglo-Normans were primarily choosing to settle and erect castles in the best agricultural lands available, a similar correlation could be expected. In the majority of Meath, where well-drained, grey-brown podzolics form the major soil types, there are no serious agricultural limitations, but in the extreme south-west corner of the county, and in the area to the south of the Hill of Tara, and in the north along the Cavan border (on the southern edge of the North Central Drumlin Belt where gleys predominate), the agricultural potential is much more limited. Theoretically then, the Anglo-Normans should have avoided these areas of poor quality soil, opting instead to settle and erect their castles in the more fertile regions.

Figure 59 shows Meath's land-use capability and its Anglo-Norman castles. It is clear from the map that far from avoiding the locales where poor soils prevailed, the Anglo-Normans erected a veritable plethora of castles in those regions; with the exception of the south-western corner. Soil quality can therefore be discounted as a variable affecting castle distribution. It has been suggested that the variation of soil types in Meath were not sufficient enough to influence settlement, and thus castle location (Graham, 1975, 237). This is unlikely however, as the soils in the north of the county are typically poorly drained, with only very minimal stoney-grey soil cover on the better drained flanks of the hill-slopes, making the region totally unsuited to arable cultivation. It is therefore likely that there were other, more influential, reasons behind the siting of castles, and the subsequent growth of settlement in those areas.

Topography and castle locations

Figure 55 shows Meath's topography and the locations of its Anglo-Norman castles. From the map four broad patterns are discernible: first, many of Meath's Anglo-Norman castles are situated in river valleys, close to and overlooking the watercourses; second, on the area of higher ground in the north of the county there is a highly visible curving band of castles running from the north-east to the south-west; third, there are no castles on the areas of highest ground; and fourth, in the south and, more especially, south-west of the county, there is a much lower density of castles. The topic of rivers will be dealt with separately below; the other three are discussed here, in turn.

The landscape of northern Meath is dominated by glacial drumlins, providing a ready abundance of naturally elevated sites ideal for castle construction. These glacial features were often exploited by the Anglo-Norman castle-builders, their castles in many instances were largely scarped away from the natural ridge, rather than built from the ground up (O'Keeffe, 1992, 61). It was not, however, the ready-made castle foundations which led to a proliferation of castles in the region, or, as demonstrated above, a particularly fertile zone, it was something far more sinister.

To the north of Meath was the kingdom of Bréifne (49 and 50), whose ruler, Tiernan O'Rourke, continually harried and annexed lands in Meath until his death in 1172. There existed then a history of tension and strife between the two kingdoms, in which armed conflict was commonplace. Therefore, if Meath was ever to be properly stabilised, a line had to be drawn between it and Bréifne, and the Anglo-Normans drew this line in characteristically spectacular fashion,

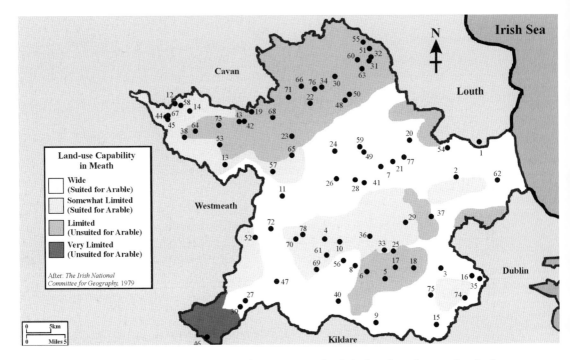

59 Meath's land-use capability and its Anglo-Norman castles. It is clear from the map that far from avoiding the locales where poor soils prevailed, the Anglo-Normans erected numerous castles in those regions

with a chain of castles stretching from Dundalk Bay in the north-east to Lough Sheelin in the north-west (*60* and *61*).

It has been suggested that the chain of castles upon the low undulating hills in the north of Meath represent a planned strategic line of defence (Orpen, 1906, 418; Graham, 1972; O'Keeffe, 1992, 60-1; McNeill, 2000, 66-70), and Graham has further argued 'that there was some defensive concept or plan for the liberty as a whole' (Graham, 1980, 45). In chapter three, one of the reasons given for a castle to exist was to control and protect a border area. A border is a purely political construct, and as a term, it is custom-built for the intangible phenomenon of a space that exists primarily in the mind. O'Keeffe has clearly demonstrated however, that the northern periphery of Meath was definitely considered a frontier or 'front tier' by the Anglo-Normans, who perceived it as the interface between native and alien populations (1992, 58). Thus, the castles in this region can discernibly be seen as the physical manifestations of a commonly conceived, but somewhat troubled, boundary.

The factors that positively demonstrate that the castles in Meath's northern region truly represent a *planned* strategic line of defence are the 'tactical

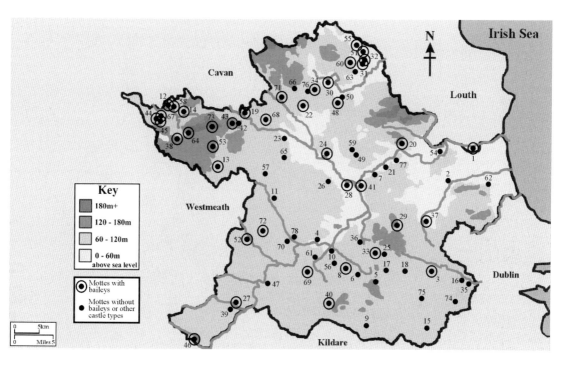

60 The majority of castles in northern Meath are mottes with baileys. The bailey would have housed a large garrison, along with its mounts. There was a history of tension and strife between Meath and Bréifne and the motte and baileys represent a planned strategic line of defence

considerations'. A landscape of glacial drumlins and kames gives rise to many corridors; add to this the fact that much of Ireland was extensively wooded in the medieval period, and it is clear that in Meath the Irish could utilise the leafy corridors to pass unnoticed into Anglo-Norman occupied territory (O'Keeffe, 1992, 61). Therefore, in order to successfully command these passes and defiles it would have been necessary to construct fortifications close together, and in Meath this is exactly what occurs on the ground. The castles in the northern chain are on average only 1.55 miles (2.50km) apart, whereas in the rest of the county the average is 2.48 miles (4km) apart. The construction of these fortifications, close together, effectively served two purposes: first, in the event of conflict the castles could act in concert, rather than as individual units; second, the castle's environs could be adequately patrolled. Based upon the figures given in chapter two, a horseman 'walking' his horse between two castles in the northern chain could have traversed the distance in just under 23 minutes, but if 'trotting' the same journey could have been made in a little over 12 minutes. Castles spaced at this distance apart then, would have enabled even a limited garrison to successfully monitor and control their section of the frontier zone; this was important as

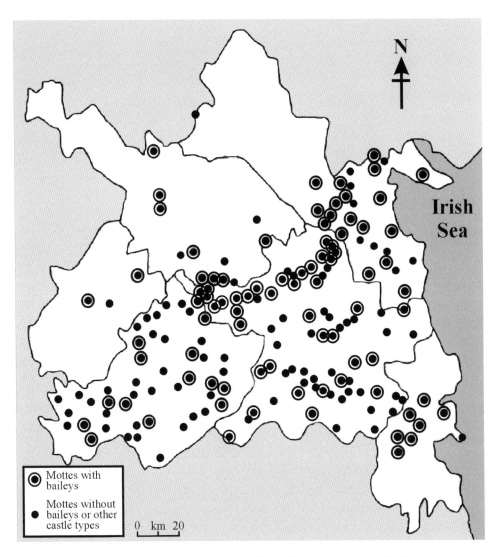

61 The distribution of mottes with baileys in the lordships of Meath and Oriel. *After: McNeill, 2000, 68*

medieval lordships would not have been able to keep permanent forces on alert indefinitely.

It is worth remembering that a castle was simply a fortified building, and as such it could not guard a river crossing, control a route or block a passage through the hills, it was the castle garrison that carried out these tasks. Turning again to the criteria in chapter two, another one of the reasons given for a castle to exist was to provide a secure base from which field armies could operate, or to provide a place of refuge in times of adversity. Thus, in a troubled frontier zone, one would expect to see castles designed specifically to accommodate and protect a sizeable garrison. Figure *61* clearly shows that the majority of castles in northern Meath are mottes with baileys: the bailey in each case would have housed a large garrison, along with its mounts. In fact, in Meath, out of 39 'mottes *with* baileys', 24 are found along the northern frontier, whilst the interior contains only 15. Also instructive is the fact that 'mottes *without* baileys' increase in size from east to west across the county, and northwards towards the periphery (Graham, 1980, 50), the general rule being, the higher the motte the more important its defensive role and capabilities.

The form and distribution of earthwork castles in the north is clearly no quirk of fate, but rather the result of a carefully planned response to a very real threat. An 1176 entry in *The Annals of Ulster* records the destruction of Richard the Flemings' motte at Slane by the Irish of the northern districts (Hennessey & McCarthy, 1887-1901). This is one of several contemporary accounts detailing Irish incursions into the area. Meath's northern region also contained lower numbers of towns and villages, due to the inherent Irish threat (Graham, 1975, 238). In the east and south of Meath the density of settlement was one to every 9.75 square miles (15.7sq km), but in the north and west the corresponding figure was only one settlement to every 16.9 square miles (27.2sq km). The claim that the form and distribution of earthwork castles in the north of Meath was the result of a planned response to Irish incursions can be further substantiated with a brief look at two of the castles in the chain.

The motte and bailey at Drumcondra [32] (*colour plate 22*) was situated at a pivotal point in the landscape (*58*) that enabled it to perform two functions: firstly, it guarded the ends of two passes through the hills, which entered Meath from the north-west and north-east; secondly, it had a clear vista down a valley to the south-east, allowing its garrison to monitor and control a section of the River Dee's environs. In addition, the castle readily embodied all of the factors listed under tactical considerations in chapter two. The defensibility of the castle was enhanced by the fact that it sat upon an area of higher ground with steep slopes on all sides, and was additionally surrounded on three sides by water. In terms of security, the castle was not overlooked by higher ground, and had good all-round visibility. In terms of accessibility, the castle could be quickly accessed by friendly troops via a ridge to the south, which also provided an elevated escape route, whilst, conversely, the castle was well protected from hostile troops arriving from the north, via the watercourse. The watercourse also provided the castle with a potable supply of fresh water. Lastly, in terms of practicality, the make-up and morphology of the hill was ideal for castle construction, and the area contained all of the required building materials.

The motte and bailey at Nobber [30] (*colour plate 23*) was also situated at a pivotal point in the landscape (*58*), which enabled the castle to guard the Dee river-valley and a gap in the hills to the north-west, down which, in all probability, an ancient route-way ran, fording the Dee to the north-west of the castle. Tactically, the castle was adequately defensible, as it sat on a pronounced ridge surrounded on all sides by water. In terms of security, the castle had good all-round visibility, and although overlooked by higher ground the castle was well outside of bow-shot range. In terms of accessibility, the castle could be accessed quickly by friendly troops via a ridge to the north-east, which also formed an elevated escape route, protected along its entire length by the River Dee. The river further provided the castle with a potable supply of fresh water. Lastly, in terms of practicality, the area again contained the necessary building materials for castle construction.

Meath's northern border was, then, a heavily militarised zone that was governed by a chain of systematically positioned castles, the stratagems behind which would have greatly pleased Giraldus, who stated: 'it is far, far better to begin by gradually connecting up a system of castles built in suitable places … than to build large numbers of castles at great distances from each other, sited haphazardly in various locations, without their forming any coherent system of mutual support or being able to relieve each other in times of crisis' (Giraldus; in Scott & Martin, 1978, 249).

It was mentioned above that there are no castles situated upon the areas of highest ground within Meath (i.e. higher than 120m above sea level [A.S.L.]). The majority of castles are in fact located between 60m and 120m A.S.L. (*60*). This may be due to the overwhelming draw exerted by the fertility of the Boyne and Blackwater valleys, but, as demonstrated in chapter two, there are many tactical advantages to be gained by securing higher ground with fortifications. These advantages only apply in cases where the high ground is close to that which the fortifications are intended to protect however, and also when the area is served with a ready supply of potable water. In Meath, the areas of highest ground are notoriously devoid of fresh-water sources and, in the majority of cases, are too secluded to be of much strategic or tactical value. It is therefore likely that in Meath the Anglo-Normans selected the areas of higher-ground close to that which they were striving to gain or protect (i.e. the fertile lowland zones), but avoided the regions of highest ground, as these were too impractical to sustain prolonged habitation, and too secluded to be of much use militarily.

Lastly here, it was also mentioned above that there is a much lower density of castles in the south and, more especially, south-west of Co. Meath. The reason for this appears to be wholly topographical in nature. Figure *60* shows that the south-west region of Meath is criss-crossed by a network of rivers, which, in combination with a few well-positioned castles, could have provided an ideal defence against attacks from that quarter. However, the more likely reason for the lack of a large defensive chain of castles, such as that in the north, is that a naturally occurring geological feature, the Bog of Allen, adequately protected the region. The Bog of Allen was once Ireland's largest raised peat bog, covering an area of around 100,000 hectares, it stretched like a brown desert through Offaly, Laois and Kildare, extending westwards almost as far as the Shannon and eastwards to within 11 miles (17km) of Dublin. Although not a completely continuous bog, it almost certainly provided excellent protection for Meath from incursions from the south, and even today, despite much of the peat bog being gradually depleted for turf-burning electricity generating stations, a large part of north-western Co. Kildare is still taken up by the bog.

CASTLES, RIVERS AND THE IRISH SEA

In Ireland mottes were used to guard navigable waterways and river crossing points.

Glasscock, 1975, 99

The physical difficulties of travel in Ireland were daunting to the traveller until relatively recently. The combination of mountains, drumlins, rivers, lakes, bogs and extensive woodland made progress difficult, and although there were roads, they were wholly inadequate in their coverage of the country and badly maintained. The rough roads that were constructed in early Ireland were not improved upon substantially until the Anglo-Norman invasion, and even then, the woods continued to bar effective progress until their virtual eradication during the seventeenth century. The most common method of travel in Ireland throughout the Middle Ages was consequently by water (Edwards, 1973, 175). Out of 78 Anglo-Norman castles in Meath, 44 of them can be directly associated with rivers (62, 63 and 64). This is unsurprising however, as in Meath one is never very far from a river, approximately 5 miles (8km) in fact; the river valleys are fertile, and were thus attractive to the Anglo-Norman settlers. The pattern of castle distribution is therefore very similar to that seen in Monmouthshire, and similarly it must again be remembered that there are some very good military reasons for positioning castles close to rivers.

It is known that the early Irish were excellent sailors. Archaeological evidence provides proof of trade and exchange between Ireland and the kingdoms of Anglo-Saxon England, before the arrival of the Vikings. Fragmentary glass

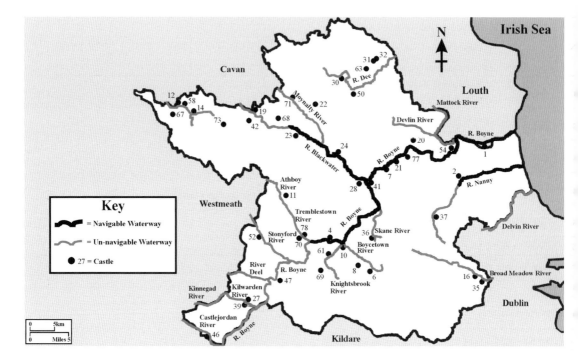

62 Meath's rivers, navigable stretches and associated Anglo-Norman castles. The most common method of travel in Ireland throughout the Middle Ages was by water and unsurprisingly out of 78 Anglo-Norman castles in Meath, 44 of them are directly associated with rivers

vessels recovered in Ireland are evidence of direct or indirect trade contacts with northern France, Belgium or the Rhineland and the importation of E ware demonstrates contacts with western France. The ninth century *Life of St Filibert* describes Irish ships arriving at the island of Noirmoutier, at the mouth of the Loire, carrying cargoes of shoes and clothes, and Giraldus mentions the importation of wine from Poitou in return for hides and skins. Christian contacts between Ireland, Rome and Spain are also in evidence (Edwards, 1999, 68-98). Before the arrival of the Anglo-Normans in Ireland, there were fleets of both Hiberno-Norse and native Irish ships at sea, and boats upon the rivers. Diarmait Mac Murchada, for example, provided Henry II with a number of ships to aid him in his foreign campaigns. Most importantly though, in both the annalistic records and the *Caithréim Chellacháin Chaisil*, there are accounts of naval warfare conducted between native Irish maritime vessels.

No.	Name	Barony	Caput	Borough type or manorial village	Ecclesiastical site	Route-way	River	Navigable section	River	Pivotal point
1	Drogheda	Lower Duleek		1 strat. Boro.		Slighe Mhidhluachra	Boyne	Yes	Yes	Yes
2	Duleek	Lower Duleek	Yes	2 strat. Boro.	Duleek	Nanny	Yes	Yes	Yes	
3	Ratoath	Ratoath	Yes	2 strat. Boro.						Near by
4	Trim	Lower Moyfen	Yes	1 strat. Boro.	Trim		Boyne	Yes	Yes	Yes
5	Culmullin	Upper Deece	Yes	Man.Vill						Yes
6	Derry Patrick	Lower Deece		Man.Vill			Boycetown	No	Yes	
7	Ardmulchan	Lower Navan		Man.Vill	Donaghmore	Slighe Assail	Boyne	Yes	Yes	Yes
8	Galtrim	Lower Deece	Yes	Man.Vill			Boycetown	No	Yes	
9	Rodanstown	Upper Deece		Man.Vill	Balfeaghan	An tSlighe Mhór				Yes
10	Scurlockstwn	Lower Deece		Man.Vill			Boyne	Yes	Yes	
11	Athboy	Lune	Yes	1 strat. Boro.			Athboy	No	Yes	Yes
12	Castlecor	Demi-Fore	Yes	Man.Vill			Oldcastle Br.	No	Yes	
13	Newtown	Demi-Fore		Man.Vill	Kilskeer	Slighe Assail				
14	Oldcastle	Demi-Fore	Yes	Man.Vill			Oldcastle Br.	No		Yes
15	Dunboyne	Dunboyne	Yes	2 strat. Boro.						
16	Donaghmore	Ratoath		Man.Vill	Donaghmore		Broad Mdw.	No	Yes	
17	Knockmark	Lower Deece								
18	Dunshaughlin	Ratoath		2 strat. Boro.	Dunshaughlin					
19	Derver	Upper Kells					Blackwater	No		Yes
20	Slane	Upper Slane	Yes	2 strat. Boro.	Slane	Slighe Assail	Boyne	Yes	Yes	Yes
21	Dollardstwn.	Skreen		Man. Vill			Slighe Assail	Boyne	Yes	Yes
22	Kilbeg Up.	Lower Kells	Yes	Man.Vill	Kilbeg		Moynalty	No	Yes	Yes
23	Kells	Upper Kells	Yes	1 strat. Boro.	Kells	Slighe Assail	Blackwater	Yes	Yes	Yes
24	Donaghpat.	Lower Kells	Man. Vill	Donaghpat.	Slighe Assail	Blackwater	Yes	Yes	Near by	

No.	Name	Barony	Caput	Borough type or manorial village	Ecclesiastical site	Route-way	River	Navigable section	River	Pivot point
25	Killeen	Skreen		Man.Vill	Trevet	Fan na gCarbad					
26	Ardbraccan	Lower Navan		Man.Vill	Ardbraccan	Slighe Assail					
27	Clonard	Upper Moyfen	Yes	Man.Vill	Clonard	An tSlighe Mhór	Kilwarden	No	Yes		
28	Moathill	Lower Navan	Yes	1 strat. Boro.	Navan	Slighe Assail	Blackwater	Yes	Yes		
29	Skreen	Skreen	Yes	2 strat. Boro.	Skreen						
30	Nobber	Morgallion	Yes	2 strat. Boro.	Nobber		Dee	No	Yes	Yes	
31	Drumcondra	Lower Slane					Dee	No	Yes		
32	Drumcondra	Lower Slane	Yes	Rural Boro.			Dee	No	Yes	Yes	
33	Dunsany	Lower Deece	Yes	Man.Vill							
34	Cruicetown	Lower Kells		Man.Vill							
35	Greenoge	Ratoath		Rural Boro.			Broad Mdw.	No	Yes		
36	Kilmessan	Lower Deece		Man.Vill	Bective & Tara	Fan na gCarbad	Skane				
37	Rathfeigh	Skreen		Man.Vill.	Kilmoon		Nanny	No	Yes	Yes	
38	Milltown	Demi-Fore		Man.Vill.		Slighe Assail			Yes		
39	Mulphedder	Upper Moyfen				An tSlighe Mhór	Kilwarden	No	Yes	Yes	

63 Table of factors associated with Meath's Anglo-Norman castles (1-39)

No.	Name	Barony	Caput	Borough type or manorial village	Ecclesiastical site	Route-way	River	Navigable section	River	Pive poi
40	Agher	Upper Deece		Man.Vill.	Rathcore						
41	Athlumney	Lower Navan				Slighe Assail	Boyne	Yes	Yes	Y
42	Balgree	Upper Kells			Castlekeeran		Blackwater	No	Yes	
43	Ballyhist	Upper Kells								
44	Ballymacad	Demi-Fore								
45	Ballymacad	Demi-Fore								
46	Castlejordan	Upper Moyfen					Castlejordan	No	Yes	
47	Castlerickard	Upper Moyfen		Man.Vill.	Rathcore	Boyne	No		Yes	

48	Castletown	Morgallion								
49	C.town Kilbry.	Morgallion				Slighe Assail				
50	C.town Kilpat.	Morgallion		Man.Vill.	Killary		Dee	No		
51	Clonbarton	Lower Slane								
52	Coolronan	Lune					Stonyford	No	Yes	Yes
53	Diamor	Demi-Fore		Man.Vill.		Slighe Assail				
54	Dowth	Upper Slane		Man.Vill.		Slighe Assail	Boyne	Yes		
55	Drumbride	Lower Slane								
56	Ginnets Gr.	Lower Moyfen								Yes
57	Girley	Upper Kells		Man.Vill.						
58	Glenboy	Demi-Fore					Oldcastle Br.	No	Yes	
59	Kilberry	Morgallion		Man.Vill.		Slighe Assail				
60	Killadden	Lower Slane								
61	Laracor	Lower Moyfen		Man.Vill.			Knightsbr.	No	Yes	
62	Lisdoran	Upper Duleek	Yes			Slighe				Yes
63	Loughbrckn	Lower Slane					Dee	No	Yes	
64	Loughcrew	Demi-Fore		Man.Vill.						
65	Milltown	Upper Kells		Man.Vill.		Slighe Assail				
66	Moat (005080)	Lower Kells								
67	Moat (008032)	Demi-Fore					Oldcastle Br.	No	Yes	
68	Moat (010039)	Upper Kells			Dulane		Blackwater	No	Yes	
69	Moat (042005)	Lower Moyfen					Knightsbr.	No	Yes	
70	Moat Town	Lune						No	Yes	
71	Moynalty	Lower Kells		Man.Vill.			Moynalty	No	Yes	
72	Moyrath	Lune			Kildalkey					
73	Patrickstown	Demi-Fore					Oldcastle Br.	No		
74	Priest town	Ratoath		Man.Vill.						
75	Rathbeggan	Ratoath		Man.Vill.						
76	Robertstown	Lower Kells		Man.Vill.						
77		Lower Duleek				Slighe Assail	Boyne	Yes		
78	Tremblestown	Lune		Man.Vill.				No	Yes	

Table of factors associated with Meath's Anglo-Norman castles (40-78)

The fact that Ireland's rivers were the main arteries for transport, communication and supply in the Middle Ages, in combination with the Irish renown for producing fine sailors capable of fighting naval battles, suggests that the appropriation, and subsequent control and defence, of the country's river systems was of utmost priority for the Anglo-Normans; a notion fully supported in Meath. Of the 44 castles associated with Meath's waterways, 18 are situated at strategic pivotal points in the landscape that relate directly to riverine control; 13 are situated upon navigable sections of those rivers; and 7 are situated at both (*58, 62, 63* and *64*). The navigable sections of Meath's rivers during the medieval period were ascertained from data supplied by *Waterways Ireland*, 'a north/south implementation body' for the inland navigable waterway systems of Ireland.

The castles of Drogheda [1] and Trim [4] admirably illustrate the Anglo-Norman strategy in regards to Ireland's rivers. At the eastern end of the River Boyne, only 4 miles (7km) inland from the Irish Sea, is the port of Drogheda. Drogheda's strategic value was immediately recognised by the Anglo-Normans, and possibly as early as 1172-4 Hugh de Lacy erected a motte and bailey on the southern side of the river, overlooking the port (*colour plate 24*). The castle was constructed at a tactically impeccable site and its presence ensured Anglo-Norman control of the Boyne estuary, thereby allowing provisions and supplies to be shipped directly from England. The Boyne was navigable as far west as Trim, and here, in 1172, Hugh de Lacy erected a second castle: today the finest extant example of an Anglo-Norman castle in Ireland (*colour plate 25*).

Over the years, the castle at Trim has been the focus for a number of studies. Recently the castle's martial aspects have been subjected to scrutiny, and current theory suggests that the castle was more 'symbolic statement' than 'military hardware'. O'Keeffe has argued that the Greek Cross plan of the great tower 'was more concerned with complex Christian symbolism and display than with defensibility' (2000, 37); and Stalley has shown that the tower had serious limitations from a defensive standpoint, since its unusual design provided no less than 12 potential points of attack (1992). McNeill has highlighted weaknesses in the north curtain wall (2000, 24), and has also suggested that the site, 'set on roughly level ground on the south bank of the River Boyne', was 'unremarkable, either strategically or tactically' (1990, 308). It must be remembered however, that the stone castle was not the first fortification erected upon the site by Hugh de Lacy.

The Song of Dermot and the Earl records the building of a 'spiked stockade' with a 'ditch around it' at Trim (lines 3220-25) (Orpen, 1892; Mullally, 2002) and recent excavations have produced definitive evidence of a ringwork castle (Sweetman, 1999, 5). Considering the hostility of the Irish in 1173, there can be little doubt that de Lacy intended his original castle to be defensible, and it may even have survived the Irish attack if Hugh Tyrrell had not simply abandoned it (Orpen, 1911-20, i, 339). The castle was strategically important, as it sat at the terminus of the navigable section of the River Boyne, at a fording point, adjacent to an important Early Christian monastery. Tactically, the castle was situated at the top of a gently sloping hill, which was protected on its northern side by a bend in the River Boyne. The local topography of the site gave the added advantage of having the high ground immediately inside the castle walls and a dramatic fall outside (Sweetman, 1999, 45). The choice of site then was anything but arbitrary.

Hugh de Lacy, with the construction of the castles at Drogheda and Trim, gained control of the majority of Meath's waterways, and his control of the port at Drogheda enabled him to supply and provision other castles further inland. In addition, 'Trim was also a frontier town and the castle protected de Lacy's newly acquired territory to the east' and 'kept the Irish under control immediately west as far as Athlone on the River Shannon' (Sweetman, 1999, 35). By positioning castles adjacent to Meath's river systems, the Anglo-Normans acquired a ready means of transport, communication and supply, whilst conversely ensuring that they were able to monitor and control enemy movement along the rivers and associated valleys, the rivers themselves further acted as physical barriers to movement.

CASTLES AND ROADS

Ireland's road network was utterly inadequate throughout the medieval period and beyond. Giraldus describes a well-wooded country with poor road communications (Scott & Martin, 1978, 251). The exact routes traversed by Meath's earliest roads (Irish 'slighe') cannot be delineated with any certainty, but figure 65 depicts the most likely courses. The roads appear to have been paved in stone, with wooden causeways constructed over bogland (Edwards, 1973, 177). The routes shown on the map (65) are: An tSlighe Mhór, 'the Great Road', which stretched from Dublin to the west coast, atop a low ridge of esker; Slighe Assail, 'the Road of Assal', considered to be the route connecting Tara with Rathcrogan, which was the capital of Connacht from a very early period; Slighe Mhidhluachra, 'the Road of Mid-Luachair', the main road north from Tara to Armagh; and Fan na gCarbad, a section of early road recorded near Tara. There were also many minor routes, but their exact whereabouts are largely unknown.

The early Irish roads were of great strategic value to the military, as they were sound enough in their construction to facilitate the movement of armies about the country, and it has been suggested that the comparative speed of progress

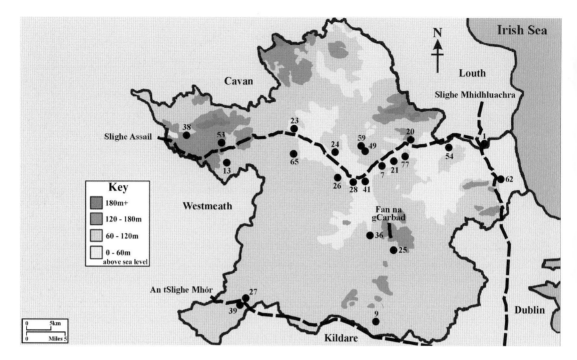

65 Meath's early roads and associated castles. The early Irish roads were of great strategic value to the Anglo-Normans, as they were sound enough in their construction to facilitate the movement of armies about the country. *After: Edwards, 1973, 177-8*

of the Anglo-Norman invasion was due, in a large extent, to the existing road systems (Edwards, 1973, 177). The acquisition and control of these road networks was vitally important, and must have ranked highly on the Anglo-Norman's agenda, twenty-one castles are associated with Meath's early roads (*63* and *64*), the majority clustering along the Slighe Assail which cuts Meath in two. There is a castle on average every 6.7 miles (10.78km) along the routes, making the journey time between castles on horseback, at a trot, 54 minutes, and as a road provides firm footing for a horse, at a gallop, 30 minutes (at a gallop a horse can typically average 13mph [21kmph]). This distribution would easily have afforded the Anglo-Normans mastery over the road networks, and in most cases the castles en route were positioned at elevated, tactically defensible, locations that afforded good views along the adjacent road in both directions.

Clonard Motte [27], in addition to being one of Meath's most enigmatic Anglo-Norman castles, is a good example of a castle built to monitor and control an early Irish roadway (*colour plate 26*). Tactically, the castle was situated on a low spur, to the north-east of, and directly overlooking, the River Kilwarden. The castle was further defended to the east by a tributary stream; the river and

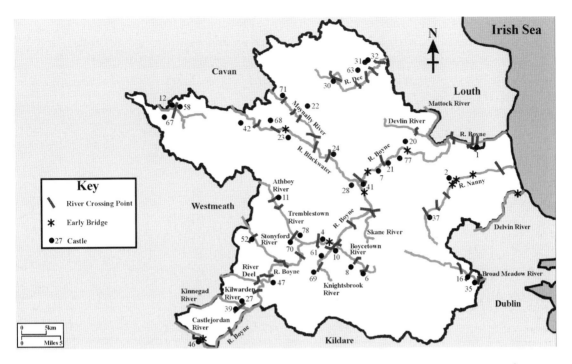

66 Meath's early bridges, river crossings, and associated Anglo-Norman castles. Forty-six per cent of Meath's castles are situated at fords or bridges, and there is a correlation between the distribution of Anglo-Norman settlements and river crossings. *After: Moore, 1987, 182 & Graham, 1975*

stream together provided the castle with an ample supply of fresh water. More importantly however, the chosen location enabled the castle to perform three strategic functions. First, it could monitor and control the river, which, although unnavigable for larger vessels, afforded easy passage for smaller watercraft. Second, the castle overlooked a north–south ford across the Kilwarden River, which in all probability formed a crossing point for an early Irish route-way that ran south from Drummond to join the An tSlighe Mhór. Third, the castle overlooked An tSlighe Mhór itself: Anglo-Norman control of the route-way being further reinforced by Mulphedder Ringwork [39] on the southern side of the road.

Although the routes traversed by Meath's early minor roads are uncertain, it is still possible to gain some indication of their whereabouts and importance. Many castles in Meath are situated at, or near, fords or bridges (66), and previous work has demonstrated a correlation between the distribution of Anglo-Norman settlements and river crossings (Graham, 1975). There is also a link between the navigable sections of Meath's rivers and Anglo-Norman settlements. In total, 36 of Meath's castles are associated with river crossings, which amounts to a surprising forty-six per cent. Although we cannot be certain that at every river crossing there was a minor road, the likelihood is very high, and in all probability nearly half of Meath's Anglo-Norman castles were positioned in the landscape in association with a network of minor roads. The strategic importance of rivers, roads and crossing places were outlined in chapter two, but it is worth repeating here the sentiments of Vauban and Maigret:

> rivers act as barriers and a skilful defender could derive much profit by combining the peculiar properties of fortresses and river barriers. He could secure the best bridges and fords and intercept the roads which follow the bank, thereby endangering the flank and rear of the enemy who was rash enough to have passed the river at some other place.

> Duffy, 1996, 25

CASTLES AND ECCLESIASTICAL CENTRES

At heart, Ireland is still a rural country, and until relatively recently it was widely believed that urbanisation was alien to the pastoral, tribal society of Celtic Ireland. An oft used quote stating that, 'the economy of this society was pastoral and agricultural. There were no cities or towns' (De Paor, 1958; cited in Graham, 1985, 9). Over the past 25 years however, as a result of both survey and excavation, knowledge of Irish medieval ecclesiastical archaeology has greatly increased, and it is now thought possible that at least some monastic centres, in essence, constituted early medieval towns.

The latter half of the sixth century witnessed the rapid spread of monasticism in Ireland, and by the beginning of the seventh century over 800 monasteries had been founded. Monastic ideals quickly took root, and with the growth of the monasteries, Ireland swiftly became a Christian country. In the secular and ecclesiastical legislation, it is possible to trace the steady assimilation of the church into early Irish society during the seventh and eighth centuries. The monasteries housed schools and well-stocked libraries and, in addition to administering to societies' spiritual and religious needs, provided a great service in educating people. A monasteries' religious community could also include women; St Brigid's at Kildare was an eminent and influential house of nuns. Most importantly however, a great number of monasteries developed into important centres for economic activity.

Land was often given to monastic houses as gifts and bequests, it was sometimes purchased, and, by the subjugation of less powerful ecclesiastical neighbours, it was occasionally won. In this way monasteries steadily acquired large estates.

These landholdings needed to be maintained and farmed, and although the monks undoubtedly participated in the manual labour, the sheer size of some of the estates meant that the majority of the work had to be done by tenants who lived, with their families, on church lands. This symbiotic partnership provided the church with the labour that it required to exploit the economic potential of its land, whilst the monastic tenants gained ready access to pastoral care. As a result of this successful relationship many of the great ecclesiastical centres became foci for significant economic activity, and from the tenth century onwards the larger monasteries developed into proto-urban complexes. These complexes housed substantial populations, which, in addition to the clergy, comprised lay men and women, estate and craft workers. In order to accommodate the numerous residents, monastic precincts were divided into different areas with streets, houses and public buildings in the form of churches, whilst outside the enclosures, markets sprang up to take advantage of the opportunity for trade and exchange (Edwards, 1999, 100).

The Anglo-Normans frequently built castles close to important ecclesiastical centres in an attempt to gain control over the existing structures of administration and power, and to take advantage of the mechanisms for trade and exchange (Graham, 1991, 1985, 1980, 1975; Bradley, 1988). In Meath, 28 monastic sites can be identified from the ecclesiastical histories, the most important of which were Ardbraccan, Clonard, Donaghpatrick, Duleek, Kells, Kilbeg, Skreen, Slane and Trim (67). At 13 of these monastic sites, there are castles in direct association, all of the major proto-urban sites have a castle, and the majority of the remaining sites have a castle within 5 miles (8.04km) (63, 64 and 67). In Meath, there is clearly a significant correlation between the distribution of Irish proto-urban ecclesiastical centres and Anglo-Norman castles. This is hardly surprising however, as 'towns are a major strategic consideration in any military campaign' (Vauban & Maigret; in Duffy, 1996, 22).

Graham has suggested that the majority of castles associated with Meath's proto-urban monastic complexes were 'major mottes with baileys' (1991, 29), arguing that the baileys were needed to house garrisons large enough to keep the residents of the complexes under control. This notion is not fully supported by the archaeological evidence however, as only 12 of the 25 castles associated with the proto-urban complexes have baileys, 11 are without, and 2 are ringworks (56, 57, 63 and 64). Furthermore, at the nine major ecclesiastical sites, five castles have baileys, three are without, and one is a ringwork. Nevertheless, the building of castles at such locations undoubtedly represents an Anglo-Norman attempt to usurp the existing political and economic roles of the proto-urban centres; although the correlation is not as significant as for the county's road and river systems, suggesting that Meath's communications networks were of far greater importance.

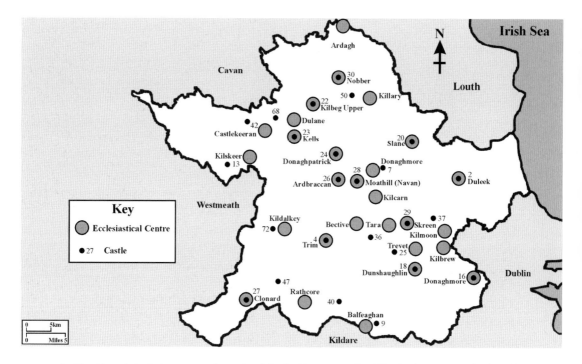

67 Meath's ecclesiastical centres and associated Anglo-Norman castles. The Anglo-Normans built castles close to the county's proto-urban monastic complexes in an attempt to gain control over the existing structures of administration and power, and to take advantage of the mechanisms for trade and exchange

POLITICAL LAND DIVISIONS, CASTLES AND CAPUTS

The early political geography of Ireland is extremely complex. In general though, from the seventh century onwards, the country was sub-divided into units of government, or small kingdoms, called *tuatha*. At the bottom end of the scale was the *tuath*, this was the land of an autonomous group of people of independent political jurisdiction – best described as a tribe – under a 'local king'. Larger units, comprising several *tuatha*, were built up by 'regional kings' whose families maintained their traditional ascendancy, and at the upper end of the scale was the 'king over kings', or the 'provincial king' (*49*). By the early twelfth century however, the smallest unit, the *tuath,* had ceased to be a political entity as such, and was merely a district under a *toísech* (a term meaning 'leader of a war-band'), whilst the *rí*, or 'regional king', ruled over an area known as a *trícha cét* (meaning 'thirty hundreds'); roughly equivalent to the *cantref* ('hundred homesteads') found in Wales (Byrne, 1993, 5).

A late twelfth-century poem entitled *Les Geste des Engleis en Yrlande* (The Deeds of the Normans in Ireland), which is also known as *The Song of Dermot*

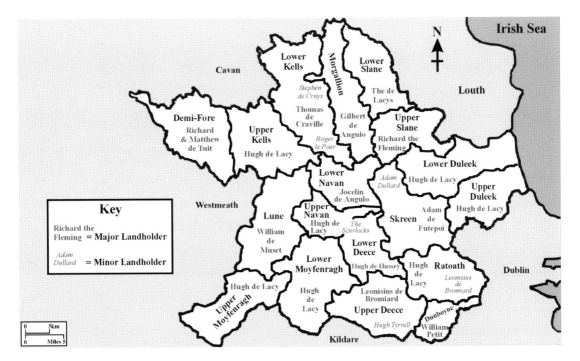

68 Hugh de Lacy's sub-infeudation of Meath is recorded in a late twelfth-century poem entitled *Les Geste des Engleis en Yrlande*. Hugh split East Meath into seven major subdivisions, and several minor ones, and retained large areas of land as seignorial manors for himself

and the Earl, records Hugh de Lacy's sub-infeudation of Meath (Orpen, 1892 & Mullally, 2002). According to the poem, Hugh split East Meath into seven major subdivisions, and several minor ones, and retained large areas of land as seignorial manors for himself (*68*). The major subdivisions – roughly equivalent to a future barony in extent – are recorded as: Skreen to Adam de Futepoi; Morgallion to Gilbert de Angulo; (Upper) Slane to Richard the Fleming; (Lower) Deece to Hugh de Hussey; Lune to William de Muset; Demi-Fore to Richard and Matthew de Tuit; and Dunboyne to William le Petit. Some smaller grants are also recorded: the lands of (Lower) Navan and Ardbraccan to Jocelin de Angulo; Emlagh Beccon (Lower Kells) to Thomas de Craville; and lands around Dollardstown and Painestown (in the barony of Skreen) to Adam Dullard. If the record of the land grants in the poem are complete, Hugh de Lacy retained the baronies of Moyfenragh (Upper and Lower) and Ratoath, plus large areas of the baronies of Kells (Upper), Navan (Lower) and Duleek (Upper and Lower) as seignorial manors.

It is often stated that the Anglo-Norman baronies created in Ireland were based upon earlier units of government established by the Gaelic Irish. Rice, for

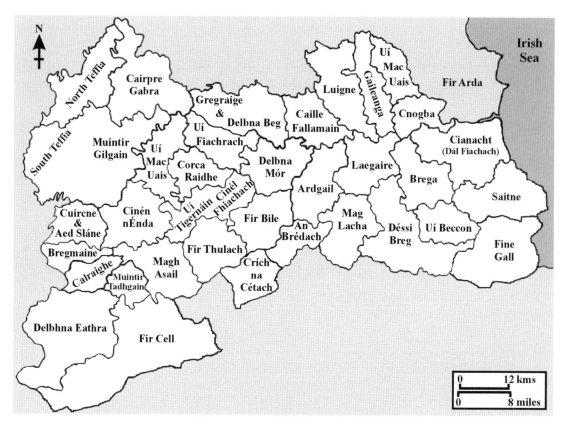

69 By the twelfth century, Midhe (Meath and West Meath) was divided into areas known as *trícha céts*, which were ruled over by a *rí*, or 'regional king'. *Trícha cét* originally meant 'thirty hundred men', but by the twelfth century applied to a measure of land or 'thirty hundreds'

example, states that 'the divisions of Meath by Hugh de Lacy reflect the structures of government of his predecessors' (2001, 15). The evidence to substantiate such claims is extremely limited however, as to date very little work has been carried out upon this topic. The standard text on early Irish land divisions is Reeves' 'On the Townland Distribution of Ireland' which was published in 1862 (PRIA, vol. 7, 473-90) and the only map available showing Meath's political landscape at the time of the Anglo-Norman invasion is a very poor quality affair in the back of Orpen's translation of *La Geste des Engleis en Yrlande*, which was published in 1892 and contains some significant errors and omissions. Fortunately, a recently published collection of works by the late Paul Walsh (2003) contains translations of many of the manuscripts which detail the *trícha céts* and the free and tributary kingdoms of Midhe (Meath & West Meath). These translations, although convoluted and fragmentary, have facilitated the construction of a new map which shows the political geography of Midhe before the arrival of the Anglo-Normans (*69*).

If the map of Gaelic Irish land divisions in Midhe (*69*) is compared to that of Hugh de Lacy's sub-infeudation of Meath (*68*), it is evident that the boundaries used to delineate the various units are practically identical. The only perceptible differences are: Upper Moyfenragh (formerly An Brédach) absorbing part of Crích na Cétach; Demi-Fore (formerly Delbna Beg) absorbing part of Gregraige; and the lands of the Déssi Breg being subdivided to form the baronies of Deece and Dunboyne. This strongly suggests that the Anglo-Normans – who were familiar with a similar system of Welsh *cantrefs* and *commotes* – simply adopted and adapted the existing political land divisions in those parts of Ireland over which they gained control. The *provinces* were subdivided into *counties* (comparable to the Anglo-Saxon *shire*), the *counties* were subdivided into *baronies* (comparable to the Anglo-Saxon *hundred* or Welsh *cantref*), and the *baronies* – whose boundaries generally corresponded to those of the earlier *trícha céts* – were subdivided into *townlands*. Whilst lower down the territorial hierarchy, the *ballybetagh* (one of the names given to the principal subdivisions of the *trícha cét*) manifested itself in the Anglo-Norman landscape as the *manor*, with the subdivisions of the *ballybetagh* (or its equivalent) manifesting themselves as *small manorial and sub-manorial holdings* (O'Keeffe, 1996, 147).

According to several contemporary accounts, following the sub-infeudation of Meath, Hugh de Lacy was instrumental in founding a number of castles within the county. Aside from the castles destroyed at Trim [4] and Duleek [2] in 1174, at least four other castles are documented as founded before 1180. In 1176, the castle at Slane [20] was attacked and destroyed, and consequently, those at Galtrim [8], Kells [23] and Derry Patrick [6] were razed and left desolate (Hennessey & McCarthy, 1887-1901, ii, 183-5). Whilst in 1182, according to Giraldus, Hugh de Lacy was building a castle at Clonard [27], and another for Adam de Futepoi, who held the barony of Skreen [29] (Scott & Martin, 1978, 195). The castles at Slane, Galtrim and Skreen formed the *capite* of principal land grants, whilst the castles at Trim, Duleek and Kells were founded within seignorial manors. The fact that Hugh de Lacy was personally involved in the castle building programme indicates that there was some defensive concept or plan for the liberty as a whole.

Between 1172 and 1200, castles were founded across nineteen baronies in Meath to act as the *caputs* of new lordships (*63* and *64*). The vast majority of these castles were built before the death of Hugh de Lacy in 1186 (*70*), and 13 of them were positioned at highly significant pivotal points in the landscape. Bearing in mind that castles often served several strategic functions simultaneously, 11 of the castles constructed can be linked to river crossings, 5 can be related to navigable

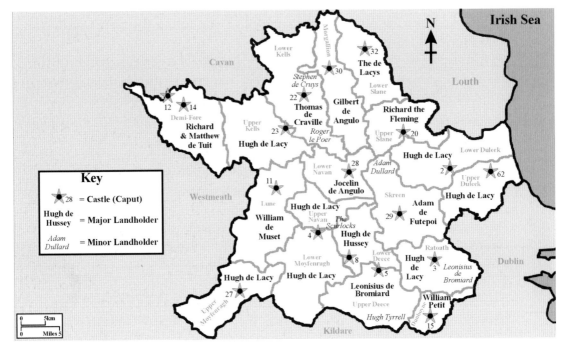

70 Anglo-Norman barons, baronies and *caputs* in the Liberty of Meath, *c.*1172–1200

river sections, 5 can be connected to routes taken by early roads, and 8 can be associated with proto-urban ecclesiastical centres. This suggests that the locations for the *caput* castles were carefully selected with strategic considerations foremost in mind.

It has been suggested that there is a link between both the principal land grants of the sub-infeudation, seignorial manors, and mottes with baileys (O'Keeffe, 2000, 17; Graham, 1980, 46). The argument is that the majority of the castles constructed to act as the *caputs* of the new lordships were large and had baileys attached, thereby reflecting the status and importance of their owners. In truth, the morphology of these castles is highly variable (56 and 57), so size does not appear to accurately represent status. However 12 of the 19 castles do have attached baileys, representing 55 per cent of all the mottes with baileys in the interior of Meath, and as such the presence of a bailey, in this instance, could be taken to indicate status. As the land grants were made to de Lacy's trusted followers, it seems clear that these fortifications were the means by which the liberty was brought under Anglo-Norman control, a necessary antecedent to colonisation and settlement.

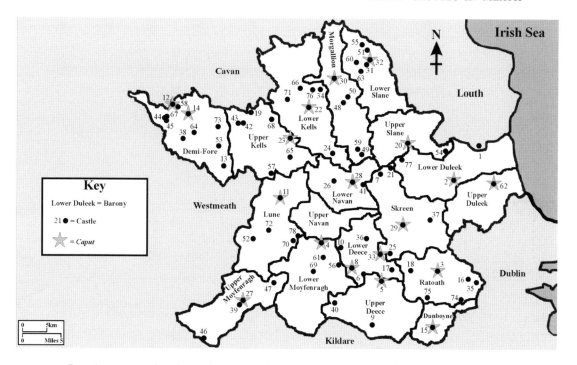

71 Baronies, *caputs* and castles in the Liberty of Meath. With powerful castles functioning as *caput* centres, the baronies were further subdivided into manors, and additional castles were erected within each. This added an auxiliary layer of defence to the barony

Once the major castles were firmly established as *caput* centres, the principal land grants were further subdivided into manors and outlying subsidiary castles were erected within them, thereby adding an auxiliary layer of defence to the barony (*71*). Each barony, on average, contained three additional castles, whilst along the more dangerous northern frontier the average was six. Interestingly, Upper Navan contained no castles whatsoever, but it can be supposed that its central location within the county afforded it adequate protection, as it was completely surrounded by castles in the adjoining lordships.

CASTLES, COLONISATION, TOWNS AND BOROUGHS

Having successfully secured Meath's northern border, gained control of the county's systems of transport, communication and supply, usurped the political and economic power of the proto-urban monastic centres, and established *caputs* within the new lordships (although not necessarily in that order), the Anglo-Normans were in a position to begin the process of colonisation. The mass of mottes and allied earthworks that are widely distributed across Meath's landscape are poignant and symbolic reminders of the establishment of Anglo-Norman military control in the area, but such action, however harsh, was deemed necessary, as it provided stable foundations for the development of the colony.

The Irish community, who had fled from their lands in Meath as a result of the continual raids and counter-raids by the Anglo-Normans and Irish since 1170, were invited to return by Hugh de Lacy, who re-established them with cattle and farms, and offered them protection. Whilst other settlers of mainly English origin with some Welsh and Flemings, who were attracted by the lure of increased social status and lessened labour services, were introduced in large numbers. The process of colonisation was for the most part controlled through a new and distinctive form of settlement in Ireland's landscape – the manor. The manor was much more than a geographical unit, it was a military, economic, social and judicial institution, and in most cases at the heart of the manor there was a castle.

Colonisation boosted the economy, which in turn led to the development of market villages, towns and boroughs. In Meath, 92 manorial villages and 18 boroughs have been identified, of which 36 of the manorial villages and 14 of the boroughs have associated castles (*63, 64* and *colour plate 27*). Graham (1975) has divided the boroughs into three classes in order of importance. 'First stratum boroughs' were the five walled towns of Trim, Kells, Navan, Athboy and Drogheda, all of which were associated with castles, and all of which remain the most important central places in Meath today. 'Second stratum boroughs' were the seven unwalled, but strategically important, settlements of Slane, Nobber, Dunshaughlin, Dunboyne, Duleek, Skreen and Ratoath, all of which were associated with castles, and each of which acted as a *capite baroniae*, monastic and market centre. 'Third stratum' or 'rural boroughs', were Syddan, Drumconrath, Greenoge, Mornington, Colpe and Newtown Trim, two of which were associated with castles, and each of which never developed beyond a manorial village. The association between the castle and both borough and manorial village clearly signifies the castle's usefulness as a centre for administration, justice and social organisation, whilst additionally underlining its continuing role as a mechanism for control.

HUGH DE LACY'S CAMPAIGN IN MEATH

Over the years a number of articles have been published on the castles of Meath, but to date there has been little attempt to reconcile the results of these empirical studies with the historical narrative Orpen's, *Ireland under the Normans:*

1169-1333 (4 vols., 1911–20) being the notable exception. Clearly then, an effective way to demonstrate the brilliance of Hugh de Lacy's castle building strategies is to combine the results of this chapter with the historical accounts of events in Meath. This is additionally useful, as the lack of consistency between the historic narrative and the conclusions drawn so far visibly supports the chapter's findings.

In 1169, the king of Midhe, Dermot O'Melaghlin – who in 1166 had aided Tiernan O'Rourke in the expulsion of Dermot MacMurrough – was killed by Donnell Bregach O'Melaghlin (*Domnall*) (51), who immediately seized the kingdom for himself. This action greatly angered Rory O'Connor, king of Connacht, who marched into Midhe, and in revenge expelled Donnell Bregach. Rory then divided Midhe into two halves, allocating East Meath to Tiernan O'Rourke, king of Bréifne, and keeping West Meath for himself, installing Art O'Melaghlin as king of West Meath under him. This event is sometimes referred to as 'The Partition of Meath'. Donnell Bregach was not going to give up the kingdom without a struggle however, and in 1170 he turned to Rory and Tiernan's old enemy, Dermot MacMurrough, for help. Dermot, with the backing of his Anglo-Norman allies, conquered East Meath, harried Tiernan O'Rourke's kingdom of Bréifne, and reinstalled Donnell Bregach as king of East Meath, under him.

When Henry II arrived in Ireland in 1171, he was faced with at least four rival claimants for the kingship of Meath: two from within the Clann Cholmáin royal dynasty (Art and Donnell), an external challenge from Tiernán O'Rourke, king of Bréifne, and a claim from Strongbow, in light of his and Diarmait Mac Murchada's military intervention in the region. Unsurprising, considering the circumstances and Meath's strategic and political importance, in 1172, Henry II granted the kingdom to Hugh de Lacy, to hold 'as Murrough O'Melaghlin or any other before or after him best held it' by the service of fifty knights (*Gormanston Reg.*, f.5, 177). Henry's grant was a double-edged sword however, as with the lands and titles came the unenviable task of capturing, subduing and securing the kingdom.

Internally, Meath was divided between two rival sibling would-be-kings of the Ua Máel Sechlainn line. To the south, sat Strongbow, effectively 'king of Leinster', who, although not obviously hostile, must have resented Hugh's appointment. Immediately to the south, in the midlands of Leinster, were the Uí Failge, who were unfriendly towards the Anglo-Normans, and refused to pay tribute to Strongbow. In 1172, Strongbow led an expedition into Uí Failge territory to extract tribute, and there plundered the land for cattle. Initially, there was no resistance to the attack, but on the return journey south Diarmait Ua Dímmusaig, king of Uí Failge, ambushed the rearguard and killed Strongbow's son-in-law,

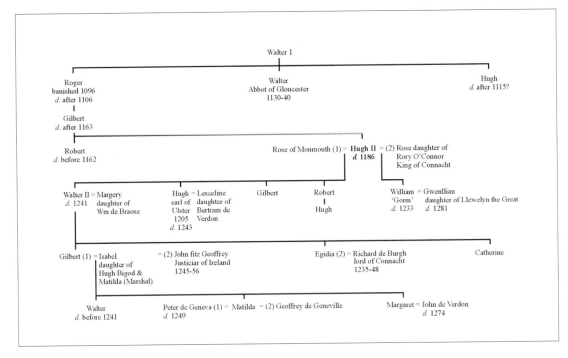

72 Genealogical table of the de Lacy's, 1066-1241. Hugh de Lacy, the 'Constable of Dublin' and 'Justiciar of Ireland' is shown in bold. *After: Hillaby, 1992/3, 6*

Robert de Quency, the constable of Leinster. To the west, was Muintir Gilgain (*69*), whose ruler, Donnell O'Farrell, was adamantly resistant to Hugh's claims over his territory; and to the west of Muintir Gilgain was Connacht, whose king, Rory O'Connor, had claims over Meath under the forced partition of 1169. To the north, and posing the greatest threat to Anglo-Norman security in the region, was Tiernan O'Rourke's kingdom of Bréifne, which also had claims over Meath under the forced partition. Early in 1171, Tiernan O'Rourke made successive raids into Meath, drove off countless cattle, and burnt the round tower of Tullyard, with its fill of human beings (Brady, 1961, 39).

Meath then, was under constant threat from internal rebellion, and was in constant danger of attacks from the north, south and west. Hugh de Lacy, who came from a family of seasoned campaigners (*72*), was an ambitious and determined individual though, and was not about to let his enemies get the better of him. Hugh set a plan into motion that proved so successful that eventually even Henry II himself grew fearful of his power. Hugh 'filled Meath, from the Shannon to the sea, with castles and foreigners' (*Annals of Loch Cé*, c.1186; Hennessey, 1871).

Meath's datable castles can be sensibly divided into four main chronological periods: 1172-5, 1175-80, 1180-1200, and 1200 onwards (56 and 57). As Hugh de Lacy died in 1186, only the castles within the first three phases will be discussed here.

1172–1175

Hugh de Lacy's first foray into Meath came shortly after Henry II's departure for the Continent. In 1172, Hugh advanced into Meath, took Fore, and raided as far as the Shannon, in an attempt to take possession of his fief. His progress was hampered, however, when he encountered strong resistance from Tiernan O'Rourke of Bréifne, who resented Hugh's claims over lands which he felt were rightfully his. Tiernan was one of those expressly named as having sworn fealty to Henry II, but it seems that he did not intend to give up his claims in Meath to Henry's grantee, and there was an inevitable clash of interests between him and Hugh (Orpen, 1911-20, i, 319-20). A meeting was subsequently arranged between the rival claimants, at a place now known as the 'Hill of Ward' near Athboy, and upon this hill Hugh struck the first major blow of his campaign – he put Tiernan O'Rourke to the sword. Chroniclers and historians have long deliberated over this event, often apportioning equal blame on both sides, or suggesting that Tiernan was slain due to a general misunderstanding (Martin, 1993, 99). It must be remembered though, that these were violent, bloody and disorderly times, and 'we must think … of fearful men seeking to control a rebellious land under the threat of hostile invasion, men ruthless and rapacious, driven by repressions and barbarous cruelties' (Pounds, 1990, 10). The killing of Tiernan was almost certainly no accident, but a deliberate act on Hugh's part. The fact that Tiernan's head was taken and spiked over the gate of the fortress at Dublin adds further credence to this argument.

With Teirnan's death, the O'Rourke kingship over Uí Briúin Bréfne and Conmaicne collapsed. Tiernan's gains in Meath were lost, and his see at Kells was extinguished and was swiftly incorporated into the Anglo-Norman diocese of Meath. Having dealt successfully, and ruthlessly, with the threat from Teirnan and the kingdom of Bréifne, Hugh turned his attentions to Muintir Gilgain. He mounted two raids into the region, which proved highly effective, as Donnell O'Farrell, the ruler of Muintir Gilgain, was killed, and the Anglo-Normans managed to carry off many cows and capture countless prisoners. It is unlikely that any serious attempt was made to establish permanent settlement in Meath at this stage however, as the area was still extremely hostile, a fact reflected by the numerous castles constructed during this period (56 and 57).

The earliest frontier in Meath appears to have been the River Boyne, as all of the datable castles built by the Anglo-Normans between 1172 and 1175 are situated on or to the east of the river (*colour plate 28*). Of the 10 castles erected, 6 were constructed at pivotal points in the landscape (*58*), all can be accounted for militarily (*63* and *64*), and the majority were erected in locations that enabled them to perform several strategic functions simultaneously: 5 castles formed the *caputs* of new lordships, and 4 were connected with the control of proto-urban ecclesiastical centres, but more importantly, 3 were connected with the monitoring and control of route-ways, and 7 were connected with the monitoring and control of waterways – with 5 castles on navigable river sections, and 7 at river crossings. One of these castles, Ardmulchan Motte [7], admirably demonstrates the Anglo-Norman propensity for selecting optimum sites for castle erection. From its commanding location, overlooking the River Boyne, Ardmulchan Motte dominated the neighbouring ecclesiastical site of Donaghmore, controlled traffic on a navigable stretch of the River Boyne, monitored movement along the nearby Slighe Assail route-way, and guarded an adjacent river-crossing (*colour plate 29*).

Hugh's strategy in this early period is clear. Several castles were erected in the landscape to the east of the Boyne in an attempt to secure a small, yet manageable, area of land against internal revolt. Other castles were constructed adjacent to the River Boyne, the river and castles, in combination, forming an effective barrier against hostile Irish incursions: a strategy that also gave the Anglo-Normans control of the area's systems of communication, transport and supply. Hugh's most important holding was Dublin, and by securing the Boyne, along with the land to the east of the river, he provided the city with a viable means of defence. Hugh literally surrounded Dublin City with a protective screen of castles (*61*).

Because of the large number of Irish kings who swore oaths of fealty to Henry II, the military ethos of the Anglo-Norman castle building programme in Meath has been questioned. Indeed, it has been stated that during Hugh de Lacy's tenure of office 'we hear of little or no fighting in Meath or in Leinster' (Orpen, 1911–20, ii, 53), and that there was much 'peaceful penetration without warfare' by the Anglo-Normans (Martin; in Cosgrove, 1993, lv). These statements are not in concordance with the contemporary accounts of events however, such as those recorded in *The Annals* or documented in the works of Giraldus Cambrensis.

Apart from the confrontations already mentioned, in 1173 Donnell Bregach O'Melaghlin, king of East Meath, was killed by his half-brother Art O'Melaghlin, king of West Meath, who was attempting to secure the entire kingdom for himself (*51*). The attempt failed, due no doubt to Anglo-Norman intervention, and East Meath passed to Manus O'Melaghlin, under Hugh de Lacy. Later in the same year, with Hugh and Strongbow both absent from Ireland (having been recalled by Henry II to aid in suppressing the great rebellion in Normandy), the Irish revolted. Giraldus states that when Strongbow returned to Ireland, after

10 August 1173, he found the majority of the princes in the country in revolt against the king and himself (Scott & Martin, 1978, 135); and in 1174, after dealing Strongbow a crushing defeat at Thurles, 'the entire population of Ireland … rose with one consent against the English' (ibid., 139).

Early in 1174, Rory O'Connor, king of Connacht, led a full-scale assault against the Anglo-Normans in Meath, probably in an attempt to win back West Meath, to which he had claims under the partition of 1169. Rory crossed the Shannon at the head of a great army, drawn not only from Connacht, but also from Leth Cuinn. The army included Irish leaders from Meath, Bréifne, Airgialla, Ulster, and (a rare phenomenon in Meath and Leinster) from the Cénél nEógain and the Cenél Conaill. The force crossed Meath and reached the outskirts of Dublin, destroying Hugh de Lacy's castles at Trim and Duleek en route. In a desperate plight, Strongbow sent a message to Raymond le Gros in Wales. Raymond returned to Ireland with 30 knights, 100 mounted soldiers and 300 archers, and after rescuing Strongbow, who was under siege at Waterford, marched north to Dublin to deal with the allied Irish force. The Irish had faced Raymond le Gros before and were well aware of his reputation, and on hearing of his, and Strongbow's approach, they melted away. Raymond and Strongbow then began the work of restoring the usurped Anglo-Normans to their castles and outposts in Meath, and an uneasy peace returned to the county. Importantly though, Hugh's castle building strategy had proved successful, as Dublin was almost certainly saved from the Irish by his defensive screen of castles.

1175–1180

In 1175, the Anglo-Normans carried out a number of reprisals against the chieftains who had taken part in the attack on Meath in the previous year. Manus O'Melaghlin was hanged at Trim for his part in the rebellion, although Art O'Melaghlin seems to have been left undisturbed in West Meath. Clonard and Durrow were plundered, and raids were made into the territories of several petty kings of West Meath who had joined in Rory's uprising: the annals record that the whole country from Drogheda to Athlone was laid waste (O'Donovan, 1848–51; Hennessey, 1871). The castles at Trim and Duleek were quickly rebuilt and reoccupied at this time, and other castles began to be erected in the landscape (*colour plate 28*). The new castles represent the beginning of the systematic occupation of Meath by the Anglo-Normans.

Fourteen castles can be securely dated to this period (*56* and *57*), six of which were erected at pivotal points in the landscape (*58*). Each of the 14 castles can be accounted for militarily (*63* and *64*), and most were clearly intended to fulfil a number of concurrent strategic roles: 7 castles formed the *caputs* of new lordships, 7 were connected with the control of proto-urban ecclesiastical centres,

5 were connected with the monitoring and control of route-ways, and 10 were connected with the monitoring and control of waterways – with 4 on navigable sections, and 8 at river crossings. The locations chosen for the new castles suggest a threefold strategy. Firstly, the chain of castles designed to protect Meath's northern border was begun. This helped to shield the newly acquired Anglo-Norman lands from further Irish incursions, which in turn helped to ensure the success of the colonisation and settlement process. Secondly, by way of three well-positioned castles, Meath's other navigable river, the Blackwater, was secured. This gave the Anglo-Normans control over virtually all of the county's systems of transport, communication and supply. Thirdly, the Anglo-Normans began to erect castles at important ecclesiastical centres. These castles, designed to function as new focal points or 'central places' in the landscape, were used to wrest political and economic power away from the 'proto-urban' monastic complexes.

The expansion of Anglo-Norman occupied territory west of the Boyne, along with the accelerated programme of castle building, appears to have triggered three events. Firstly, early in 1176, Art O'Melaghlin, king of West Meath, was deposed, and the remnants of the O'Melaghlin family finally gave up hope of ruling Meath and retreated into the south-western part of present Co. Westmeath, settling in the modern barony of Clonlonan, where they remained until the time of Cromwell (Walsh, 2003, 101). Secondly, again in 1176, Richard the Fleming's motte at Slane was destroyed by Máel Seclainn Mac Lochlainn, who was probably angered by the growing chain of castles along Meath's northern border. The Irish annals state that immediately after the destruction of Slane, the castles of Kells, Galtrim, and Derrypatrick … were razed or left desolate through fear of the Cénél nEógain (Hennessey & McCarthy, 1887-1901). Thirdly, in 1177, probably in direct response to the destruction of Slane castle, and the continued threat posed by the Cénél nEógain, John de Courcy invaded and conquered Ulaid (*49, 50* and *53*).

On 1 June 1176, the battle-scarred veteran Richard fitz Gilbert de Clare – also known as Strongbow, and described as brave, courteous, generous and lavish in *The Song of Dermot and the Earl* (Orpen, 1892, 27) died of a 'mortal illness'. Strongbow was temporarily replaced by William fitz Audelin, but in 1177, having been made 'Procurator-general of Ireland' by Henry II, Hugh de Lacy returned to take control. Henry II, in addition, reconfirmed Hugh's grant of Meath, and the castle and city of Dublin.

1180–1200

There are nine castles that can be safely attributed to the period 1180 to 1200 (*56* and *57*), and again each castle can be accounted for militarily (*63* and *64*), with 3 constructed at pivotal points in the landscape (*58*), and the majority performing more than one strategic function (*colour plate 28*). 6 castles formed the *caputs* of new lordships, 6 were connected with the control of proto-urban ecclesiastical centres, 4 were connected with the monitoring and control of route-ways, and 4 were connected with the monitoring and control of waterways – with 1 on a navigable section, and 4 at river crossings. Anglo-Norman control of Meath's rivers and road systems was thus reinforced via the erection of several new castles, and the chain of castles designed to protect Meath's northern border was further strengthened around the River Dee area, probably in response to the attack on Slane castle in 1177. As the majority of castles constructed at this time were associated with either proto-urban ecclesiastical centres or *caputs* however, it is clear that the focus for the castle building programme was gradually shifting away from the necessity to control the region's communications networks towards the need to control the region's economy and, on a slightly smaller scale, the territory in each lordship.

After 1180, the process of sub-infeudation in Meath began apace, with Hugh de Lacy constructing a number of castles upon the principal land grants of his favourite barons. In 1182, Hugh built the castles of Clonard [27] and Skreen [29], and it is likely that he was also responsible for the construction of the castles at Killeen [25], Navan [28] and Nobber [30]. The majority of these fortifications were designed to fill gaps in the network of castles forming the *caputs* of lordships – making the Anglo-Normans masters of Meath – or to gain control of the remaining Irish economic and administrative structures – in the form of the proto-urban ecclesiastical centres. The fortifications thereby provided the means to bring the liberty under full military control: a necessary precursor to the process of colonisation and settlement.

With Meath captured, subdued and secured, Hugh implemented the next stage of his plan. Giraldus states that Hugh went to great trouble to conciliate those who had been conquered and forcibly ejected from their lands, by restoring the countryside to its rightful cultivators and bringing back cattle to the pastures which had formerly been deserted, enticing the Irish still further to his side by mild rule, and by agreements on which they could rely (Scott & Martin, 1978, 191). Colonisation followed conquest, and the Anglo-Norman barons turned their lordships to profit. In the words of Giraldus, 'when they [the Irish] had been hemmed in by castles and gradually subdued, he [Hugh de Lacy] compelled them to obey the laws. Thus he succeeded in reducing to an ordered condition all that his predecessors had either destroyed or thrown into confusion, and was the first to succeed in deriving any profit from that which had brought others nothing but trouble' (ibid.).

In 1180, Hugh sealed his pact with the Irish by marrying the daughter of Rory O'Connor, and in doing so won their unmitigated support. Unfortunately his marriage, and his overwhelming success in the region, brought him into conflict with Henry II, who suspected him of 'wanting to throw off his allegiance and usurp the government of the kingdom, and with it the crown and sceptre' (Scott & Martin, 1978, 191). As a result, in 1181, Hugh was deprived of his custody of Dublin, and although he was reinstated after a year, he was finally superseded as governor of Dublin by Philip of Worcester in 1184.

In 1186, as part of his plan to pacify West Meath, Hugh de Lacy was busy supervising the construction of a castle at Durrow. There, he was approached by an Irish youth, named Gilla-gan-inathair Ua Miadhaigh, who, 'having his axe hidden under his cloak ... gave de Lacy one blow, so that he cut off his head, and he fell, both head and body, into the ditch of the castle' (*Annals of Loch Cé, c.*1186; ed. Hennessey, 1871). In this way Hugh, the 'King of Midhe and Bréifne and Airghiall' (ibid.), and one time Constable of Dublin, and Justiciar and Procurator-general of Ireland, passed into shadow, dying before the final part of his plan could be completed. West Meath was never fully pacified, and with Hugh's death, the lordship was effectively divided into two, a land of peace and a land of war. Walter de Lacy eventually succeeded to his father's estates when he came of age in 1194, but paled against his father's achievements. In his lifetime, Hugh de Lacy proved himself a great warrior, competent campaigner, proficient strategist, and effective statesman and politician, and with his death, the last real hope for complete Anglo-Norman domination in Ireland died also. Consequently, for many centuries, the 'country was divided into two cultures and two 'nations'' (Martin; in Cosgrove, 1993, xlviiii).

CASTLES IN MEATH AND IRELAND: A CONCLUSION

Judging by the evidence, there can be little doubt that the Anglo-Normans, under the capable direction of Hugh de Lacy, implemented a deliberate and carefully considered plan of action for the conquest, consolidation and colonisation of Meath, which was based upon the strategic use of castles. This plan was undoubtedly hatched out of the various lessons learnt by at least three generations of Norman campaigners involved in the conquest and colonisation of first England, and later Wales, and the plan proved so successful that Meath became the most heavily Anglo-Normanised territory in the whole of Ireland. Indeed, it is tempting to state that in Meath, at least, we are witnessing the pinnacle of the Norman castle building achievement. This statement is somewhat controversial however, and in order to justify the assertian it is necessary to briefly assess the conclusions of several other castellologists.

Regarding the nature of the Anglo-Norman castles erected in Ireland, it has been suggested that the motte and bailey was out of date and almost obsolete as a castle type by 1200 (O'Keeffe, 1992, 59; McNeill, 2000, 56 and 76). This may be true in terms of the motte and bailey as a comfortable lordly residence, but it is not true in terms of the motte and bailey as an item of military hardware: the role for which it was originally intended. This notion was fully supported by Brown, who stated, 'in the expediency of conquest and settlement … [the motte and bailey's] effectiveness and ease of construction were as indispensable to the Angevins in Ireland in the late twelfth and thirteenth centuries as to Duke William in England in 1066' (1980i, 139).

It has also been suggested that many of Ireland's earthwork castles appear to be militarily weak in comparison to their Anglo-French contemporaries (McNeill, 2000, 76). Ignoring Ireland's heavy annual rainfall and prolonged agricultural background – both of which must have caused heavy erosion at many castle sites over the years – it must be remembered that it is nearly impossible to accurately judge the strength of a castle from the surviving earthworks. Mottes that now appear as isolated insignificant monuments in the landscape may once have been surrounded by vast palisaded enclosures, features now undetectable without geophysical prospecting, excavation or close scrutiny of aerial photographs (O'Keeffe, 1990 & 1992; Glasscock, 1975). Indeed, O'Conor has recently emphasised the fact that many Irish mottes could have displayed sophisticated, almost Hen Domen-like, earth and timber defences (2002, 173-82). In truth, the Anglo-Normans knew from experience that motte and baileys would adequately serve their purposes in Ireland, and were confident enough to base their conquest upon them.

Concerning the positioning of castles in Ireland's landscape, it has been argued that in many areas there is little sign of an overall strategic pattern or plan against either external attack or internal revolt (McNeill, 1989-90; Flanagan, 1996). McNeill has suggested that the proliferation of castles along the borders of territories are not the result of strategic planning, but rather of a phenomenon occurring after the process of conquest was complete, which was concerned with the stabilisation of lordships, further adding that there was no systematic building of castles at points in the landscape that could be considered 'strategic pressure points' (2000, 76). Such arguments are entirely contrary to what has been discovered in Meath, where the castles form discernible strategic patterns in the landscape, most likely due to an overall strategic plan, with 23 of the county's castles located at 'pivotal points', and the abundance of castles on the northern border resulting from a steadily unfolding military strategy. Therefore, it is perhaps fairer to state that in Ireland individual territories can exhibit differing castle strategies, which result from localised considerations and requirements or independent lordly planning.

McNeill has also argued that in order to hold down the countryside and suppress the native population within a lordship, a baron would have required a 'blanket coverage' of castles, and that even knights in possession of less than half a fee should have been erecting castles, in case they too were attacked. As Ireland's landscape does not contain this high density of castellation, McNeill concluded that the castles did not act together as part of a lordly scheme, but served only to hold land already won, or to provide administrative headquarters for lords in their lordships (2000, 76-77). Based upon the findings from Meath, it can be conversely argued that if castles are properly positioned in the landscape, at locations with tactical or strategic value, there is simply no need for 'blanket coverage' one well-positioned castle is worth a dozen poorly positioned ones. Moreover, as Meath contains at least 78 Anglo-Norman castles, with an average distance between them of 2.48 miles (4km), it could just as easily be argued that there was 'blanket coverage' anyhow. As for the poor castle-less knight with less than half a fee, it was not uncommon in times of danger for such men to seek refuge in the castle of the lord to whom they owed service (Pounds, 1990, 44-52).

Ultimately, if the Anglo-Norman campaign was to succeed, colonisation and settlement had to follow conquest and consolidation. For colonisation and settlement to succeed, there are two essential requirements: a sound material base and adequate security (Luttwak, 1981, 1). The challenge for the Anglo-Normans in Meath was to provide the necessary level of security without prejudicing the vitality of the county's economic base, and without compromising the stability of the rapidly evolving political order: both of which could have easily led to the failure of the colony. Drawing upon years of military experience, the Anglo-Normans devised a strategy that covered practically all eventualities, and one which utilised the best tool for the job – the castle. This strategy proved to be highly effective and, in the words of Giraldus, 'quickly succeeded in reducing to an ordered condition all that ... had [previously been] either destroyed or thrown into confusion' (Scott & Martin, 1978, 191).

The strategy employed in Meath may have been a little too successful however, as it brought Hugh de Lacy into conflict with Henry II. The king, who had grown fearful of Hugh's steadily increasing power, deprived him of his custody of Dublin and replaced him as governor. This act may have inadvertently led to Hugh's demise, as he removed himself to West Meath, where he was later murdered. Hugh was truly the last of the great old-style Anglo-Norman campaigners, and his death ended any possibility of complete Anglo-Norman domination in Ireland as 'there was no place further for the old warriors to go ... they settled down to the thankless task of garrison duty along a frontier which no longer meant opportunity, but toil. Their frontier had come to an end' (Nelson, 1966, 150).

6

A few well-positioned castles

If you have built castles in the air, your work need not be lost; that is where they should be. Now put the foundations under them.

Henry David Thoreau (1817–62)

The Norman army included amongst its ranks large numbers of highly skilled knights (*milites*), who were trained to fight as cavalry, with lance and sword, from the backs of nimble, specially bred and trained war-horses. The knights were divided into two classes: landholding *milites* or *mediae nobilitatis*, who were vassals and leading followers, and landless *gregarii* or *stipendiarii* who served for wages. In addition, the army comprised heavy and light infantry and the *arrière-ban*, or general levy of freemen, all skilled in the use of spear, bow and crossbow. What is often overlooked however is that the Norman army also included a number of specialists, the most important of which were the military engineers.

Domesday Book contains references to at least two types of engineer. In the Exon Domesday Book, it is recorded that 'Gerard the ditcher (*fossarius*) holds Lopen from Roger of Corcelle' (21:38). It is probable that 'Gerard the ditch-digger' was Robert of Mortain's chief engineer; the use of the word 'ditcher' indicating that he was a specialist in the construction of earthworks. Gerard appears to have been responsible for the construction of the huge and visually striking motte and bailey castle at Montacute, and as a reward for his efforts, he was given the nearby holding of Lopen by Roger of Corcelle, who was one of Robert of Mortain's most trusted knights. Domesday Book also mentions 'Waldinus Ingeniator', who held ten properties in the county of Lincolnshire (the lands of Waldin Engaine) [47]. Waldinus is a personal name, but Ingeniator (or Engaine) translates as engineer.

Norman military engineering skills were also in demand in other countries. By the mid-eleventh century, for example, there were many Normans in the employ of the Byzantine Empire, where they are recorded in the role of siege engineers (Janin, 1930, 64; Nicolle, 1999, 21).

The Norman invasions of England and Wales, and the Anglo-Norman campaign in Ireland, thrust men into unfamiliar, difficult and hostile environments. Conquest could bring land, and with it status, wealth and power, but it was a risky business and was equally likely to result in violence and death. Greatly outnumbered by their enemies, men in such situations were forced to place their trust in strong leadership, the ability and comradeship of their companions, and an infallible plan for victory, which in the case of the Normans was the deployment of castles. It is not difficult to imagine small scouting parties of engineers covertly surveying enemy territory in order to establish the whereabouts of the best sites for the construction of their castles. Each site would have been carefully examined and assessed, to ensure that it met the necessary requirements, and these decisions would not be made in haste, as a poorly chosen site could easily render a castle useless or, worse still, lead to the death of many men. To inform their choice of site, the engineers would have relied upon their detailed knowledge of the strategic and tactical principals of warfare, and this knowledge, in combination with their skill and experience, would have made them a very valuable asset indeed.

A study of historic military manuals, texts and treatise, in chapter two, led to the compilation of a set of strategic and tactical principles which relate to the positioning of fortifications in the landscape. These principles, which comprise factors that any military engineer would consider when selecting a site upon which to erect a fortification, essentially indicate *where* castles should be constructed in the landscape, and consequently can be used as a framework to test the positioning of historic (or real) castles. The two sets (strategic and tactical) can both be broken down into four groups. The tactical considerations can be summarised as follows:

Defensibility: the chosen position must be strongly fortified by nature; sites protected by the presence of natural obstacles, such as steep slopes, cliffs, rivers, marshes or shorelines are ideal.

Security: the site should not be overlooked, or be within range of missile weapons or artillery, and ideally should provide good all-round visibility, hence higher ground is preferable.

Accessibility: while it is essential to exclude hostile forces, it is also important to ensure relatively easy access for friendly troops and supplies, and, in case of an emergency, an escape route.

Practicality: there must be locally available construction materials, the site must have firm foundations upon which to build, be close to a potable water supply, and be well-drained and 'healthy'.

The strategic considerations for a castle to exist may include one or more of the following:

Borders: to control and protect a border, or border area.

Communications: to command lines of communication, transport and supply, particularly rivers and river crossings, roads, defiles and passes.

Assets: to dominate a locality or region of perceived value, such as a commercial centre, rich agricultural land, or a resource-producing area.

Safety: to provide a secure base from which field armies may operate, or a place of refuge in times of adversity.

It is clear, looking at the above groups, that the Norman military engineers, when selecting sites for their castles in the landscapes of Somerset, Monmouthshire and Co. Meath were basing their decisions upon knowledge of similar tactical and strategic principles.

In Somerset, the first castles built by the Normans were constructed upon a rough semi-circle of hills that form a natural perimeter enclosing the county. These early castles, which made good use of tactically defensible positions, were built at carefully selected locations in a strategy designed to secure the border. Around the same time the coastline was secured, west and north, with a chain of castles stretching from Portbury to Dunster. The county was vulnerable to seaborne invasion and these castles were clearly intended to counteract this threat. This barrier was in many respects similar to the coastal defences of Alfred and Edward the Elder. The line of castles stretching down the coast, along with those on the hills bordering the county, in addition to fencing in the Saxon population of Somerset and severing their supply routes in and out of the county, clearly outlined the Norman 'grounds of contention'.

With the borders of the county more or less secure, and a number of castles in place to retreat to if attacked, the Normans gained the luxury of time, which was presumably used to survey Somerset's waterlogged, reed-filled and treacherous interior for other suitable sites for castles. The strategic consideration that exerted the most influence upon the Norman castle building programme in Somerset was the county's many rivers. This is unsurprising however, given that in the low-lying Somerset Levels transport was predominately by water. At no point was a castle located more than 2.5 miles (4.02 km) away from a river, whilst 13 out of the county's 27 castles were situated on, or less than a quarter of a mile (0.4km) away from a navigable stretch of water. The vast majority of these castles were located at tactically significant sites, on areas of higher ground, overlooking rivers, and in many cases upstream, which is the prime location for a castle designed to control a river. A number of castles were also built at strategic locations associated with overland portage routes that run between the rivers.

At strategic locations overlooking Somerset's Roman roads and Saxon *herepaðs*, the Normans also constructed castles, and the positions of these castles indicate that the *herepaðs* were the more important consideration. This arrangement of castles quickly handed control of the county's rivers, major ports and road networks over to the Normans, which in turn gave them command of the county's systems of communication and supply, and with them jurisdiction over the passage of goods and people in and out of the county. With the territory firmly in their grasp, the Normans were free to press home their advantage. They founded castles to dominate the county's commercial centres and rich agricultural lands, and thereby secured the region's assets, turning their conquest into profit.

Perhaps the most surprising discovery in Somerset was that Normans chose to largely ignore the existing Saxon 'central places'. This was an unusual occurrence, considering that many of these central places were burhs, and burhs were located to take advantage of natural defensive features such as rivers, and were surrounded by earthwork defences. This decision must have been intentional, and appears to have formed part of the Norman strategy in the county. The Normans redistributed the old Saxon estates in order to form new baronies, and replaced the Saxon central places with new centres that revolved around castles. In this way, the Normans created new administrative centres, and successfully transferred power away from the old Saxon central places, which in turn led to the destruction of the Saxon hundred system. With the destruction of the Saxon 'political landscape', the Normans were free to institute a political landscape of their own, a 'landscape of feudalism', which effectively spelled the end for the traditional Anglo-Saxon way of life.

Robert of Mortain's castle at Montacute is also of note, as it appears to have been designed to fulfil a symbolic rather that function role. The castle was constructed upon a hill which, according to near contemporary sources, was a Saxon holy site. In addition, it appears that the landscape surrounding the castle was intentionally manipulated to graphically portray the Norman lord's god-given right over the biblical facets of dominion, which suggests that the Normans were attempting to utilise symbolism to psychologically suppress the local Saxon population.

Between 1067 and 1202, the Normans founded 27 castles in Somerset, and this economic scheme, which employed the use of a few well-positioned castles, was incredibly successful, as the relatively trouble-free pacification of the county, the suppression of the rebellion at Montacute, the defeat of Harold's marauding sons, the capture of Exeter, and the resulting fall of Devon and Cornwall show.

In Monmouthshire, although the strategic considerations were roughly equivalent to those in Somerset, the Normans appear to have employed a very different strategy. Between 1066 and 1262, the Normans founded 58 castles in the county, but overall the scheme appeared to lack cohesion or direction. The first concern of the Normans in Monmouthshire was to secure England's western border, and to that end, they constructed a chain of castles on the banks of the Dore, Monnow and Wye Rivers. The castles on the Monnow were regularly spaced at intervals of 5 miles (8.04km) apart, and as such were well placed to defend England's border. The Dore and Wye Rivers were, initially, inadequately defended however, and could easily have been crossed by the Welsh. It has been argued that the larger the castle, and the more numerous its garrison, the larger the area around it that could be protected (King, 1983, xvii). By this reckoning, a castle as large as Chepstow would hold a garrison substantially large enough to adequately defended the Wye. The argument is flawed however, as a garrison can only travel as far as their mounts will carry them in a day. In reality, many castles are required to adequately defend an area. Shortly after the initial attempts to protect England's western border, several castles were constructed overlooking the coastline, indicating that the Norman invasion came from both land and sea. Two castles were also founded on Monmouthshire's western border, guarding a crossing of the River Rhymney into neighbouring Glamorgan. At this stage though, the north and west of the county remained virtually undefended.

Logically, the next step in the Norman campaign in Monmouthshire should have been to secure the largely undefended north and west of the county, but this is not what occurred. In the south, emphasis shifted towards securing the river and road systems, whilst in the north, castles were already being constructed to take advantage of the fertile narrow parallel valleys of the Olchon, Escley Brook, Upper Monnow, Dulas and Dore, which were ripe for economic exploitation. This clearly indicates that the campaign was fragmentary, and did not represent a concerted effort on the part of the Normans. The river and road systems were eventually secured in the south, and the few castles constructed in the Olchon and Escley valleys afforded the north a modicum of protection from the Welsh. The northern upland area of the Newport lordship was never adequately secured however, and remained under Welsh rule until the late thirteenth century.

Monmouthshire's castles, almost without exception, displayed the Norman talent for choosing tactical sites to maximum military and territorial advantage, but the overall campaign was protracted and, in terms of castle usage, inefficient. Of the castles built in Monmouthshire, the largest proportion were located in the fertile river valleys, or upon the lands overlooking the profitable coastal regions, which suggests that individual greed overtook military obligation. Unsurprisingly, the Norman attempts to secure the county were never wholly successful.

The failure of the Norman castle building strategy in Monmouthshire can be attributed to two factors. Firstly, the conquest of Monmouthshire was not a single campaign planned and co-ordinated by a king, or powerful lord, but rather, many campaigns, carried out over the course of 120 years, by numerous individuals, in various locations. The direct opposite, in fact, of the situations in both Somerset and Meath, as the campaign in Somerset appears to have been the brainchild of Robert of Mortain, and the campaign in Meath seems to have been devised by Hugh de Lacy. Secondly, all three campaigns appear to reflect the military climate of the day.

The decisive part of the campaign in Somerset took place during the reign of William the Conqueror, whose personal influence over his men was the keystone of his achievements. He successfully harnessed the energies of the Norman baronage to his purposes, held his army together through supply shortages and disease, fought one of the most demanding battles of the Middle Ages, and pacified a hostile nation. In the 10 years following the conquest he tirelessly defended his realm, his strategy was generally brilliant, and he showed a keen appreciation of where the greatest threats to his security lay (Morillo, 1994, 187). In contrast, the majority of the campaign in Monmouthshire took place during the reigns of William II, Henry I and Stephen. William II's offensive campaigns exhibited uniform caution and conservatism to the point of ineffectiveness; he had little daring, concentration of effort, or success, and generally displayed a complete lack of battle tactics. Henry I was a skilful diplomat, but a poor strategist, and his policies exhibited the same caution that characterised William II's offensive strategies. Stephen was a capable soldier, but made many political mistakes, and can be criticised for his continual lack of judgement. Conversely, the campaign in Meath took place during the reign of Henry II, who was one of England's most capable and energetic medieval rulers. Henry was a brilliant diplomat, competent strategist and accomplished tactician, who was active in a number of fields and succeeded in extending his rule over many territories.

The failure of the Norman castle building strategy in Wales was translated into success by the Anglo-Normans in Ireland, as the lessons learnt were not quickly forgotten. In Meath, the strategy in the early period is clear. Several castles were erected in the landscape to the east of the River Boyne in an attempt to secure a small, but manageable, area of land against internal revolt, whilst other castles were constructed adjacent to the river. This gave the Anglo-Normans a means of transport, communication and supply, and in addition, formed an effective defensive barrier against hostile Irish incursions. The principal concern of the Anglo-Normans in the initial stages of their campaign was Dublin, and by securing the Boyne, along with the land to the east of the river, the city was furnished with a viable means of defence. Dublin was literally surrounded by a protective screen of castles. This strategy proved invaluable, as it successfully saved Dublin from a full-scale Irish assault in 1174.

With Dublin and the Boyne secured, the Anglo-Normans pressed on into the interior of Meath. To shield their newly acquired lands from further Irish incursions, the Anglo-Normans began the construction of a chain of castles along Meath's northern border. By way of three well-positioned castles, the Anglo-Normans also succeed in securing the Blackwater, Meath's other navigable river. The early Irish roads were indubitably of great strategic value, and although their exact routes cannot be delineated with any certainty, the likelihood is that many of Meath's castles were associated with their appropriation and subsequent control. With their castles overlooking the principal rivers and roads, the Anglo-Normans successfully gained control of Meath's systems of transport, communication and supply. Many of Meath's ecclesiastical centres were also furnished with a castle. From the ecclesiastical histories, 28 monastic sites can be identified in Meath, and at 13 of these sites, there were castles. All of the major proto-urban sites had a castle, and the majority of the remaining sites had a castle within 5 miles (8.04km). These castles were designed to function as new focal points or 'central places' in the landscape, and were intended to wrest political and economic power away from the 'proto-urban' monastic complexes.

Anglo-Norman control of the county's rivers and road systems was then further reinforced via the erection of several new castles. The chain of castles designed to protect Meath's northern border was additionally strengthened around the River Dee area. More castles were constructed to ensure Anglo-Norman domination over the remaining ecclesiastical proto-urban centres and following the sub-infeudation process, castles were constructed across the 19 baronies to act as the *caputs* of new lordships. Having successfully secured Meath's northern border, gained control of the systems of transport, communication and supply, usurped the political and economic power of the proto-urban monastic centres, and established *caputs* within the new lordships, the Anglo-Normans set the colonisation process in motion. This process was controlled by way of the manor, which was a new and distinctive settlement type in Ireland's landscape, and at the core of most manors was a castle, which acted as a centre for administration, justice and social organisation, as well as a mechanism for control.

Between 1172 and *c.*1275, the Anglo-Normans erected 78 castles in Meath and, although the strategy can hardly be considered economic in terms of the number of castles used, it was incredibly successful. The castles provided the means to bring the Liberty under full Anglo-Norman control, and with Meath captured, subdued and secured, the Irish were restored to the countryside and cattle were returned to the pastures. Colonisation followed conquest, and the Anglo-Norman barons were able to turn their lordships to profit.

When discussing the various Norman conquests it is all too easy to get caught up in the detail and overlook the impetus behind each successive campaign.

Intrinsically, conquest is all about the acquisition of land. Admittedly, conquest brings status, power and wealth, but it should not be forgotten that these aspects are firmly rooted in the soil of the land, and the land must first be taken before any such benefits are gained. The Normans, with their wealth of military experience and knowledge, would have known that it was impossible to hold onto captured areas of land for any length of time by troops alone, as such a practice entails 'too much division and frittering away of the army' (Shaw & Pilkington, 1872, 3). Such territory had, instead, to be secured using the minimum number of troops, so as to leave as many men as possible available for active operations in the field, and the best way to achieve this was to construct a few well-positioned castles. The Normans were not the first to learn this valuable lesson either, as during a series of bitter campaigns intended to expand the borders of his lands, Fulk Nerra of Anjou (995-1031) developed the strategy of establishing wooden strongholds to exploit the strategic or tactical potential of each newly won patch of Angevin terrain he captured. The fortifications, in addition, served as springboards for the acquisition of the next area of land on his programme.

The foremost strategic function of a castle was the winning and holding of territory and the Normans exploited this function to great advantage. Employing the castle's supreme offensive capabilities, the Normans erected fortifications deep within enemy territory. This gave them a safe base from which to mount their military operations, and they could sally forth to subdue local hostilities knowing that, should anything untoward happen, they had a safe place to retreat to. Once the area was secured, it could be permanently occupied as long as the castles held out. Moreover, the Normans did not build their castles in random locations, but at sites chosen either for their tactical or strategic potential; or in many cases for both. The tactically significant locations, which were selected because they were topographically or geologically strong, helped to bolster the castle's defences, whilst the strategically significant locations, due to their geographical positions, afforded the Normans control over the all important 'key strategic elements', such as rivers and roads, valley and passes, the possession of which meant the difference between victory and defeat.

Having followed the development and progress of Norman castle building through three different countries, across a time span of 120 years, it has been possible to provide answers to the four questions posed in the introduction to this book.

Study of the Norman campaigns in Somerset, Monmouthshire and Co. Meath has clearly shown that in the vast majority of cases factors of a tactical and or strategic nature did indeed provide the main incentives for the successive castle building programmes. Gaining control of strategic factors like borders or supply routes was essential to the success of a campaign, and as a result, strategic considerations generally dictated that a castle should be built. Tactical considerations, on the other hand, dictated where a castle should be built.

The tactical considerations that most influenced castle siting, in order of importance, were found to be Defensibility, Security, Practicality and Accessibility. Most sites seem to have been chosen because they were strongly fortified by nature, the presence of natural obstacles affording additional layers of defence for the castle. Higher ground was the next significant consideration, as an elevated site provided the castle with good all-round visibility, as well as placing it outside of the range of missile weapons. Sites close to sources of potable water and suitable construction materials ranked third, whilst easy access to a site seemed to be the least important factor. Sites which offered a number of tactical advantages were of course the most favoured.

The strategic considerations which dictated that a castle should be built were discovered to be Safety, Borders, Communications and Assets. Depending upon the situation, the order of these considerations could change but, in general, castles were first constructed to provide shelter for Norman soldiers on campaign, which also gave them a safe base from which to launch fresh attacks. The next castles erected were generally those intended to secure and then control a border area. Following this, castles were often built to command lines of transport, communication and supply. The last castles to be erected were usually those designed to dominate commercial centres, rich agricultural lands, or resource-producing areas.

A comparison between the Norman campaigns in Somerset, Monmouthshire and Co. Meath, has shown how the castle building programme developed over time as a result of the lessons learned and experiences gained from each successive campaign, and how the programme was adapted from region to region in response to localised conditions and requirements. It is also apparent that the castle building programme was ultimately successful because it was founded upon a sound understanding of – and adherence to – the strategic and tactical principles of warfare.

This book has concentrated on the castle building programmes in three counties, and it could be argued that many of its findings are regionally specific. The only way to be certain of this is to apply the 'Strategic Approach' to the study of castles in other counties in the future. In the meantime, a brief examination of the results of other regional castle studies is instructive. Figure *73* shows the results of 15 regional castle studies. In each case, the results show the percentage of castles in the regions which were interpreted as social, economic, political or military foundations. It is clear that in the majority of the regions the 'military castle' was the predominant foundation. Figure *74* shows the total results from the regions, highlighting the fact that 48 per cent of the castles examined were seen as military foundations, whilst 20 per cent were social, 18 per cent were political and 14 per centwere economic. There is a good probability then, that in most

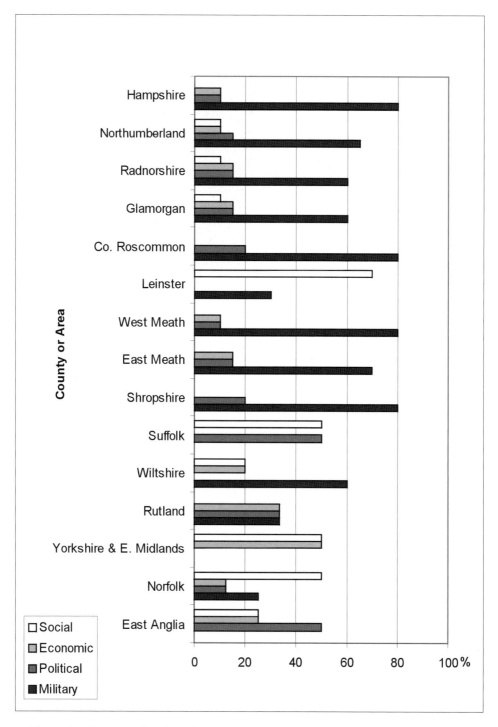

73 The results of 15 regional castle studies. In each case, the results show the percentage of castles in the region which were interpreted as social, economic, political or military foundations

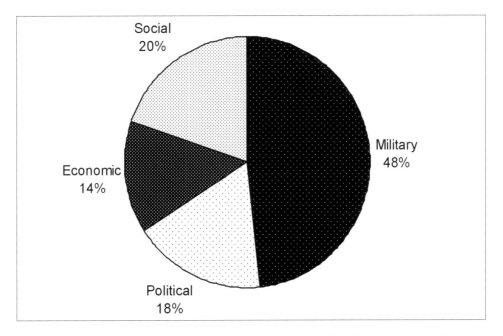

74 The combined results of 15 regional castle studies. The pie-chart highlights the fact that the
majority of the castles examined were seen as military foundations

counties, the majority of castles were strategically or tactically positioned in the
landscape to achieve a military objective.

Norman culture was born in battle and weaned on war, conquest and martial
virtue formed the mainstays of Norman society, and the Norman Army was
one of the most cohesive and effective fighting forces of the eleventh century.
The Normans were the first to appreciate the true value of the castle, and
the strategies, tactics and stratagems that they developed for their deployment,
not only ensured the success of their campaigns, but served to established the
reputation of their army as a 'force-majeur par excellence'. This, however, raises two
final questions: Where did the Normans acquire their detailed knowledge of
military principals and what inspired their usage?

THE NORMANS AND THE ROMANS

The continuing influence of *Romanitas* runs like a bright thread through the rich
tapestry of the period AD 800-1600.

Steane, 2001, 7

233

In an attempt to destroy the 'military orthodoxy' that allegedly surrounds castle studies, Liddiard states, 'the Norman Conquest [of England] was not an invasion akin to that of the Romans, but the second occasion in the eleventh century that a foreign king had taken the throne by force' (2000, 5). It is conversely possible however, that the Norman Conquest of England was exactly akin to the Roman invasion of Britain because it was deliberately based upon it, and further, it is conceivable that the Normans actually drew their inspiration, and the bulk of their military knowledge, from the Romans themselves. This argument is somewhat speculative, but the evidence is overwhelmingly in its favour.

The Normans did not call themselves 'Norman', and did not know that they were 'feudal' or 'medieval'. The term 'Middle Ages' was not invented until the fifteenth century, and the 'feudal system' was not conceptualised until the seventeenth century. Rather, the Normans considered themselves 'French' and lived in *tempore moderno*. In the tenth century, Normandy was carved out of the western edge of the Frankish kingdom, and the Vikings who settled in Normandy were absorbed into the Frankish population. By the eleventh century, Normandy was more Frankish in its customs and culture than it was Viking (Bradbury, 1997, 23-4). Thus, the Normans formed the vanguard of a wider European movement of Frankish conquest.

The Frankish system of governance derived from two basic models. The first, which was thoroughly heterogeneous in its composition, came from classical antiquity: there were some classical sources gleaned from surviving texts, whilst others were mediated by and through the later Roman Empire and the Romano-German kingdoms of Gaul, and were also merged with contemporary Byzantine, ecclesiastical and western secular influences to create a corpus of information. The second was provided by the Holy Scriptures with the vast commentary which had been developing for almost a millennium (Bachrach, 1993, xiii-xiv). The Franks as a result inherited many of the characteristics of the Roman Empire, and in the eighth century were on the verge of reconstituting the pan-European empire of the Romans, particularly after Charlemagne was crowned Emperor of the Romans by Pope Leo III on Christmas day 800: an event that marked the beginning of the 'Holy Roman Empire'. The Franks, in effect, claimed for themselves what they could of the Roman legacy, and by the end of the tenth century, Normandy had adopted many of these characteristics. Indeed, Barlow states that in England the Anglo-Norman kings instituted 'governmental procedures that came from the Roman Empire by way of the Franks' (1999, 90-1). William the Conqueror was born within a well-established and essentially Frankish territorial principality that drew inspiration from the bygone glory of the Roman Empire.

Another principality that was greatly inspired by the Roman legacy was Anjou. In northern France, during the early eleventh century, there was incessant war between rival princes, and foremost among them was count Fulk Nerra of Anjou (995-1031). During his lifetime, Fulk began an aggressive campaign to expand Anjou's borders, a policy that continued under his son Count Geoffrey Martel (1040-60). Eventually, the principality stretched from the southern frontiers of Normandy in the north to Poitou and the Saintonge in the south, and from near Nantes in the west to Tours in the east (Bates, 2001, 20). Fulk's early use of castles has already been mentioned, but he is important for several other reasons. Fulk's military strategies and tactics were informed by Roman military science, most likely Vegetian in inspiration, which he modified according to his needs. He adopted Roman, or Neo-Roman, rituals and ceremonies, erected Romanesque stone towers, studied Roman law and made numerous visits to Rome. His use of a highly eclectic collection of techniques, images and ideas, which in a broad sense can be traced to the Roman past, were of the utmost importance in legitimising his exercise of political power within the Angevin state (Bachrach, 1993, xi-xiv). Indeed, John of Marmoutier calls Fulk 'The Neo-Roman Consul' more than a century after his *adventus*. Fulk was a near contemporary of William the Conqueror, and it is quite feasible that Fulk's success inspired William to adopt the use of castles and Roman military science for his conquest of England. As Bates suggests, Fulk Nerra was a dominant personality and 'might well have provided a role-model for the young William to emulate' (2001, 21-2).

If Fulk Nerra's creative use of *Romanitas* did not encourage the Norman adoption of Roman military principles, then it is equally possible that they were inspired by surviving Roman literature. Contemporary authors drew upon Vergil, Suetonius, Sallust, Statius, Lucan, Scipio, Pompey, Cato, Ovid, Tacitus and Julius Caesar, to shape Norman history. Livy's account of early Roman history was utilised extensively by the authors of the *Royal Frankish Annals*, and the Normans were familiar with the Roman military authors Vegetius and Frontinus. Shrader (1979) has located 324 copies of Vegetius' *Epitoma rei Militaris* dating from the seventh century to the seventeenth, and 32 of them date to before the thirteenth century. Vegetius' *Epitoma rei Militaris*, was one of the most influential military treatises in the western world from Roman times to the nineteenth century and was used, amongst others, by Charlemagne (742-814), Count Everard de Frejus (837), Fulk Nerra (995-1031), Henry II (1133-89) and Richard the Lionheart (1157-99). Hrabanus Maurus, a ninth-century archbishop of Mainz, produced a revised version with additions intended to adapt it to Frankish warfare, and Bishop Frechulf of Lisieux produced a copy for the library of Charles the Bald.

Norman knowledge of Roman history is probably most evident in William of Poitiers' *Gesta Guillelmi*, in which William the Conqueror is continually compared with the great generals of antiquity. The biography, albeit incomplete, ends with a lengthy comparison between the Norman invasion of England and the Roman invasion of Britain, emphasising that William had faced far greater challenges than Julius Caesar and yet had achieved a much more impressive victory.

If the Normans were utilising a form of *Romanitas*, or drawing upon Roman literature and military treatise to inform their military policy, several aspects of the Norman Conquest of England acquire new meaning. Before the invasion of England, William sent a mission to seek the support of Rome. It is customarily believed that this mission was sent to win the support of the Pope – and so of the wealthy and powerful Norman Church – for the enterprise. The Pope endorsed the invasion and sent a blessed banner to Normandy. But rather than seeking funding, it is equally possible that William was emulating Charlemagne and Fulk Nerra, and was attempting to establish himself in the role of a 'Neo-Roman Consul'.

The fact that William did not land at Dover, but chose instead to stage his landing at Pevensey, Sussex, has long been debated. The Romans clearly recognised the strategic value of Pevensey and erected a Saxon shore fort in the area, but more importantly, Bird has recently suggested that 'Romanists' may be incorrect in their assumption that the landing site for the Roman invasion of Britain was in Kent. He argues that 'there is no mention of Kent in … [the] sources and there is no need to assume that any part of the invasion force landed there', suggesting instead that 'the Roman invasion of AD 43 took place in Sussex' (2000, 91-2). It is perhaps possible then that William was privy to knowledge and information pertaining to the Roman invasion that is now lost, choosing his landing site in Sussex in order to follow in the footsteps of the Claudian invasion force.

The advanced structure of the Norman army, comprising knights, heavy and light infantry and the *arrière-ban*, or general levy of freemen, has been a moot point for generations of historians. In light of the above arguments, its structure can perhaps be seen as a Norman attempt to mirror the make-up of the Roman army, which also comprised cavalry, heavy and light infantry, and auxiliaries. Indeed, it is even possible that the number of troops in William's invasion force, estimated at between 5,000-6,000 men, is directly comparable to a Roman Legion, which consisted of approximately 6,000 men. In addition, the 'feigned flight' reputedly used by the Normans at Hastings is a classic Vegetian manoeuvre.

In chapter three, it was stated that the initial phase of Norman castle building in England, between 1066 and 1071, appeared to follow a pattern similar to the spread of the Roman Conquest of Britain (75). Castles were constructed along the south coast from Exeter to Dover. In the Midlands, a scatter of fortifications stretched up as far as Lincoln and York. There was a concentration in the West

Midlands, and in the Welsh Marches, where Chester formed the north-western point of attack and, at the estuary of the River Wye, Chepstow the southernmost. The north-western chain of the Norman defences coincided roughly with the line of Icknield Street, which the Romans originally intended as the north-western boundary for their occupied territory in Britain (Rowley, 1999, 88-9). It is feasible then that this distribution is significant, and that the Normans were intentionally positioning their castles along Roman lines.

The strongest evidence for the Norman adoption of *Romanitas* comes from their use of symbolism. At Colchester (*Camvlodvnvm*), in the first century AD, the Romans constructed a large classical style temple to the Emperor Claudius (AD 41-54). The podium for the temple measured 32m x 24.4m, and survives today beneath the donjon of a Norman castle. The donjon at Colchester was the first to be built in England (*c*.1075-80), is by far the largest, and in plan is similar to the White Tower of London. Its dimensions are 46.2m north–south, 33.5m east-west, and 27.4m in height, with corner turrets rising to between 32m and 33.5m (*colour plate 30*). The reason generally given for the construction of this colossal donjon is that it was built in response to a serious Danish raid on the town. This is highly unlikely however, as a much smaller castle would easily have sufficed. It is far more likely that this vast and imposing castle was built upon the site of the Roman temple to serve as a symbol of Norman power and supremacy.

In Roman Britain, Colchester was the first site to be permanently settled. A *Colonia* was established by AD 49, and this rapidly developed into the first Roman town, which in time became the headquarters of the imperial cult. As the only settlement before the Roman invasion that could, with some justification, be called the 'capital' of Britain, it was the ideal choice for a cult centre, as there the cult would have made its greatest impression upon the native Britons. The cult temple became a symbol of oppression for the Britons, and unsurprisingly, during the Boudican revolt in AD 60, the town was attacked and burnt to the ground. There is little doubt that the Normans knew of Colchester's former importance in Roman Britain. They were familiar with the works of Tacitus, and he mentions Colchester three times in Agricola: 'the Britons … hunted down the Roman troops in their scattered posts, stormed the forts, and assaulted the colony itself, which they saw as the citadel of their servitude' (Handford, 1970, 66).

An extract from the *Colchester Chronicle* for 1076 states: 'Eudo Dapifer built the Castle of Colchester on the foundation of the Palace of Coel, once king, and restored the chapel of St Helen which she built herself, it is said, and gave it to St John' (Crummy, 1999, 143). Excavations in 1958 proved unequivocally that the Norman castle encased the temple precinct wall, which was located within the Norman bailey bank and was found to stand to a height of just over 3m from the Roman ground level. The massive donjon that the Normans constructed

75 The extent of Roman occupation in Britain *c.* AD 40 and major Norman castles built in England by 1086

atop the remains of the headquarters of the imperial cult, in the former heart of Roman Britain, was undoubtedly intended to act as a symbol of Norman dominion and Anglo-Saxon oppression. Its construction also suggests though that the Normans were identifying with the Roman past and were attempting to claim a part of the Roman legacy for themselves, William perhaps seeing himself as the 'Neo-Roman Consul of Britain'.

Colchester was not the only Roman site to be furnished with a castle, the Normans continued the pattern across England, building 12 royal castles in towns of Roman origin, and on into Wales, where in Monmouthshire alone five castles were founded at important Roman sites. Traditionally, it is suggested that the association between castles and Roman sites was due largely to the protection afforded the castle by the surviving Roman defences. It is equally possible however, that the Normans were styling their conquest on the Romans' and, in addition to any military advantages gained, were occupying these sites in order to connect with the past. Furthermore, the Normans would have been well aware of the fact that the Romans consistently occupied the best sites in any given area, so logic would dictate that they do the same.

Following the completion of the conquest, the Normans sought to impress their religious fervour upon England, and in an unparalleled spate of ecclesiastical building, nearly every cathedral and abbey church was rebuilt. This heralded the introduction of a new architectural style, and this style visibly emphasises the Norman predilection for the Roman past. The style was known as 'Roman' in France and 'Norman' or 'Romanesque' in England. The term 'Romanesque' was applied to the architecture of the eleventh and twelfth centuries because it revived classical precedents established by the Romans, chief among which was the emergence of the rib vault, which was later adopted in Normandy and across the Continent by the early thirteenth century. Furthermore, at Chepstow, in order to accentuate an elaborate entranceway, Norman builders stripped Roman floor tiles from nearby Caerwent and incorporated them into the fabric of the keep. This practice was also adopted at Colchester, where Roman materials were used as architectural decoration, and in both instances, it appears that a conscious effort was being made to link present to past, and Norman to Roman.

In conclusion, it is likely that Norman familiarity with Roman history and military science helped to shape their army, strengthen their combat skills, aid their planning and logistics for the Conquest, inform their strategies and tactics, inspire their image-making and eventually assist them in the political governance of the lands which they conquered. In light of the overwhelming success of their military endeavours and conquests, the triumph of their castle building programme and their adoption of *Romanitas*, perhaps the statement that best sums up the Normans is '*venimus, vidimus, vincimus*'.

Appendix: A gazetteer of the castles studied

SOMERSET

No.	Name	National Grid Reference
1	Castle Neroche	ST 2720 1580
2	Montacute Castle	ST 4935 1699
3	Wimble Toot	ST 5605 2800
4	Dunster Castle (Torre)	SS 9911 4344
5	Cockroad Wood Castle	ST 7461 3218
6	Culverhay Castle	ST 7190 6302
7	Stowey Castle	ST 5970 5920
8	Hales Castle	ST 7976 4424
9	Burrow Mump	ST 3590 3052
10	Castle Batch	ST 3617 6370
11	Cary Castle	ST 6411 3214
12	Edithmead	ST 3286 4932
13	Locking Head Castle	ST 3638 6087
14	Over Stowey Castle	ST 1862 3854
15	Bury Castle	SS 9385 2698
16	Richmont Castle	ST 5610 5580
17	Ballands Castle	ST 7534 3105
18	Downend Earthworks	ST 3092 4135
19	Nether Stowey Castle	ST 1870 3958
20	Fenny Castle	ST 5078 4357
21	Croft Castle	ST 4206 1075
22	Taunton Castle	ST 2260 2464
23	Swallow Cliff Mound	ST 3262 6603
24	Breach Wood Castle	ST 7040 4120
25	Portbury Mound	ST 5094 7467
26	Stogursey Castle	ST 2030 4260
27	Bridgwater Castle	ST 2987 3717

MONMOUTHSHIRE

No.	Name	National Grid Reference
1	Ewyas Harold Castle	SO 3846 2876
2	Monmouth Castle (Mingui)	SO 5070 1293
3	Chepstow Castle	ST 5334 9411
4	Caldicot Castle	ST 4867 8851
5	Caerwent Motte	ST 4707 9031
6	The Bage (Bach Motte)	SO 2982 4337
7	Mouse Castle (Cusop)	SO 2483 4247
8	Walterstone	SO 3395 2497
9	Grosmont Castle	SO 4052 2445
10	Skenfrith Castle	SO 4570 2027
11	Raglan Castle	SO 4145 0830
12	Rumney Castle	ST 2102 7894
13	Caerleon Motte	ST 3425 9054
14	The Berries, Ballan Moor	ST 4873 8951
15	Abergavenny Castle	SO 2995 1394
16	Caer Castle – St Mellons	ST 2265 8034
17	Dixton Mound	SO 5179 1372
18	Mynydd-brith	SO 2805 4147
19	Snodhill Castle	SO 3220 4030
20	Urishay Castle	SO 3230 3756
21	Beiliau Llangwm	ST 4275 9980
22	Dorstone Castle	SO 3122 4165
23	Nant-y-Bar (Dorstone)	SO 2784 4102
24	Stow Hill Castle	ST 3046 8734
25	The White Castle	SO 3794 1679
26	Pont-Hendre	SO 3258 2813
27	Usk Castle	SO 3768 0109
28	Dinham Castle	ST 4802 9234
29	Penhow Castle	ST 4237 9086
30	Cothill Tump	SO 3386 3630
31	Chanstone Tumps	SO 3657 3590
32	Bacton (Newcourt Farm)	SO 3713 3356
33	Llancillo Motte	SO 3671 2554
34	Rowlestone Motte	SO 3750 2718
35	Longtown Castle	SO 3210 2920
36	Mill Wood Castle Mound	SO 4597 1038
37	Twyn-Bar-Lwm Castle	ST 2439 9266
38	Coed-y-Mount, Penrhos	SO 4094 1321
39	Goytre Wood Castle Mound	SO 3532 2330
40	Newcastle	SO 4477 1728
41	Cwrt-y-Gaer Ringwork	ST 4492 9988
42	Pen-y-Clawdd Motte	SO 3100 2010
43	St. Mary's Yard Mound	SO 3498 0693
44	Wern-y-Cwrt Castle Mound	SO 3939 0880
45	New House Ringwork	SO 4243 0110

46	Trecastle (Llangovan)	SO 4517 0702
47	Wentloog Castle	ST 2513 8347
48	Graig Wood Motte	ST 3190 9249
49	Langstone Court Mound	ST 3703 8953
50	Kemeys Inferior Motte	ST 3892 9392
51	Rockfield Castle	SO 4830 1420
52	St. Illtyd's Motte	SO 2170 0195
53	The Moat – Treveddw	SO 3304 2177
54	Caer Licyn	ST 3897 9285
55	Graig Foel	SO 3695 0102
56	Hendre Hafaidd	SO 3437 1277
57	Trostrey	SO 3590 0430
58	Llangibby Castle Mound	ST 3695 9735

CO. MEATH

No.	Name	National Grid Reference
1	Drogheda	O 0902 7480
2	Duleek (Commons)	O 0490 6861
3	Ratoath	O 0214 5186
4	Trim (Manorland)	N 8025 5670
5	Culmullin	N 9150 4985
6	Derry Patrick	N 8839 5120
7	Ardmulchan	N 9081 7026
8	Galtrim	N 8618 5210
9	Rodanstown	N 9019 4168
10	Scurlockstown	N 8331 5637
11	Athboy	N 7200 6500
12	Castlecor (Typermessan)	N 5237 8126
13	Newtown (Killallon)	N 6203 7036
14	Oldcastle	N 5512 7966
15	Dunboyne	O 0140 4190
16	Donaghmore	O 0785 5035
17	Knockmark	N 9350 5193
18	Dunshaughlin	N 9700 5188
19	Derver	N 6698 7997
20	Slane	N 9604 7511
21	Dollardstown	N 9304 7112
22	Kilbeg Upper (Kilbeg)	N 7760 8176
23	Kells	N 7400 7500
24	Donaghpatrick	N 8194 7290
25	Killeen	N 9328 5484
26	Ardbraccan	N 8268 6797
27	Clonard (Anneville)	N 6576 4506
28	Moathill (Navan)	N 8598 6765
29	Skreen	N 9530 6006
30	Nobber	N 8220 8669

31	Drumcondra	N 8830 8980
32	Drumcondra	N 8873 9021
33	Dunsany	N 9151 5481
34	Cruicetown	N 7962 8461
35	Greenoge	O 0957 4990
36	Kilmessan	N 8875 5744
37	Rathfeigh	O 0028 6127
38	Milltown (Moylagh)	N 5445 7512
39	Mulphedder	N 6565 4493
40	Agher	N 8319 4556
41	Athlumney	N 8746 6739
42	Balgree	N 6536 7826
43	Ballyhist	N 6446 7817
44	Ballymacad	N 5069 7888
45	Ballymacad (Killeagh)	N 5103 7836
46	Castlejordan	N 5875 3869
47	Castlerickard	N 7174 4894
48	Castletown	N 8406 8233
49	Castletown Kilberry	N 8763 7293
50	Castletown Kilpatrick	N 8470 8280
51	Clonbarton	N 8839 9181
52	Coolronan	N 6792 5705
53	Diamor	N 6090 7393
54	Dowth	O 0290 7390
55	Drumbride	N 8728 9398
56	Ginnets Great	N 8402 5298
57	Girley	N 7083 6908
58	Glenboy	N 5316 8092
59	Kilberry	N 8680 7370
60	Killadden	N 8626 8986
61	Laracor (Knightsbrook)	N 8080 5371
62	Lisdoran	O 1258 6806
63	Loughbrackan	N 8713 8816
64	Loughcrew	N 5638 7631
65	Milltown	N 7447 7208
66	Moat (ME005 080)	N 7602 8469
67	Moat (ME008 032)	N 5108 7895
68	Moat (ME010 039)	N 7075 7907
69	Moat (ME042 005)	N 7910 5130
70	Moat Town	N 7513 5685
71	Moynalty	N 7352 8253
72	Moyrath	N 7054 5860
73	Patrickstown	N 6070 7743
74	Priest town (Kilbride)	O 0671 4638
75	Rathbeggan	O 0001 4695
76	Robertstown	N 7840 8430
77	Thurstianstown	N 9524 7196
78	Tremblestown	N 7602 5758

Bibliography

Abrams, L. 1996 *Anglo-Saxon Glastonbury*. Boydell: Woodbridge

Adkins, L. & R. 1992 'Mons Acutus and the Miraculous Cross'. *Somerset Magazine*, 22-5

Albu, E. 2001 *The Normans in their Histories*. Boydell: Woodbridge

Armitage, E.S. 1912 *Early Norman Castles of the British Isles*. John Murray: London

Aston, M. & Lewis, C. 1994 *The Medieval Landscape of Wessex*. Oxbow: Oxford

Aston, M. 1986 'Post-Roman Central Places in Somerset'; in Grant, E. (ed.) 1986, 49-77

Aston, M. & Leech, R. 1977 *Historic Towns in Somerset*. Somerset Books: Tiverton

Austin, D. 1984 'The Castle and the Landscape'. *Landscape History*, 6, 69-81

Austin, D. 1982 'Barnard Castle, Co. Durham'. *Château-Gaillard*, 9-10, 293-300

Bachrach, B.S. 1993 *Fulk Nerra, The Neo-Roman Consul, 987-1040*. Uni. of California Press: London

Bachrach, B.S. 1983 'The Angevin Strategy of Castle-Building in the Reign of Fulk Nerra, 987-1040'. *American Historical Review*, 88, 533-60

Barlow, F. 1999 *The Feudal Kingdom of England, 1042-1216*. Longman: London

Barlow, F. 1961 *The Feudal Kingdom of England, 1042-1216*. Longman: London

Barrett, G. 1982 'Problems of Spatial and Temporal Continuity of Rural Settlement in Ireland, AD 400-1169'. *Journal of Historical Geography*, 8:3, 245-60

Bartlett, T. & Jeffery, K. (eds) 1996 *A Military History of Ireland*. Cambridge Uni. Press

Bates, D. 2001 *William the Conqueror*. Tempus: Stroud

Beeler, J.H. 1956 'Castles and Strategy in Norman and Early Angevin England'. *Speculum*, Boston, 31, 581-601

Beeler, J.H. 1971 *Warfare in Feudal Europe; 730-1200*. Ithaca: New York

Beeler, J.H. 1966 *Warfare in England; 1066-1189*. Ithaca: New York

Beeler, J.H. 1951 *The Military Significance of the English Castle; 1066-1175*. Unpublished PhD Thesis, Cornell Uni. Ithaca: New York

Bennett, C.E. & McElwain, M.B. 1925 *The Stratagems and the Aqueducts of Rome – by Frontinus*. William Heinemann: London

Beresford, M. 1967 *New Towns of the Middle Ages: Town Plantation in England, Wales and Gascony*. Lutterworth: London

Blair, J. forthcoming *Water Transport and Management in Medieval England*. Oxford Uni. Press

Bradley, J. 1988 'The Medieval Towns of County Meath'. *Riocht na Midhe*, 8:2, 30-49

Brady, Rev., J. 1961 'Anglo-Norman Meath'. *Riocht na Midhe*, 2:2, 38-45

Braun, H. 1936 *The English Castle*. Batsford: London

Britnell, R.H. 1978 'English Markets and Royal Administration before 1200'. *Economic History Review*, 31:2, 183-96

Brown, R.A. 1989 *Castles, Conquests and Charters*. Boydell: Woodbridge

Brown, R.A. 1985 *Castles*. Shire Archaeology Series (no. 36): Aylesbury

Brown, R.A. 1984 *The Norman Conquest: Documents of Medieval History 5*. Edward Arnold: London

Brown, R.A. 1980i *Castles – A History and Guide*. Blandford Press: Poole

Brown, R.A. 1980ii 'The Battle of Hastings'; in Brown, R.A. (ed.) 1989, 264-89

Brown, R.A. 1976 *English Castles*. Batsford: London

Brown, R.A. 1976 *The Normans and the Norman Conquest*. Constable: London

Brown, E.A. 1974 'The Tyranny of a Construct: Feudalism and Historians of Medieval Europe'. *American Historical Review*, 79, 1063-88

Brown, R.A. 1970 'A Historian's Approach to the Origins of the Castle in England'; in Brown R.A. (ed.) 1989, 1-18

Brown, R.A. 1969 'A Historian's Approach to the Origins of the Castle in England'. *Archaeological Journal*, 126, 131-48

Brown, R.A. 1962 *English Medieval Castles*. Batsford: London

Brown, R.A. 1959 'A List of Castles, 1154-1216'. *English Historical Review*, 74, 249-80

Brown, R.A. 1954 *English Medieval Castles*. Batsford: London

Bradbury, J. 1997 *The Medieval Archer*. Boydell: Woodbridge

Brice, M.H. 1984 *Stronghold – A History of Military Architecture*. Batsford: London

Butler, R. 1849 *The Annals of Ireland* – by Friar John Clyn and Thady Dowling. Dublin

Byrne, F.J. 1993 'The Trembling Sod: Ireland in 1169'; in Cosgrove, A. (ed.) 1993, 1-42

Calendar of Documents Relating to Ireland, 1171-1307; Sweetman, H.S. (ed.) 1875-86 (5 vols.) PRO: London

Calendar of the Gormanston Register; Mills, J. & McEnery, M.J. (eds) 1916, Dublin

Calendar of Justiciary Rolls, Ireland; Mills, J. & Griffith, M.C. (eds) 1905-14 (3 vols.), Dublin

Calendar of Patent Rolls of Henry III, 1232-47; Dublin

Cambell, J., John, E. & Wormald, P. 1982 *The Anglo-Saxons*. Oxford Uni. Press

Carley, J.P. 1985 'Chronica Sive Antiquitates Glastoniensis Ecclesie' (*The Chronicle of Glastonbury Abbey*): an addition, translation and study of John of Glastonbury's … [From the 1375-90 Cambridge Trinity College Manuscript]. Boydell: Woodbridge

Chambers' Etymological English Dictionary; Findlater, A. (ed.) 1900

Chater, A.G & Major, A.F. 1908 'Excavations at Downend, near Bridgwater, 1908'. *PSANHS*, 1910, 56, 162-74

Chibnall, M. 2003 'Orderic Vitalis on Castles'; in Liddiard, R. (ed.), 2003, 119-32

Chibnall, M. (ed.) 1969-80 *The Ecclesiastical History of Orderic Vitalis* (6 vols.). Oxford Medieval Texts

Chibnall, M. & Davis, R.H.C. 1998 *The Gesta Guillelmi of William of Poitiers*. Oxford Medieval Texts

Clark, G.T. 1910 *Liber Landaviensis – Cartae et Alia Munimenta Quae ad Dominion de Glamorgan Pertinent* (6 vols.). Cardiff

Clark, G.T. 1884 *Medieval Military Architecture in England*. Wyman: London

Clark, J. & Phillips T.R. 1985 *The Military Institutions of the Romans – by Flavius Renatus Vegetius*. Greenwood: Westport, Connecticut

Cleary T. (trans.) 1998 *The Art of War- by Sun Tzu*. Shambhala Dragon Edition: Boston

Cosgrove, A. (ed.) 1993 *A New History of Ireland: Medieval Ireland, 1169-1534*. (vol. 2) Clarendon: Oxford

Costen, M. 1994 'Settlement in Wessex in the Tenth Century: The Charter Evidence'; in Aston & Lewis (eds), 1994, 97-111

Costen, M. 1992 *The Origins of Somerset*. Manchester Uni. Press

Coulson, C. 2003 *Castles in Medieval Society: Fortresses in England, France and Ireland in the Central Middle Ages*. Oxford Uni. Press

Coulson, C. 1998 'The Sanctioning of Fortresses in France: Feudal Anarchy or Seigneurial Amity?' *Nottingham Medieval Studies*, 42, 38-104

Coulson, C. 1996 'Cultural Realities and Reappraisals in English Castle-Study'. *Journal of Medieval History*, 22:2, 171-208

Coulson, C. 1992 'Some Analysis of the Castle of Bodiam'. *Medieval Knighthood*, 4, 79-83

Coulson, C. 1991 'Bodiam Castle, Truth and Tradition'. *Fortress*, 10, 3-15

Coulson, C. 1982 'Heirarchism in Conventual Crenellation: An Essay in the Sociology and Metaphysics of Medieval Fortification'. *Medieval Archaeology*, 26, 69-100

Coulson, C. 1979 'Structural Symbolism in Medieval Castle Architecture'. *Journal of the British Archaeological Association*, 132, 73-90

Courtney, P. 1983 *The Rural Landscape of Eastern and Lower Gwent – c.1070 to 1750*. Unpublished PhD Thesis, Uni. College Cardiff

Creighton, O.H. & Higham, R. 2003 *Medieval Castles*. Shire Archaeology Series (no.83): Aylesbury

Creighton, O.H. 2002 *Castles and Landscapes*. Continuum: London

Creighton, O.H. 2000 'Early Castles in the Medieval Landscape of Wiltshire'. *The Wiltshire Archaeological and Natural History Magazine*, 93, 105-19

Creighton, O.H. 1999 'Early Castles in the Medieval Landscape of Rutland'. *Leicestershire Archaeological and Historical Society Proceedings*, 73, 20-33

Creighton, O.H. 1999 'Early Castles and Rural Settlement Patterns: Insights from Yorkshire and the East Midlands'. *The Medieval Settlement Research Group's Annual Report*, 14

Creighton, O.H. 1998 *Castles and Landscapes: an Archaeological Survey of Yorkshire and the East Midlands*. Unpublished PhD Thesis, Uni. of Leicester

Creveld, M.V. 2000 *The Art of War – War and Military Thought*. Cassell & Co: London

Cruickshank, D. 2001 *Invasion – Defending Britain from Attack*. Boxtree: London

Crummy, P. 1997 *City of Victory: The Story of Colchester, Britain's First Roman Town*. Colchester Archaeological Trust

Davidson, B.K. 1972 'Castle Neroche: An Abandoned Norman Fortress in South Somerset'. *PSANHS*, 116, 16-58

Davidson, B.K. 1969 'Early Earthwork Castles: A New Model'. *Château-Gaillard*, 3, 37-47

Davis, O. & Quinn D.B. 1941 'The Irish Pipe Roll of (14) John: 1211-1212'. *Ulster Journal of Archaeology*, 3:4, supplement

Davies, R.R. 2000 *The Age of Conquest – Wales 1063-1415*. Oxford Uni. Press

Davis, W. 1982 *Wales in the Early Middle Ages*. Leicester Uni. Press

Dean, D. 1973 *The Legend of the Miraculous Cross of Waltham*. Waltham Abbey Historical Society

Dixon, P. & Marshall, P. 1993 'The Great Tower in the Twelfth Century: The Case of Norham Castle'. *Archaeological Journal*, 150, 410-33

Dixon, P. 1990 'The Donjon of Knaresborough: The Castle as Theatre'. *Château-Gaillard*, 14, 121-39

Duffy, C. 1996 *Fire & Stone – The Science of Fortress Warfare, 1660-1860*. Greenhill: London

Dunning, R. 1995 *Somerset Castles*. Somerset Books: Tiverton

Dyer, C. 1998 *Standards of Living in the Later Middle Ages: Social Change in England, c.1200-1520*. Cambridge Uni. Press

Edwards, J.G. 1956 'The Normans in the Welsh March'. *Proceedings of the British Academy*, 42, 155-77

Edwards, N. (ed.) 1997 *Landscape and Settlement in Medieval Wales*. Oxbow Monograph 81: Oxford

Edwards, N. 1999 *The Archaeology of Early Medieval Ireland*. Routledge: London

Edwards, R.D. 1973 *An Atlas of Irish History*. Methuen & Co: London

Field Service Pocket Book (FSPB). Published in 1914 by His Majesty's Stationary Office for the British Army

Flanagan, M.T. 1996 'Irish and Anglo-Norman Warfare in Twelfth-Century Ireland'; in Bartlett & Jeffery (eds), 1996, 52-75

Fletcher, M. 2000 *An Archaeological Survey of St Michael's Hill, Montacute, Somerset.* Unpublished English Heritage Report: Exeter

Fox, C. 1932 *The Personality of Britain.* Cambridge Uni. Press

Freeman, E.A. 1867-79 *The History of the Norman Conquest of England* (6 vols.), Oxford

Garmonsway, G. (ed.) 1990 *The Anglo-Saxon Chronicle.* J.M. Dent & Sons Ltd: London

Gesta Regis Henrici Secundi (Gesta Henrici); Stubbs, W. (ed.) 1867, Roll Series (2 vols.), London

Gilbert, J.T. *c.*1900 *The Register of the Abbey of St Thomas the Martyr in Dublin.* Dublin

Gillmor, C.M. 1981 'The Introduction of the Traction Trebuchet into the Latin West'. *Viator*, 12, 1-8

Giraldus Cambrensis Itinerary and Description of Wales; Dimock, J.F. (ed.) 1868, Rolls Series 21 (vol. 6), London

Glasscock, R.E. 1975 'Mottes in Ireland'. *Château-Gaillard*, 7, 95-110

Golding, B. 1994 *Conquest and Colonisation: The Normans in Britain, 1066-1100.* St Martin's Press: New York

Golding, B. 1991 'Robert of Mortain'. *Proceedings of the Battle Conference*, 13, 119-44

Graham, B.J. 1991 'Twelfth and Thirteenth Century Earthwork Castles in Ireland: an assessment'. *Fortress*, 9, 24-34

Graham, B.J. 1985 'Anglo-Norman Settlement in Ireland'. *Group for the Study of Irish Historical Settlement, Athlone*, 2-40

Graham, B.J. 1980 'The Mottes of the Norman Liberty of Meath'. *Irish Midland Studies – Essays in commemoration of N.W. English.* The Old Athlone Society, 1980, 39-56

Graham, B.J. 1975 'Anglo-Norman Settlement in County Meath'. *PRIA*, 75c, 223-48

Graham, B.J. 1972 *The Settlement Pattern of Anglo-Norman Eastmeath: 1170-1660.* Unpublished PhD thesis, Queens Uni. of Belfast

Grant, E. (ed.) 1986 *Central Places, Archaeology and History.* Dept. of Archaeology & Prehistory, Sheffield

Gravett, C. 2000 *Medieval Siege Warfare.* Osprey: London

Gray, H. St G. 1903 'Excavations at Castle Neroche, Somerset, June-July, 1903'. *PSANHS*, 49, 23-53

Great Pipe Roll, 1155-1158. Hunter, J. (ed.) 1931, Record Commission: London

Halsall, T.J. 2000 'Geological Constraints on the Siting of Fortifications: Examples from Medieval Britain'; in Rose & Nathanail (eds) 2000, 3-31

Halsall, T.J. 2000 'Geological Constraints on Battlefield Tactics: Examples in Britain from the Middle Ages to the Civil Wars'; in Rose & Nathanail (eds) 2000, 32-59

Handford, S.A. 1970 *Tacitus: The Agricola and The Germania.* Penguin: Harmondsworth

Harvey, A. 1925 *The Castles and Walled Towns of England.* Methuen: London

Hennessey, W.M. 1871 *The Annals of Loch Ce* (2 vols.). Dublin

Hennessey, W.M. & McCarthy, B. 1887-1901 *The Annals of Ulster* (4 vols.). Dublin

Heslop, T.A. 1991 'Orford Castle, Nostalgia and Sophisticated Living'. *Architectural History*, 34, 36-58

Higham, R. & Barker, P. 1992 *Timber Castles.* Batsford: London

Hill, D.R. 1973 'Trebuchets'. *Viator*, 4, 99-114

Hillaby, J. 1992/3 'Colonisation, Crisis-Management and Debt: Walter de Lacy and the Lordship of Meath, 1189-1241'. *Riocht na Midhe*, 8:4, 1-50

Hollinrake, C. & N. 1991 *Wincanton By-pass Report.* Unpublished Report in SRO

Hope, W.H. St J. 1910 *The Strategical Aspects of English Castles.* Royal United Service Institution

Howard, M. & Paret, P. 1984 *Carl Von Clausewitz – On War.* Princetown Uni. Press

Hughes, M. 1989 'Hampshire Castles and the Landscape 1066-1200'. *Landscape History*, 11, 27-60

Houts, van, E. 1987 'The Ship List of William the Conqueror'. *Anglo-Norman Studies*, 10, 159-84

Houts, van, E. (ed. & trans.) 1992-5 *The Gesta Normannorum Ducum of William of Jumièges, Orderic Vitalis and Robert of Torigni* (2 vols.): Oxford

Inquisition – Post Mortem, Edward I, 1307. Chancery Collection, PRO: London

Janin, R. 1930 'Les Francs au service des Byzantines'. *Echos d'Orient*, 29, 61-72

Johnson, M. 2002 *Behind the Castle Gate – From Medieval to Renaissance*. Routledge: London

Johnson, M. 1996 *The Archaeology of Capitalism*. Blackwell: Oxford

Jones, T. 1952 Brut y Tywysogion - Peniarth MS.20. *Uni. of Wales, History and Law Series*, 11, Cardiff

Jones, T. 1955 Brut y Tywysogion - Red Book of Hergest. *Uni. of Wales, History and Law Series*, 16, Cardiff

Kenyon, J. R. & Avent, R. (eds) 1987 *Castles in Wales and the Marches: Essays in Honour of D.J. Cathcart-King*. Uni. of Wales Press, Cardiff

King, D.J.C. 1983 *Castellarium Anglicanum* (2 vols.). Kraus International Publications: New York

Kightly, C. 1975 *Strongholds of the Realm*. Thames and Hudson: London

Knight, J.K. 1987 *The Three Castles: Grosmont, Skenfrith and White Castle*. Cadw – Welsh Historic Monuments, Cardiff

Leach, P. & Ellis, P. 2004 'Roman & Medieval Remains at Manor Farm, Castle Cary'. *PSANHS*, 147, 80-128

Leach, P. 2001 *Roman Somerset*. Dovecote Press: Wimborne

Lenoir, M. 1979 *Pseudo-Hygin – Des Fortifications Du Camp*. Uni. of France, Paris

Lester G. (ed.) 1988 *The Earliest English Translation of Vegetius' De Re Militari*. Carl Winter: Universitätsverlae

Lewis, C., Mitchell-Fox, P. & Dyer, C. 1997 *Village, Hamlet and Field: Changing Medieval Settlements in Central England*. Manchester Uni. Press

Liddiard, R. (ed.) 2003 *Anglo-Norman Castles*. Boydell: Woodbridge

Liddiard, R. 2000 *Landscapes of Lordship – Norman Castles and the Countryside in Medieval Norfolk, 1066-1200*. BAR – British Series (no. 309): Oxford

Lilley, K.D. 2002 *Urban life in the Middle Ages, 1000-1450*. Palgrave: Basingstoke

Lloyd, J.E. 1954 *A History of Wales from the Earliest Times to the Edwardian Conquest* (2 vols.). Longmans & Co: London

Luttwak, E.N. 1981 *The Grand Strategy of the Roman Empire*. Johns Hopkins Uni. Press: London

Manual of Field Fortification – Military Sketching and Reconnaissance (MFF), 1871, British Army Publications

Marten-Holden, L. 2001 'Dominion in the Landscape: Early Norman Castles in Suffolk'. *History Today*, 51:4, 46-52

Martin, F.X. 1993 'Overlord Becomes Feudal Lord – 1172-85'; in Cosgrove, A. (ed.), 1993, 98-126

McNeill, T.E. 2000 *Castles in Ireland – Feudal Power in a Gaelic World*. Routledge: London

McNeill, T.E. 1992 *Castles*. English Heritage & Batsford Books: London

McNeill, T.E. 1990 'Trim Castle, Co. Meath; The First Three Generations'. *Archaeological Journal*, 147, 308-36

McNeill, T.E. 1989/90 'Early Castles in Leinster'. *The Journal of Irish Archaeology*, 5, 57-64

Meade, Rev. P. 1877-8 'History of Castle Cary'. *PSANHS*, 24, 50-2

Meade, Rev. P. 1856-7 'Castle Cary'. *PSANHS*, 7, 82-99

Ministers Accounts 1262-3; Special Collection 6, PRO: London

Moore, J. 1798 *A list of the Principal Castles and Monasteries in Great Britain*. Egerton: London

Morillo, S. 1994 *Warfare under the Anglo-Norman Kings, 1066-1135*. Boydell: Woodbridge

Mullally, E. 2002 *Les Geste des Engleis en Yrlande* (The Deeds of the Normans in Ireland), 'A new edition of The Song of Dermot and the Earl'. Four Courts Press, Dublin

Murphy D. 1896 *The Annals of Clonmacnoise*. Dublin

Neaverson, E. 1947 *Medieval Castles in North Wales; a Study of Sites, Water Supply and Building Stones*. Liverpool Uni. Press

Nelson, L.H. 1966 *The Normans in South Wales, 1070-1171*. Uni. of Texas Press: Austin & London

Nicolle, D. 1999 *Arms and Armour of the Crusading Era 1050-1350: Islam, Eastern Europe and Asia.* Greenhill Books: London

Oakeshott, R.E. 1960 *The Archaeology of Weapons.* Lutterworth Press: London

O'Conor, K.D. 2002 'Motte Castles in Ireland: Permanent Fortresses, Residences and Manorial Centres'. *Château Gaillard*, 20, 173-82

O'Donovan, J. 1848-51 *The Annals of the Kingdom of Ireland by the Four Masters* (7 vols.): Dublin

O'Dwyer, S. 1937 *The Roman Roads of Wales – Brecknock and Glamorgan.* Montgomeryshire Printing Co. Ltd: Newtown

O'Dwyer, S. 1934 *The Roman Roads of Wales – Denbigh and Flint.* Montgomeryshire Printing Co. Ltd: Newtown

O'Keeffe, T. 2000 *Medieval Ireland – An Archaeology.* Tempus: Stroud

O'Keeffe, T. 1996 'Rural Settlement and Cultural Identity in Gaelic Ireland, 1000-1500'. *Ruralia I, Památky archeologické* – Supplementum 5, Praha, 1996, 142-53

O'Keeffe, T. 1992 'Medieval Frontiers and Fortification: The Pale and its Evolution'; in Aalen & Whelan (eds) 1992, 57-78

O'Keeffe, T. 1990 'The Archaeology of Norman Castles in Ireland' (Part 1: Mottes and Ringworks). *Archaeology Ireland*, 4:3, Autumn, 15-17

O'Keeffe, T. 1990 'The Archaeology of Norman Castles in Ireland' (Part 2: Stone Castles). *Archaeology Ireland*, 4:3, Winter, 20-22

O'Meara, J. 1985 *Gerald of Wales: The History and Topography of Ireland.* Penguin: Harmondsworth

Orpen, G.H. 1892 *Song of Dermot and the Earl.* Oxford (Reprinted by Llanerch, 1994)

Orpen, G.H. 1911–20 *Ireland Under the Normans: 1169-1333* (4 vols.). Clarendon Press: Oxford

Orpen, G.H. 1907 'Motes and Norman Castles in Ireland'. *English Historical Review*, 22, 228-54 & 440-67

Orpen, G.H. 1907 'Motes and Norman Castles in Ireland'. *JRSAI*, 37, 123-52

Orpen, G.H. 1906 'Mote and Breteshe Building in Ireland'. *The English Historical Review*, 21:83, 417-44

Page, W. (ed.) 1911 *Victoria County Histories* (vol. 2). Constable: London

Painter, S. 1935 'English Castles in the Early Middle Ages: their number, location and legal Position'. *Speculum*, Boston, Mass., 10, 321-32

Patent Rolls of Henry III, 1216-1232

Pettifer, A. 2000 *Welsh Castles.* Boydell: Woodbridge

Plantagenet Somerset Fry 1996 *Castles of Britain and Ireland.* David & Charles: Newton Abbot

Platt, C. 1995 *The Castle in Medieval England and Wales.* Chancellor Press: London

Pooley, C. 1877 *A Historical and Descriptive Account of the Old Stone Crosses of Somerset.* Longmans Green: London

Potter, K.R. (ed. & trans.) 1955 *Gesta Stephani, the Deeds of Stephen.* Nelson Medieval Texts: London

Pounds, N.J.G. 1990 *The Medieval Castle in England and Wales: A Social and Political History.* Cambridge Uni. Press

Prévost, A. le 1838-55 *Ordericus Vitalis' Historia Ecclesiastica.* Paris

Prior, S.J. 2000 *A Desk-top Study and Photographic Survey of a Motte and Bailey Castle and its Environs; at St.Michael's Hill, Montacute, Somerset.* Unpublished MA Dissertation, Uni. of Bristol

RCAHMW 1991 *An Inventory of the Ancient Monuments in Glamorgan, The Early Castles – from the Norman Conquest to 1217.* HMSO: London

Rees, W. 1930 'Medieval Gwent'. *The Journal of the British Archaeological Association*, 35, 189-207

Rees, W. 1840 *Liber Landaviensis – The Book of Llandaff.* Llandovery

Reeves, W. 1862 'On the Townland Distribution of Ireland'. *PRIA*, 7, 473-90

Remfry, P.M. 1997 *Longtown Castle – 1048 to 1241.* SCS Publishing: Malvern Link, Worcester

Renn, D. 1987 'Chastel de Dynan: The First Phases of Ludlow'; in Kenyon & Avent (eds), 1987, 55-74

Renn, D. 1968 *Norman Castles in Britain.* John Baker: London

Rice, G. 2001 *Norman Kilcloon – 1171 to 1700*. Kilcloon Jubliee Committee: Kilcloon

Richards, M. 1969 *Welsh Administrative and Territorial Units – Medieval and Modern*. Uni. of Wales Press, Cardiff

Roche, R. 1995 *The Norman Invasion of Ireland*. Anvil Books Ltd: Dublin

Rose, P.F. & Nathanail, C.P. (eds) 2000 *Geology and Warfare – examples of the influence of terrain and geologists on military operations*. Geological Society: Bath

Round, J.H. 1899 *Calendar of Documents Preserved in France, Illustrative of the History of Great Britain and Ireland*. PRO: London

Round, J.H. 1888 Ancient Charters Prior to A.D. 1200. *Pipe Roll Society* 10, London

Rowley, T. 2001 *The Welsh Border – Archaeology, History and Landscape*. Tempus: Stroud

Rowley, T. 1999 *The Normans*. Tempus: Stroud

Sauvage, E.P. 1882 *Etienne de Fougères: Vitae BB Vitalis et Gaufridi Analecta Bollandiana* (vol. 1)

Saxe, M. de 1732 *Reveries of Memoirs upon the Art of War*. Published in English in 1787, London

Scott, A.B. & Martin, F.X. (eds) 1978 *Expugnatio Hibernica – The Conquest of Ireland – by Giraldus Cambrensis*. Royal Irish Academy, Dublin

Shaw, H. & Pilkington, H. (eds) 1872 *Principles of Fortification – by Captain Reinhold Wagner*. Staff College of the Royal Engineers, Chatham

Shrader, C.R. 1979 'A Handlist of Extant Manuscripts Containing the De Re Militari of Flavius Vegetius Renatus'. *Scriptorium*, 33, 280-350

Spurgeon, C. J. 1987 'Mottes and Castle-Ringworks in Wales'; in Kenyon & Avent (eds), 1987, 23-50

Stalley, R.A. 1992 'The Anglo-Norman Keep at Trim: Its Architectural Implications'. *Archaeology Ireland*, 6:4, 22, 16-19

Steane, J.M. 2001 *The Archaeology of Power*. Tempus: Stroud

Sweetman, D. 1999 *The Medieval Castles of Ireland*. Boydell: Woodbridge

Taylor, C.C. 2000 'Medieval Ornamental Landscapes'. *Landscapes*, 1:1, 38-55

Taylor, C.C., Everson, P. & Wilson-North, R. 1990 'Bodiam Castle, Sussex'. *Medieval Archaeology*, 34, 155-7

Thomas, R. 1977 *South Wales*. Bartholomew & Son Ltd: Edinburgh

Thompson, A.H. 1912 *Military Architecture in England during the Middle Ages*. Oxford Uni. Press

Thorpe, B. 1848-9 *Florence of Worcester*, 'Chronicon ex Chronicis' (2 vols.): London

Thorpe, L. 1978 *Gerald of Wales: The Journey Through Wales* (6 vols.): London

Trask, C. 1898 *Norton Sub-Hamdon*. Barnicott & Pearce: Taunton

Turvey, R. 2002 *The Welsh Princes, 1063-1283*. Longman: London

Walsh, P. 2003 *Irish Leaders and Learning through the Ages*. Edited by Ó'Muraíle, N., Four Courts Press: Dublin

Walters, W.D. 1968 *Royal Policy and English Castle Distribution, 1154-1216*. Unpublished MA Thesis, Indiana Uni.

Warbis, A.T. 1921 *Fragments of South Somerset – Montacute*. Murry: Yeovil

Webster's New World Dictionary, 1998

Welch, M. 1994 *Anglo-Saxon England*. English Heritage & Batsford Books: London

Wheatley, A. 2004 *The Idea of the Castle*. York Medieval Press, Boydell & Brewer: Suffolk

Williams, A. & Martin, G.H. (eds) 2002 *Domesday Book – A Complete Translation*. Penguin: Harmondsworth

Whitelock, D., Douglas, D.C. & Tucker, S.I. 1961 *The Anglo-Saxon Chronicle*. Eyre & Spottiswoode: London

Yule, Lieut. H. 1851 *Fortifications for Officers of the Army and Students of Military History*. Chatham

Index

Abergavenny **14,** 124, 136, 137, 139, 140, 141, 142, 144,
  147, 151, 152, 158, 159, 241
Adam de Futepoi 183, 207, 209
Adam Dullard 21, 207
Aelfgar, Earl of East Anglia 113, 114
Afon Llwyd, River 135, 154
Alfred d'Epaignes 71, 107
Alfred, king of England 76, 89, 96, 105, 225
An tSlighe Mhor 187, 197, 198, 201, 203
Anglo-Saxon Chronicle 20, 37, 111, 113
Annals of Loch Ce 184, 214, 220
Annals of Ulster 184, 193,
Antioch 35, 46
Ardbraccan 183, 198, 205, 207, 242
Ardmulchan **29,** 182, 186, 197, 216, 242
Art O'Melaghlin 213, 217
Art of War The 39, 40, 41, 42, 43
Artillery, medieval 64, 65, 67, 224
Athboy 183, 186, 197, 212, 215, 242
Athelney 98, 100, 102, 103
Athlumney 184, 186, 198, 243
Avon, River 74, 84, 85, 86, 89, 95, 108, 137
Axbridge 96, 97, 99
Axe, River 82, 85, 86, 90

Bacton (Newcourt Farm) 125, 148, 158, 241
Baldwin de Redvers 71, 98
Balgree 184, 198, 243
Ballands Castle 71, 76, 85, 240
Ballons, the 123, 124, 144, 146, 159
Ballyhist 184, 198, 243
Ballymacad 184, 198, 243
Ballymacad (Killeagh) 184, 198, 243
Baronies **27,** 98, 99, 178, 207, 209, 210, 211, 226, 229
Bath 30, 74, 90, 95, 96, 97, 106, 137
Battle of Hastings 35, 103
Beiliau Llangwm 124, 146, 158, 241

Bernard de Neufmarché 121, 144
Bishop of Llandaff 142, 147, 149
Black Mountains 111, 118
Blackwater, River 194, 197, 198, 199, 218, 229
Bodiam Castle 21, 22
Bog of Allen, the 176, 195
Boyne, River 179, 194, 197, 198, 199, 200, 201, 215,
  216, 218, 228
Breach Wood Castle 71, 85, 90, 95, 240
Brecon 137, 142, 156
Breicheiniog 144, 146
Brian, earl of Cornwall 80, 81
Bridgwater Castle 71, 74, 85, 108, 240
Bristol 49, 80, 95, 97, 108, 171, 172
Bristol Channel 53, 74, 76, 82, 84, 86, 89, 108, 118,
  132, 135, 136, 139, 141, 144, 156
Brue, River 61, 82, 84, 86, 88, 89
Brut y Tywysogyon 112, 143, 144
Brynbuga, commote 158, 159, 161
Burhs 96, 97, 98, 99, 226
Burrow Mump **8,** 71, 84, 85, 98, 240
Bury Castle 71, 85, 240

Caer Castle (St Mellons) 124, 135, 136, 139, 144, 159,
  241
Caer Licyn 126, 135, 140, 153, 242,
Caerleon Motte 123, 134, 135, 136, 139, 140, 141, 144,
  158, 241
Caerwent Motte **11,** 123, 134, 139, 159, 241
Caldicot Castle **10,** 123, 134, 159, 241
Cale, River 84, 85, 86, 88
Cannington **5,** 30, 108
Cantrefs 117, 118, 119, 157, 160, 161, 209
Cao Cao 41, 45, 46, 56
Caputs 98, 99, 108, 209, 210, 211, 216, 217, 219, 229
Caradog ap Gruffydd 143, 148
Cardiff 139, 140, 157

Carl von Clausewitz 25, 43, 45, 48, 50, 54, 55, 57, 58, 60, 62, 63, 95, 132
Cary Castle **5**, 71, 84, 86, 87, 88, 240
Cary, River 82, 84, 86, 87, 88, 92, 93, 105
Castelries 159, 161
Castle Batch 71, 81, 240
Castle Neroche 70, 73, 75, 76, 77, 79, 81, 84, 88, 96, 104, 105, 108, 240
Castlecor (Typermessan) 183, 197, 242
Castlejordan 178, 184, 198, 243
Castlerickard 184, 186, 198, 243
Castletown 185, 199, 243
Castletown Kilberry 185, 243
Castletown Kilpatrick 185, 243
Chandos', the 71, 108, 124, 148, 149
Chanstone Tumps **17**, 125, 139, 148, 158, 241
Charlemagne 36, 234, 235, 236
Chepstow 49, 90, 123, 126, 132, 134, 135, 136, 137, 139, 140, 141, 143, 146, 151, 154, 159, 174, 227, 237, 239, 241
Chester 90, 115, 121, 142, 188, 237
Chew, River 84, 85
Cirencester 74, 137
Clare's, the 125, 126, 144, 146, 148, 154, 161, 172, 218
Clifford Castle 115
Clonard **26**, 183, 198, 202, 205, 209, 217, 219, 242
Clonbarton, 185, 199, 243
Cockroad Wood Castle **4**, 71, 73, 75, 76, 84, 85, 86, 240
Coed-y-Mount, Penrhos **21**, 125, 152, 241
Colchester **30**, 237, 239
Columbers, the 71, 89
Commotes 117, 118, 119, 146, 147, 148, 149, 150, 154, 155, 157, 158, 159, 160, 161, 209
Conor O'Melaghin 166
Coolronan 185, 186, 199, 243
Cothill Tump 125, 148, 158, 241
Crewkerne 86, 88, 90, 91, 97, 98, 100, 101
Croft Castle 71, 85, 86, 90, 91, 98, 240
Crossbow 64, 65, 223
Cruicetown 184, 198, 242
Culmullin 182, 186, 197, 242
Culverhay Castle **6**, 71, 73, 84, 90, 95, 108, 240
Cwrt-y-Gaer Ringwork 125, 153, 241

David fitz Gerald, Bishop 172
De Munitionibus Castrorum 256
Dee, River 194, 198, 199, 219, 229
Demi-Fore, barony 197, 198, 199, 207, 209
Dermot MacCarthy 174
Dermot MacMaelnamo 166
Dermot MacMurrough 169, 171, 172, 173, 174, 184, 200, 206, 213, 218
Dermot O'Melaghlin 169, 171, 213
Derry Patrick 182, 197, 209, 242
Derver 183, 186, 197, 242

Diamor 185, 199, 243
Diarmait Mac Murchada 196, 213
Diarmait O'Brien 166
Diarmait Ua Dímmusaig 213
Dinham Castle 125, 146, 159, 241
Dixton Mound 124, 135, 139, 146, 158, 241
Dollardstown 183, 187, 207, 242
Domesday Book 36, 70, 81, 86, 92, 93, 101, 102, 121, 146, 161, 223
Domnaill MacLochlainn 166
Donaghmore 183, 197, 216, 249
Donaghpatrick 183, 186, 205, 242
Donal Mor O'Brien 174
Donn Sleibhe MacDunleavy 174
Donncadh O'Carroll 169, 171
Donnell Bregach O'Melaghlin 213, 216
Donnell O'Farrell 214, 215
Donnell O'Melaghlin 169
Dorstone Castle 124, 148, 158, 241
Dover 49, 69, 70, 72, 90, 236
Down End Earthworks 61, 71, 85, 88, 89, 90, 240
Dowth 185, 199, 243
Drogheda **24**, 182, 186, 188, 197, 200, 201, 212, 217, 242
Drumbride 185, 199, 243
Drumcondra **22**, 184, 186, 193, 198, 242
Du Mu 41, 45, 52, 57, 59
Du You 41, 54
Dublin 15, 150, 171, 173, 174, 175, 178, 179, 181, 195, 201, 214, 215, 216, 217, 218, 220, 222, 228
Duleek 182, 186, 197, 199, 205, 207, 209, 212, 217, 242
Dunboyne 183, 197, 207, 209, 212, 242
Dundalk Bay 176, 178, 190
Dunsany 184, 198, 242
Dunshaughlin 183, 197, 212, 242
Dunster Castle (Torre) **2**, 71, 76, 84, 85, 108, 225, 240
Durrow 15, 217, 220

Ebbw, River 55, 134, 135, 139, 142, 146, 155, 156
Edithmead 71, 74, 75, 84, 99, 240
Edmund (Harold's son) 79
Edward III, king of England 33
Edward the Elder, king of England 68
Engineers, Military 40, 43, 66, 67, 223, 224
Epitoma rei Militaris 42, 235
Eudo Dapifer 237
Eustace of Boulogne, Count 70
Everard de Frejus, Count 235
Ewias, commote 118, 129, 143, 146, 147, 148, 149, 150, 151, 157, 158, 159, 161
Ewyas Harold 111, 115, 123, 143, 158, 241
Exe, River 85, 107
Exeter 70, 79, 80, 81, 90, 91, 101, 107, 226, 236
Exmoor 79, 82, 106, 107
Expugnatio Hibernica 175, 184

Fan na gCarbad 198, 201
Fenny Castle **3**, 63, 71, 85, 86, 240
Flavius Renatus Vegetius 42, 44, 47, 48, 49, 52, 235
Florence of Worcester 111, 113
Folkestone 20, 72
Fosseway 90, 91, 93, 96, 101
Franks, the 34, 234
Fulk Nerra of Anjou 23, 230, 235, 236

Galtrim 183, 197, 209, 218, 242
Geoffrey de Ivry 125, 146
Geoffrey of Coutances, Bishop 81, 105
Gerard the ditcher 223
Gesta Guillelmi 20, 36, 37, 70, 235
Gesta Regis Henrici Secundi 121
Gesta Regum 81
Gilbert de Angulo 183, 207
Gilbert de Clare 126, 148, 161, 172
Gilbert de Lacy 149, 150, 151, 152
Gilbert Marshall 157
Gilla-gan-inathair Ua Miadhaigh 220
Ginnets Great 185, 186, 199, 243
Giraldus Cambrensis 121, 150, 164, 166, 169, 171, 172,
   173, 174, 175, 184, 186, 194, 196, 201, 209, 216,
   219, 222
Girley 185, 199, 243
Glastonbury 63, 86, 89, 90, 102, 103
Glenboy 185, 199, 243
Gloucester 74, 80, 137, 154, 156
Godwin (Harold's son) 79
Golden Valley, the 141, 149
Gower 116, 148
Goytre Wood Castle Mound 125, 140, 151, 241
Graig Foel 126, 129, 135, 152, 242
Graig Wood Motte 126, 135, 154, 242
Greenoge 184, 198, 212, 243
Grosmont Castle **13**, 123, 139, 141, 143, 147, 150, 151,
   158, 161, 241
Gruffydd ap Cynan 121
Gruffydd ap Llewelyn 110, 111, 112, 113
Gruffydd ap llywelyn Gruffydd ap Rhydderch 143
Gruffydd ap Rhydderch 110, 111, 112, 113
Gruffydd ap Rhys 148
Gwent Is Coed, cantref 118, 143, 144, 147, 157, 158,
   159, 161
Gwent Uwch Coed, cantref 118, 143, 144, 146, 152,
   157, 158, 159, 161
Gwynllwg (Morgannwg), cantref 157, 159, 161
Gytha (Harold's mother) 79, 80, 81

Hales Castle 71, 84, 90, 240
Ham Hill 92, 101, 102, 103
Hamelin de Ballon 124, 144, 159
Harold, king of England 15, 68, 70, 74, 76, 79, 80, 81,
   103, 105, 107, 113, 226
Harrowing of the North 38

Hastings 35, 68, 70, 72, 79, 103, 172, 236
Hendre Hafaidd 126, 152, 242
Henry I, king of England 121, 123, 148, 150, 154, 228
Henry II, king of England 17, 103, 123, 149, 150, 172,
   174, 175, 196, 213, 214, 215, 216, 218, 220, 222,
   228, 235
Henry III, king of England 157
Henry Yule, Lieutenant 52
Hereford 69, 111, 113, 115, 126, 127, 137, 141, 142, 148
Herepaðs 93, 95, 96, 97, 226
Herluin of Conteville 81
High-kingship 166, 171
Hill of Slane 179
Hill of Tara 169, 179, 188
Hill of Ward 215
Historia Ecclesiastica 36, 37
Ho Yanxi 41, 57
Holy Roman Empire 234
Hugh d'Avranches 115, 121, 142,
Hugh de Hussey 183, 207
Hugh de Lacy I 124, 147, 148, 149, 161, 214
Hugh de Lacy II (Constable of Dublin & Justiciar of
   Ireland) 15, 125, 149, 150, 174, 175, 178, 182, 183,
   186, 200, 201, 207, 208, 209, 212-220, 222, 228
Hugh de Lacy III 184, 214
Hugh Tyrrell 201
Hundreds 29, 34, 49, 96, 98, 99, 206, 208
Hyginus Gromaticus 42, 48, 52, 53, 57, 59, 61, 62, 89
Hywel ap Edwin 111

Icknield Street 90, 237
Ilchester 30, 89, 91, 92, 93, 94, 96, 97, 98, 99, 101
Ilminster 97
Iorwerth ab Owain ap Caradog ap Gruffydd 148
Is Coed, commote 159
Isabel de Chandos 71, 108
Isle, River 82 84

Jia Lin 41, 59
Jocelin de Angulo 183, 207
John de Courcy 218
John, king of England 93, 144, 175

Kells 169, 183, 186, 197, 198, 199, 205, 207, 209, 212,
   215, 218, 242
Kemeys Inferior Motte 126, 135, 140, 154, 242
Kenchester 137, 139, 141
Kilbeg 197, 205
Kilbeg Upper 183, 186, 197, 242
Kilberry 185, 199, 243
Killadden 185, 199, 243
Killeen 183, 198, 219, 242
Kilmessan 184, 198, 243
Kilwarden, River 198, 202, 203
Knights fees 153, 144, 161, 222
Knockmark 183, 197, 242

Langport 88, 89, 96, 97
Langstone Court Mound 126, 140, 154, 242
Laracor (Knightsbrook) 185, 199, 243
Leonisius de Bromiard 182, 183
Les Geste des Engleis en Yrlande 206, 207, 208
Li Quan 41, 46, 56
Liber Landaviensis 121, 143, 146, 149
Lincoln 30, 90, 236
Lisdoran 185, 186, 199, 243
Llancillo Motte 125, 140, 149, 151, 241
Llandeilo Fawr 142
Llangibby Castle Mound 126, 135, 152, 153, 161, 242
Llanthony Priory 148
Llantilio Crossenny 142, 147, 158
Llys 157
Locking Head Castle 71, 74, 84, 107, 240
London 51, 68, 72, 78, 79, 137, 237
Longbow 64
Longtown Castle **19**, 125, 149, 150, 158, 241
Loughbrackan 185, 243
Loughcrew 179, 185, 199, 243
Lower Deece, barony 197, 198
Lower Duleek, barony 197, 199, 207
Lower Kells, barony 197, 198, 199, 207
Lower Moyfenragh, barony 207
Lower Navan, barony 197, 198, 207
Lower Slane, barony 198, 199
Lune, barony 197, 199, 207
Lyng 96

Machen, commote 146, 154, 155, 157, 161
Máel Seclainn Mac Lochlainn 218
Magnus (Harold's son) 79
Mangonel 65
Manors 32, 78, 81, 93, 98, 102, 104, 105, 107, 111, 131, 161, 187, 207, 209, 210, 211, 212, 229
Manus O'Melaghlin 216, 217
Maredudd ap Gruffydd 157
Markets 31, 32, 97, 131, 205, 212
Matilda, Queen (wife of William the Conqueror) 80
Matthew de Tuit 183, 207
Maurice de Prendergast 173
Maurice de Saxe, Count 42, 43, 47, 48, 59, 63, 137
Maurice fitz Gerald 172, 173
Mei Yaochen 41, 52, 54
Melaghlin O'Melaghlin 169
Meredud ap Owain 143
Milborne Port 96, 97
Miles of Gloucester 149, 150, 151
Mill Wood Castle Mound **20**, 125, 151, 241
Milltown 184, 185, 186, 198, 199, 243
Milltown (Moylagh) 243
Moat (ME005 080) 185, 199, 243
Moat (ME008 032) 185, 199, 243
Moat (ME010 039) 185, 199, 243
Moat (ME042 005) 185, 199, 243

Moat Town 185, 199, 243
Moathill (Navan) 183, 186, 198, 242
Monmouth 116, 118, 132, 136, 137, 139, 141, 144, 146, 151, 158
Monmouth Castle (Mingui) 123, 126, 134, 135, 136, 141, 143, 158, 241
Monnow, River 118, 132, 134, 135, 139, 140, 142, 147, 148, 149, 151, 152, 161, 227
Montacute **9**, 31, 70, 71, 75, 76, 79, 81, 84, 91, 92, 93, 96, 99, 100–105, 107, 146, 223, 226, 240
Morgallion, barony 198, 199, 207
Morgan ap Hywel 157
Morgan ap Owain 154
Morgannwg 143, 144, 154, 156, 157, 159, 161
Mouse Castle (Cusop) 123, 143, 158, 241
Mowbray Rebellion 147
Moynalty 185, 197, 199, 243
Moyrath 185, 199, 243
Muchelney Abbey 88
Muirchertach MacLochlainn 169, 171
Muirchertach O'Brien 166
Mulphedder 184, 186, 187, 198, 203, 243
Murchad Ua Mael Sechlainn 175
Murchadh O'Carroll 174
Murrough O'Melaghlin 169, 213
Mynydd-brith 124, 148, 158, 241

Nanny, River 197, 198
Nant-y-Bar (Dorstone) 124, 148, 158, 241
Navan 179, 197, 198, 207, 211, 212, 219, 242
Nedern Brook 134, 135, 136, 139
Nether Stowey Castle **1**, 71, 85, 108, 240
New House Ringwork 126, 152, 241
Newcastle 125, 141, 151, 241
Newtown (Killallon) 183, 197, 242
Newtown Trim 212
Nigel de Gourney 71
Nobber **23**, 183, 186, 194, 198, 212, 219, 242
Normandy 21, 34, 36, 46, 69, 70, 74, 78, 79, 80, 83, 86, 111, 166, 172, 216, 234, 235, 236, 239

Odo, Bishop of Bayeux 37, 69, 74, 81
Oldcastle 179, 183, 186, 197, 242
Oldcastle Brook 197, 199
Orderic Vitalis 36, 37, 46, 49, 70, 79, 80, 101, 121
Osbern Penticost 111, 123
Ostmen (Norsemen) 171, 174
Over Stowey Castle 71, 84, 99, 107, 108, 240
Owain Gwynedd 148

Palatinates 114, 115, 142
Parrett, River 61, 82, 84, 85, 86, 88, 89, 90, 92, 108
Patrickstown 185, 243
Payn fitz John 124, 147, 148, 149, 150, 151, 161
Penhow Castle 125, 129, 139, 146, 159, 241
Penselwood 75, 76

Pen-y-Clawdd Motte 125, 152, 241
Pevensey 72, 78, 79, 236
Philippe Maigret 43, 54, 55, 57, 58, 62, 63, 96, 204, 205
Polden Hills 61, 88, 89, 90
Pont-Hendre 124, 148, 150, 158, 241
Port Way, the 129, 136, 137, 140, 141, 157
Portage routes 86, 90, 91, 225
Portbury Mound 71, 85, 108, 225, 240
Priest town (Kilbride) 185, 199, 243

Raglan Castle **12**, 123, 139, 143, 158, 241
Rathbeggan 185, 199, 243
Rathfeigh 184, 186, 198, 243
Ratoath 182, 186, 197, 198, 199, 207, 212, 242
Raymond le Gros 173, 217
Reinhold Wagner, Captain 44, 45, 46, 47, 50, 57, 63, 127
Rhydderch ap Caradog 143
Rhymney, River 118, 134, 135, 136, 139, 143, 144, 227
Rhys ap Gruffydd 172
Rhys ap Tewdwr 121, 144
Rí 206, 208
Richard de Clare 125, 144, 172,
Richard de Tuit 183
Richard fitz Gilbert de Clare (Strongbow) 172, 173, 174, 213, 216, 217, 218
Richard fitz Godebert 173
Richard I, king of Normandy 172
Richard Redvers 71, 98
Richard the Fleming 183, 207
Richmont Castle 71, 85, 95, 107, 240
Robert de Chandos 71, 149
Robert de Quency 214
Robert fitz Hamon 123, 124, 136, 141, 144, 146, 154, 161
Robert fitz Stephen 172, 173
Robert of Bampton 71, 107
Robert of Hay, 124 146, 154
Robert, Count of Mortain 69, 70, 74, 75, 76-82, 93, 101, 102, 104, 105, 106, 107, 228
Robertstown 185, 243
Rockfield Castle 126, 142, 151, 242
Rodanstown 183, 186, 187, 197, 242
Roger de Breuteuil 143, 161
Roger de Lacy 123, 149
Roger fitz Osbern 143
Roger le Poer 183
Roger of Corcelle 223
Roger of Montgomery 69, 76, 115, 121, 143,
Roman invasion, the 234, 236, 237
Roman roads 51, 85, 89, 90, 91, 92, 93, 94, 136, 137, 138, 139, 140, 141, 146, 153, 226
Romanesque architecture 235, 239
Romanitas 233, 235, 236, 237, 239
Rory O'Connor 169, 171

Rowlestone Motte 125, 140, 241
Rufus, king 121, 147
Rumney Castle 123, 134, 135, 136, 139, 144, 157, 159, 241

Salisbury 82, 86, 90
Scotney's (Escotot's), the 125, 149
Scurlocks, the 183
Scurlockstown 183, 242
Sébastien le Prestre de Vauban 43, 54, 55, 57, 58, 62, 63, 96, 204, 205
Seignorial manors 207, 209, 210
Selwood Forest 76, 101, 106
Severn, River 111, 132, 136, 137, 143
Sextus Julius Frontinus 40, 41, 42, 52, 54, 59, 60, 62, 235
Shannon, River 169, 175, 176, 178, 186, 195, 201, 214, 215, 217
Sheppy, River 85, 86
Sherborne 91, 96, 101
Shires 79, 81, 82, 105, 110, 116, 209
Shortbow 64
Sicily 34, 46
Skenfrith Castle **16**, 123, 143, 147, 151, 158, 161, 241
Skreen 183, 197, 198, 205, 207, 209, 212, 219, 242
Slane 169, 179, 183, 186, 193, 197, 198, 199, 205, 207, 209, 212, 218, 219, 242
Slighe Assail 187, 197, 198, 199, 201, 202, 216
Slighe Mhidhluachra 178, 197, 199, 201
Snodhill Castle 124, 148, 158, 241
Sock Dennis 92, 93, 94, 96, 98
Sollers, the 124, 148
Somerset Levels 63, 82, 84, 86, 225
Song of Dermot and the Earl 184, 200, 206, 218
South Cadbury 96, 97
South Petherton 88, 97
Springal 65
St. Illtyd's Motte 126, 135, 242
St. Mary's Yard Mound 125, 140, 241
Stamford Bridge 103
Stephen de Cruys 184
Stephen, king of England 86, 123, 148, 149, 150, 151, 152, 172, 228
Stogursey 30, 71, 74, 85, 108, 109, 240
Stour, River 85, 86
Stow Hill Castle 124, 139, 146, 159, 241
Stowey Castle 71, 84, 240
Strategemata 40, 41
Sub-infeudation 207, 209, 210, 219, 229
Sun Tzu 39, 41, 47, 51, 52, 54
Swallow Cliff Mound 71, 85, 240
Swegen Godwinson, earl 111

Tadg MacCarthaigh 166
Tara 169, 179, 187, 188, 198, 201
Taunton Castle 71, 85, 95, 98, 100, 108, 109, 240

Teirtref, commote 158, 159, 161
The Bage (Bach Motte) 123, 143, 158, 241
The Berries, Ballan Moor 123, 135, 144, 159, 241
The Moat (Treveddw) **18**, 126, 140, 242
Thomas de Craville 183, 207
Thurstianstown 185, 243
Tiernan O'Rourke 169, 171, 173, 174, 189, 213, 214, 215
Toirrdelbach O'Brien 166
Toísech 206
Tone, River 82, 85, 89
Topographia Hibernica 175, 184
Tovi, Sheriff of Somerset 80, 102, 103
Townlands 208, 209
Trebuchet 65
Trecastle (Llangovan) 126, 140, 153, 241
Tregrug, commote 153, 160
Tremblestown 185, 243
Trevet 187, 198
Trícha céts 206, 208, 209
Trim 21, 24, **25**, 182, 186, 187, 197, 200, 201, 205, 209, 212, 217, 242
Trostrey 126, 140, 153, 242
Tryleg, commote 159, 160, 161
Tuatha 206
Turbeville's, the 125, 149
Turlough O'Connor 166, 169
Turstin fitz Rolf 123, 144, 146, 159
Twyn-Bar-Lwm Castle 53, 55, 125, 154, 156, 241
Tywysog, the 157, 158

Upper Deece, barony 197, 198, 209
Upper Duleek, barony 199, 207
Upper Kells, barony 197, 198, 199, 207
Upper Moyfenragh, barony 207, 209
Upper Slane, barony 197, 199, 207
Urishay Castle 124, 148, 158, 241
Usk Castle 124, 135, 136, 139, 141, 146, 158, 241
Uwch Coed, commote 158, 159

Waldinus Ingeniator 223
Walter Bloet 123, 143
Walter de Lacy 123, 143, 147, 148, 161,
Walter de Lacy II 150, 184, 220
Walter fitz Richard de Clare 125, 146, 161
Walter of Douai 71, 74, 83, 86, 106, 107
Walterstone 8, 139, 141, 143, 147, 151, 158, 241
Waltham Abbey 103
Wang Xi 41, 44, 56
Warkworth 32, 33
Watchet 96, 97, 99
Wells 63, 86
Wentloog Castle 126, 140, 155, 157, 241
Wentwood Ridge 118, 146
Wern-y-Cwrt Castle Mound **15**, 125, 141, 152, 241
Weston under Penyard 137, 141

White Castle 124, 147, 150, 151, 152, 158, 161, 241
White Tower, the 237
Wigmore Castle 115, 127
William de Briwerre 71
William de Curci, 71 108
William de Lacy 184
William de Mohun 71, 74, 76, 83, 106
William de Muset 183, 207
William de Say 71, 107
William fitz Audelin 218
William fitz Osbern 74, 115, 121, 123, 124, 126, 128, 135, 143, 159, 161
William Gifford 71, 98, 108
William I, the Conqueror 35, 36, 37, 38, 46, 68, 69, 70, 74, 76, 78, 79, 80, 81, 83, 86, 101, 102, 103, 106, 114, 142, 143, 144, 147, 221, 228, 234, 235, 236, 239
William II, king of England 228
William le Petit 183, 207
William of Falaise 71, 107,
William of Jumièges 81
William of Malmesbury 70, 81, 102
William of Poitiers 49, 70, 79, 235
William of Worcester 20
William Petit 183, 207
Wimble Toot **7**, 71, 84, 88, 92, 93, 94, 98, 240
Winchester 30, 51, 69, 72, 80
Winebald de Ballon 144, 146
Wolvesnewton 153
Wye, River 49, 90, 115, 118, 132, 134, 135, 136, 139, 143, 146, 227, 237

Yeo, River 82, 84, 89, 92, 93,
Y-Gaer, St. Nicholas 72
York 30, 79, 90, 236
Ystradyw 143

Zhang Yu 41, 44, 56